Get the F*#k Off My Quarterdeck

Becoming a Vietnam-Era P-3 Pilot

Randy Hotton

Black Rose Writing | Texas

©2025 by Randy Hotton
All rights reserved. No part of this book may be reproduced, stored in a retrieval system or transmitted in any form or by any means without the prior written permission of the publishers, except by a reviewer who may quote brief passages in a review to be printed in a newspaper, magazine or journal.

The author grants the final approval for this literary material.

First printing

The author has tried to recreate events, locales and conversations from his/her memories. In order to maintain anonymity in some instances, the author may have changed the names of individuals and places. The author may have changed some identifying characteristics and details such as physical properties, occupations and places of residence.

ISBN: 978-1-68513-608-6
PUBLISHED BY BLACK ROSE WRITING
www.blackrosewriting.com

Printed in the United States of America
Suggested Retail Price (SRP) $21.95

Get the F#k Off My Quarterdeck!* is printed in Book Antiqua

*As a planet-friendly publisher, Black Rose Writing does its best to eliminate unnecessary waste to reduce paper usage and energy costs, while never compromising the reading experience. As a result, the final word count vs. page count may not meet common expectations.

The anecdotes and stories in this book are based on my memories and records. These accounts are truthful to the best of my knowledge.

Praise for
Get the F#k Off My Quarterdeck!*

"Strap in for an extraordinary ride as a directionless youth from the tumultuous `60s transforms into a decorated Navy combat pilot in Vietnam. Hotton's the real deal!"

–Cam Torrens, award-winning author of the *Tyler Zahn suspense series*

"This fast-paced account recognizes the many mentors helping Hotton, leading to his highly successful military and civilian career."

–Barry D Levine, author of *Yankee Air Museum*

"Not everyone with childhood dreams lives them out. But Randy Hotton did. His origin story, *Get the F*#k off My Quarterdeck*, details the sacrifices and challenges he faced to realize his boyhood dream: escaping the `surly bonds of earth.' To fly!"

–Patti Brehler, author of *Facing Sunset: 3800 Solo miles; A Woman's Journey Back and Forward.*

This book is dedicated to all my fellow active and reserve Patrol Squadron crews who kept watch in the skies over the world's oceans. We were almost always alone and a thousand miles from our base. During the Cold War, we played a continuous cat-and-mouse game with the Soviet Fleet. Navy squadrons patrol these same skies today. Our decades of diligence contributed to the Soviet Union's downfall and still contribute to America's safety today.

ACKNOWLEDGMENTS

The help of so many was crucial in making my memoir "Quarterdeck" a reality. Luckily, I've had wholehearted support on the journey to finishing my book. To my wife, Lou, for allowing me the countless hours isolated in our basement to finish the book. Also, to my son Andy and his wife Marty, who let vacations at their home in New Mexico turn into book writing exercises. Particular thanks go to Patti Brehler Anderson, a fellow author and Lou's bicycle buddy, who recommended Max Frazier to me. A special recognition for MaxieJane Frazier. The ideal editor at the right time. Without Maxie's extraordinary editing skills, my manuscript might have been dead on arrival. She was an immeasurable resource for me in putting this memoir together. My thanks to fellow former squadron members Gregg Pappas and Mike Theodore, who beta read my work and pointed areas for improvement. To the USMC Drill Instructors in Pensacola who showed me a new world of possibilities. To a steady flow of P-3 Squadron mentors who guided me into qualification as a Patrol Plane Commander. And last but not least, acknowledgement to my former employer, USA Jet Airlines. They locked me in hotel rooms at the various glamor spots across the US, like Laredo, Del Reo, and McAllen, waiting for the phone to ring with another trip. With nothing but spare time on my hands during the lock ups, writing my autobiography preserved my sanity. Finally, Black Rose Writing for believing in my work.

Get the F*#k Off My Quarterdeck

OPENING
"Poopieville"

The Transition Indoc Battalion Building 699, "Poopieville"

SERGEANT SANDERS

Three of us from NAS Grosse Ile, Michigan, walked through Bldg. 699's front door with me leading. Little did we know that we had crossed a threshold into the unknown. *What am I supposed to do now? What would happen next?* Once in the building, the room appeared dimly lit after coming in from the bright sunlight. As my eyes adjusted, I observed a meticulously polished floor with large bullets neatly arranged and wrapped in white roping. In the room's middle, a staircase marched out of sight. To my left stood a wall with a small opening like a fast-food checkout window. That opening adjoined a hallway leading deeper into the building. While we gazed around the room, a short-haired Marine sergeant stuck his head out of the small window. I said "Hi, Sarge." and then reeled in shock when he unleashed his voice.

"GET THE FUCK OFF OF MY QUARTERDECK!" he screamed.

I paused mid-stride, my mouth agape after a friendly "Hi, Sarge." *What had we done to draw his screaming introduction? What made up a quarterdeck?* I had never heard of a quarterdeck. Later

I would learn a quarterdeck was an official Navy term for an entrance to a ship or a building. My brain was looking for answers. In a panic, I didn't know what to do. What brought on the sergeant's wrath? Being a math student, I thought *Oh! He wants us off his 25% of the floor.* The three of us shuttled to the right, trying to put distance between us and the sergeant.

Naval Air Station Pensacola Building 699 housed the Indoctrination Battalion (Batt) where I would begin my Navy career. They called it "Poopieville" because the new inductees wore baggy dark green WWII flight overalls called "poopiesuits." We lived there through our indoctrination in the military that would lead successful trainees into the world of Naval Aviation. The new world would be a minefield of unfamiliar words and new ways for me.

The Marine sergeant screamed again: "WHAT DON'T YOU UNDERSTAND ABOUT GET THE FUCK OFF OF MY QUARTERDECK!?"

Why is he screaming? I have done something wrong? What is going on? He must have me confused with someone else. I am here to be a Navy pilot.

The time was 2:30 p.m. on Wednesday, June 29, 1966. At his bellow, it became 1430 on 29JUN66 and my life changed forever.

Things weren't going well. The Marine sergeant disappeared from the fast food window and came out the adjacent passageway's hatch. Soon I would learn these Navy terms for door and hallway. USMC Drill Instructor (DI) Sgt. Sanders was a classic DI: medium height, about five feet eight inches tall and 160 pounds. A cleanly tapered body in a perfectly fitting khaki uniform gave the impression of no fat, as if he'd ordered it off his body the same way he ordered us off his quarterdeck. He had three olive drab chevrons on his sleeve; his uniform was spotless, and the creases in his shirt and trousers were perfect. A highly polished brass belt buckle perfectly aligned with the button line on his shirt and the fly on his trousers. His glossy polished black shoes were mirrors, enhancing the image of excellence. With his short cropped blond hair, he came across as all business. Everything about Sgt. Sanders commanded our attention. He personified the ideal Marine.

Again, he screamed and pointed down the passageway yelling "Get in here, get in here!"

The quarterdeck was off limits to AOCS Candidates. Ten long, arduous weeks that turned me into a candidate officer would pass before I walked on the Bldg. 699 quarterdeck again. I thought, *What have I gotten myself into?*

Three of us from NAS Grosse Ile arrived a day late, through no fault of our own. Our class, 25-66, had already reported and was busy with in-processing. Sgt. Sanders now had a couple of hours to blow off and play with us. They wouldn't serve evening chow until 1700. As we entered the passageway, he asked for our orders. He took our the papers, looked them over and snarked, "I didn't know how 'hard up' the Navy must be to send me losers like you."

He took us to a space, Navy term for room, off the passageway just opposite his office. The space had built-in counters set at desk height along both left and right walls, with two chairs at each counter. Slotted wooden compartments were above counters and held various official forms. Desktops held pencil holders with pencils. Sergeant Sanders reached into a compartment. He pulled out some forms to draw towels and sheets for our room. Then he handed these forms to us and said, "Fill these out and bring them to me."

I filled out my form, name, serial number, date, etc. With my paper, I walked across the passageway to his office. Sergeant Sanders's office hit me as an ordinary, stark, and sterile space. He sat behind a standard Navy wooden desk centered on the hatch three steps back from the opening. The desktop was bare except for a name tag centered, facing me, embossed with the USMC Eagle, Globe, and Anchor emblem and his name. Behind him there was a bare table holding only an in and out basket. He placed our orders there after collecting them. Above the table taped to the wall was a large, hand-drawn eyeball with red lines running through it, giving a blood shot effect. A wastebasket sat on the right side of the desk. To the left was the opening where he had bellowed his admonition moments ago.

I stepped into his office and said, "Here are the forms."

He stood up and yelled, "Don't you ever come into my fucking office again without being invited! Now go out and do it correctly." His volume never softened.

What is going on? Why is he so mad at me? What have I done wrong?

Shocked, I returned to the passageway and stood by his door. "Request permission to enter your office."

"How stupid can you be? You don't know shit." Sergeant Sanders walked around his desk toward the entrance to his office. He called the two other NAS Grosse Ile recruits, Larry and Bruce, over from the space across the passageway. Then he showed us how to enter an office for the next 10 weeks.

Office entrance instructions: I approached the door with my right shoulder, one fist off the starboard bulkhead, Navy term for a wall. Then I took one step forward and performed a right face maneuver. Centered in the hatch, as he instructed, I pounded the door jamb three times and said, "Sir, Candidate Hotton requests permission to enter the office, sir." Over the years, countless candidates "pounding the pine" have worn out the door jamb.

Sergeant Sanders didn't answer me, but screamed, "I cannot hear you!"

I pounded harder and screamed at the top of my lungs

"SIR, AVIATION OFFICER CANDIDATE HOTTON REQUESTS PREMISSION TO ENTER THE OFFICE, SIR"

I was now looking at him, and he yelled, "Don't you eyeball me! Use your peripheral vision."

Eyeballing? What the hell is eyeballing?

Sergeant Sanders pointed to a piece of paper above his desk with a bloodshot eyeball. He told me to keep my eyes on that eyeball. He told me to start over.

Again, I banged on the doorjamb. I kept my eyes focused on the eyeball and screamed for permission to enter his office.

He granted permission to enter.

I handed him my form. He looked at it and ripped it in half. He told me "You did not do it right, now go back and do it correctly."

Back then, I went and started filling out the forms again. All I wanted to do was avoid ever being seen by the DI again. *I need to find a place to hide and not be his center of attention.* Meanwhile, Larry and Bruce went through the same experiences learning how to enter the sergeant's office. He ripped up what they handed him and sent them back to redo their forms. We went through the frustrations of trying to turn our linen request forms three times.

Finally, after about an hour of trying to turn in our linen request cards, Sgt. Sanders walked into the room across from his office. He had a look of disgust on his face and said in a straightforward, accusatory voice, "How fucking stupid can you be? You cannot follow directions. You have absolutely no hope in this program. The form instructions tell you to write between the lines. Your pencils have touched the lines."

Oh! Now we filled out the forms correctly and got our towels and sheets. An introduction to "attention to detail."

SHITHOLE ROOM

Sergeant Sanders took us to our room around the corner from his office, near the south end of the passageway. A spartan, uninviting space with two sets of bunk beds next to the left and right walls, with a window on the wall opposite the door would briefly be our home. An empty table filled the center of the room. By the entrance hatch was a washbasin. The sergeant showed us how to make a bed to military standards with taut sheets and square corners. Then he said, "This room is a shithole. I want it cleaned to military standards right now. I will be back to inspect it."

We thought the room was spotless. But to please him and avoid his rage, we got cleaning supplies and started washing the floor, walls, door jambs, etc. I started working on the window frames and then I noticed the window blinds. They had dust on them. They needed to be dusted. Obviously, no one had dusted them for a long time. Any attempt to dust them would expose parts of the blinds we couldn't clean. That would draw unwanted attention and the sergeant's wrath. We discussed it and chose not to touch the blinds. Our first inkling of teamwork. We elected to stop cleaning our room; it was already in good shape. Sgt. Sanders returned to inspect the room. He did not inspect the blinds, and we dodged a bullet. After two hours with the sergeant, he left us alone. It was now around 1630. We sat on our bunks, discussing what the hell we had gotten into and what would come next.

EYE-BALLING

Fifteen minutes later, class 25-66 showed up in formation behind Poopieville. The parking lot behind the Indoc Battalion was known as the "Grinder" because it was where new recruits practiced military drills and formations. They combined Class 25-66 with 75 Aviation Reserve Officer Candidates (AVROC) poopies at Poopieville. AVROCs completed AOCS in two six-week sessions while still in college. They were doing their first six-week summer program. Sergeant Sanders ordered us out to join the formation. Everyone had shaved heads and was wearing poopiesuits. When Larry, Bruce, and I joined the ranks in our civilian clothes, we stood out like flashlights on a dark night. Right away, we got the attention of a USMC DI. He started screaming at us, "So you did not have to dress like everyone else? No, you want to be different."

Everyone around me was standing stiff as a board, eyes locked straight ahead. I looked around, unsure of what I should be doing. My wandering eyes caught the DI's attention. No one wanted to draw a DI's attention. Drawing a DI's attention could cause the imposition of physical training (PT). He saw me looking around and walked toward me, screaming, "ARE YOU EYE-BALLING ME?" Then he yelled, "GIVE ME 50."

What is he talking about? Does he want 50 cents?

He yelled, "Get down and give me 50 pushups."

Fifty pushups, are you kidding me? I had never done 50 pushups. Dropping to the ground, I started cranking them out. After 25, my pushups became sloppy.

He yelled for me to do jumping jacks. I cranked out about 25 of those.

The DI then screamed for me to do flip-flops on the ground. Flip-flops are where candidates roll from belly to back to belly in repeated motion. My two buddies were getting similar treatment.

The rest of the poopie herd was standing ramrod tall and looking straight ahead. At well over 90 degrees, close to 100% humidity, the PT combined with the Florida sunshine, had me soaking wet and melting. Dirt covered my clothes. I looked like a rag doll they dragged through a mud puddle.

DOR DEMANDS

Finally, we stopped doing PT and formed up for dinner. The DI marched us to the chow hall about half a mile away. Two years of military drills in AFROTC at MSU came in handy as I responded easily to the cadence and commands of the DI. We got to the chow hall and lined up single file on the porch. We waited for our turn to enter the building. After all the unwanted attention our civilian clothes caused on the Grinder, now the candidate officers noticed us standing in line. Candidate officers were candidates in their last week of AOCS. They assumed leadership roles and assisted the DIs in managing AOCS rotations. Again, I got "You are different, you don't fit in, you should DOR (Drop, Own Request) right now." Followed by "You are a loser who has no chance to make it in this program. I want your DOR." They asked me to DOR three times.

By now, I learned to keep my eyes "caged" straight ahead. I signed the paperwork to train for the Navy. If I DORed, I would still owe the Navy time as an enlisted sailor. My hope of becoming a Navy pilot depended on successfully completing my training. I was living my childhood dream. No way would I DOR. I would fight tooth and nail to stay in Navy Flight Training. They would have to kick me out to get rid of me.

We approached the door, going into the chow hall. Over the entrance there was a black and white handwritten sign: "303." A candidate officer said to me, "That is how many airplanes have been shot down in North Vietnam. Those pilots were all better men than you. You can't live up to their standards. Quit right now, before you get killed. I want your DOR." I stood silent; eyes locked straight ahead.

In the summer of 1966, the number over the door went up every day as losses in Vietnam mounted. They removed the sign at some point while I was in class 25-66. Perhaps the number was getting too big to be motivating.

I got in line and picked up a standard military five-compartment metal tray. I'd never seen foods like this before:

collard greens, black-eyed peas, and hominy grits. The stewards slopped the food into the compartments on my tray. A gooey, delicious-looking peach cobbler dessert was the part I most looked forward to eating. I sat down at a table with my classmates. They were jamming food into their mouths. No one was talking, just eating as fast as they could. I asked, "What's going on?"

No one answered. Finally, one guy said, "Shut up and eat as fast as you can. They are going to kick us out of here in a couple of minutes."

I started jamming food into my mouth.

When I was about half done, a DI suddenly came to our table and started yelling "GET UP, GET OUT, GET UP, GET OUT." We rapidly exited the chow hall. I didn't even touch my peach cobbler. We formed up outside and marched back to the Indoc Battalion.

LIFE AT POOPIEVILLE

Back at Poopieville, we had slack time. We used the bathroom and had time to meet other candidates. Poopieville had no privacy. If I had to take a dump, it would be right in front of everyone on toilets with no doors on the stalls. A big change from my mom's admonition at home "No one wants to see you going to the bathroom, close the door." I quickly got over the lack of privacy and elimination of individuality. We were being molded into identifying as a military unit.

That evening, we attended a mandatory meeting in Poopieville's upstairs classroom. We met above the infamous quarterdeck, where six hours ago I met Sgt. Sanders. They gave us instructions on upcoming schedules and our responsibilities.

After the meeting, I went back to my room in my beat-up civilian clothes. We were dog tired and hit our racks, navy term for bed. At 2200 hours, they called lights out. I slept like a rock that night. Nothing would wake me up. Joe, a 25-66 late arrival, came into our room even later. I did not hear him. They stashed another late show, Chuck, elsewhere in Poopieville. I finished my first day in the Navy. It became one of the most unforgettable days of my life. I knew despite the harassment; this was where I wanted to be. On Thursday June 30, 1966, at 0530, a loudspeaker played a wake-up call followed by an announcement Grinder.

Once in formation, PT followed pushups, sit-ups, jumping jacks, and flip-flops. We may have run a short distance. As one of yesterday's five late arrivals, I had no PT gear, and any distance running in loafers would have been challenging. We marched to the Chow Hall for breakfast. The harassment wasn't as bad as yesterday, and we had time to finish our meal. After breakfast, we marched back to Poopieville, and they separated the five late shows from the poopie herd.

There had been talk of holding late arrivals back a week for class 26-66, but Schools Command had us stay with 25-66. A sign of the times, Vietnam demanded a greater output of pilots. We weren't squared away as poopies, and that had to be fixed. Our class officer turned us over to Sgt. Sanders, who marched us down to the barbershop. Sergeant Sanders chatted with the barber about dealing with late arrivals, while the man quickly shaved our heads. We became hairless wonders.

We marched back to Poopieville, where they issued us two poopiesuits. I donned my new uniform and threw away my civilian clothes I had worn for the last 24 hours. My clothes were near rags and seeing them go into the trash can would be another separation from who I had been only yesterday morning. It seemed like a million years ago. We could now join the herd and look like every other poopie.

That afternoon, class 25-66 had to draw uniforms, to include PT gear. I walked down the uniform issue line that they set up like an assembly line. When I came to a station, they would ask my size. I gave them my size, and they would plop something in front of me. We got underwear, khaki and white uniforms, blues, belts, buckles, hats, insignia, socks, and shoes. We put these items in a gigantic pile and hand carried them back to Poopieville. There, candidate officers gave us instructions on how to store our uniform items, and how to wear everything.

NAVAL AVIATION MEDICAL INSTITUTE (NAMI)

Friday July 1, we were up early again: clean the room, shave, make my bed, PT, and march to breakfast. Now part of the herd, I would keep my mouth shut, not eyeball anyone, and hide in the open. After breakfast, we marched to the Naval Aviation Medical Institute (NAMI) for our flight physicals. My class marched as a group everywhere we went. They confined us to a small area around Poopieville.

We spent the day at NAMI. The Navy gave us a complete physical to include eyes, hearing, and vitals. The Corpsmen took our blood pressure three different ways: standing, sitting, and lying down. NAMI also measured the lengths of elbow, knees, sitting height, and leg length. These measurements determined how we would fit into the various Navy cockpits. That morning, I was 156 pounds when only six weeks prior, at my entrance physical at NAS Grosse Ile, I weighed 162 pounds. In my brief stay at AOCS, I lost six pounds.

Some men did not pass their flight physical. The Navy dropped them from our class. A flight physical failure resulted in what was called the "NAMI Whammy." It removed people from flight training and possibly into two years of enlisted Navy service. After going through these various screening events, they cut down our class. I passed, and they found me PQ & AA DIACA SNA (Physically Qualified and Aeronautically Adopted for Duty Involving Actual Aircraft Control as a Student Naval Aviator).

The heat and humidity I encountered on my first day in Pensacola when I stepped off the airplane took a toll on me. A giant rash developed under my poopiesuit, from my neck down to my ankles. They sent me to Sick Bay, a Navy term for the emergency medical clinic. The corpsman recommended I get out of my poopiesuit and wear only my PT gear. In formation, I stood out in my PT gear with everyone else wearing poopiesuits. I feared being different would draw the same unwanted attention as I experienced the first day in civilian clothes. But I experienced no more harassment than the rest of my classmates.

Saturday, July 2, started a three-day weekend to celebrate the Fourth of July. The Navy would observe the Fourth as a holiday on Monday. Most DIs took the long weekend off, limiting our DI encounters. However, candidate officers made the weekend a blur of PT, sweating, marching, harassment, and learning about our responsibilities. We went through a variety of inspections of our rooms, bunks, and personal gear.

Saturday evening Jerry Kevitt, a laid-back senior candidate officer from class 15-66, came in and spoke to us in the upstairs classroom. He told us it was all a game. We should just stick to it. We would all get through. He went into the honors violations that would get someone thrown out of AOCS. Any lying, falsifying records, or similar unethical acts were unacceptable. These violations would eliminate us from the program. The standards of acceptable military behavior were being drilled into us. During flight training, I would cross paths with him again. Jerry would become a lifelong friend.

Our class spent the weekend shining our shoes, polishing our brass, and getting ready for the next inspection. We learned some short cuts from the candidate officers. They told us not to sleep under the sheets; sleep on top and on one side of the bed. That way, it is easy to make the bed in the morning and save time. We had five sets of underwear; three sets were supposed to be in our drawer display. To avoid building a drawer display every day. We would wear a set of our underwear into the shower and then let it dry in our locker overnight. The next day we had clean underwear without touching our drawer display. We started working as a Navy team.

We marched to church in our poopiesuits on Sunday. As the junior class, we sat in the front row. The chapel was air-conditioned, and no one harassed us while we were there. The reprieve was welcome.

After a slow day for the Fourth of July holiday, our screening continued Tuesday morning. We marched back to NAMI and took a battery of psychological tests. Taking the tests in an air-conditioned room was an escape from the constant AOCS demands.

The rest of our time at Poopieville became routine: PT, marching, daily inspections of our uniforms, rooms, and personal gear. In between inspections, they pushed us in PT. The summer sun came up early in Pensacola and woke me up at 0430, an hour before reveille. I had a routine to shine my shoes and polish my brass to prepare for the day. Tuesday evening, we met Staff Sgt. Montemeyer in the upstairs classroom. A big, mean-looking, intimidating DI with a booming voice, he commanded our attention. He came in to tell us how to spit shine our shoes. His shoes were like looking glass, and he wanted our shoes to look the same. To him, the honor of a man was the shine on his shoes. If a woman offered to kiss him in return for stepping on that perfect shine, he said he would tell her to pound sand. Staff Sgt. Montemeyer was serious about shining shoes, and he wanted us to have the same level of pride in our appearance.

SWIM TESTING

Wednesday morning, July 6, after breakfast, we put on our swimming suits at Poopieville and marched to the Enlisted Pool for our swim assessment. It was located right across the street from Poopieville. The screening tests would determine if we possessed the swimming skills to complete water survival. We got a break, just hanging out while we waited for our turn to jump into the water. Getting into the pool in the hot weather was refreshing. I grew up with a swimming pool at my home on Beach Road and was comfortable in the water. They tested us on our ability to tread water, swim the crawl stroke, sidestroke, backstroke, and breaststroke. We were told if we touched the pool' side, we had to start over. My swimming was not as good as some of my classmates who swam in college, but good enough to move into water survival training. Candidates who couldn't meet Navy swimming standards had to do extra swimming practice in their free time, known as "Stupid Swim."

ACADEMIC PLACEMENT TESTING

In the afternoon, we took our math and physics placement examinations. The math exam had a time limit and covered different subjects like arithmetic, algebra, geometry, and trigonometry. The physics evaluation dealt with the gas laws, momentum, and conservation of energy. I had no problem and breezed through the math and physics tests with passing scores. About a third of those taking the test did not pass. If a candidate didn't achieve a minimum score, they pushed him back a class for Math/Physics "Stupid Study." They pushed back many candidates from our class to later classes. I had little time to find out about anyone other than the four guys in my Poopieville room.

THE ADMIRAL

Thursday afternoon, I picked up the duties of Regimental Messenger (RM). An RM acted as a messenger for Schools Command and delivered correspondence between the various buildings at AOCS. Everyone took a turn as RM. I wore the required RM uniform: Tropical Khaki Long, with a fore-and-aft cap. Later in the day, they assigned me a run from Poopieville to Battalion I, Bldg. 623, right across the street from the Chow Hall. I had to deliver papers in an envelope. Most likely it was the roster of class 25-66 scheduled to move into Battalion I the next day.

The run was in the late afternoon, approaching chow time. I was double timing back to Poopieville, and I saw an officer walking toward me. He was an older man in a khaki uniform with wings on his chest. I couldn't make out his rank. When he was closer, I saw two stars on his collar. *Oh My God! An Admiral.* Here I was, a rookie, shaved head and all. My brain was spinning. *An Admiral is almost higher than God. He has the power to crush anyone who acts improperly in his presence.* The DIs had drilled proper military protocol into us, but I was in a real-world encounter that I could blow. If the DIs found out, I screwed it up and embarrassed them, they would kill me. So, I stopped three paces from the Admiral, came to attention feeling the stress of this encounter, gave a crisp salute, and said, "Good Afternoon Sir."

He smiled at me with a twinkle in his eye, returned a casual salute and said, "Carry on, candidate."

I answered, "Aye, Aye sir" and resumed my double time back to Poopieville.

Looking back, I had encountered Rear Admiral John J. Lynch, Chief of Naval Air Basic Training. He was in the first class of Aviation Cadets at Pensacola in 1935 and the first Naval Aviation Cadet to hold flag rank. Hence his smile on seeing me. He was probably thinking of his younger days as a cadet and how he might have reacted had he met an admiral. The Navy awarded him the Navy Cross, the second highest honor in the Navy, for hitting an enemy cruiser during the Battle of Midway.

BASEBALL AND BEERS

Thursday evening, we were semi-secured after dinner. Secured is a navy term for time off with no duties and the ability to come and go as we want. Being secured gave us relief from Indoc Battalion's relentless oppression. But we were only semi-secured to go to a baseball game, not free to go to other places. The Naval Academy Grads were playing the AOCS team. We put on our khaki uniforms and went to the game. It was a night match up under the lights. The class enjoyed a soothing evening out from under the pressure experienced in Poopieville. We could unwind out from under the thumb of the candidate officers and DIs. We could also have beer. I drank two at ten cents a can. Larry and I talked about an airplane flying overhead in the pattern at Sherman Field. He quizzed me about the navigation lights on the airplane. Larry would find out he did not pass the Math/Physics placement test. They put him back a class, and he joined 26-66, housed in Batt 3, the USMC Battalion. But for that night, we enjoyed the camaraderie while watching the AOCS team win. Larry would also become a lifelong friend.

THE QUIZ

On Friday, July 8, our last day in Poopieville, we went to breakfast in our poopiesuits. After breakfast, we marched back to Poopieville and turned in our poopiesuits. We had worn these ripe, hideous bags unwashed for ten days. Thankfully, we would never wear them again. Ditching the suits was a graduation moment; we were no longer poopies dressed in poopiesuits.

We performed uniform drills the rest of the morning. First, we would put on a uniform, (dress blues, tropical white short, choker whites, etc.) get inspected, and then go back into Poopieville, put on another uniform, only to be inspected again. The inspection's last part, just before lunch, was a quiz by our class officer, Captain Cody, USMC. Captain Cody was a Marine Aviator and wore the same Wings of Gold as Navy pilots and was a product of Naval Aviation Training. His job was to oversee and evaluate the members of class 25-66. He quizzed us on the chain of command.

We stood abreast at parade rest on the sidewalk opposite Poopieville with our backs to the Enlisted Pool. Captain Cody approached each person. We snapped to attention, and he asked about the chain of command like "Who is the Head of U. S. Naval School Pre-Flight?" *Who the hell knew who that guy was?* A wrong answer resulted in PT. I wanted nothing to do with PT and was sweating my question.

Captain Cody approached me, and I snapped to attention. He asked, "Who is the Secretary of Defense?"

My luck held. Everyone knew Robert McNamara was the Secretary of Defense. He was on the news every day. My answer was "The honorable Robert S. McNamara, sir."

"Very good," he said and moved on to the next candidate.

I had dodged a bullet while most of the class was doing PT.

BATAAN DEATH MARCH

We had our final room inspection after lunch. To pass, we had to fold everything perfectly, arrange uniforms in lockers with hangers spaced just right, and make our beds with military precision. Our room passed the inspection with no issues. Our class, combined with the AVROC class, made about one hundred candidates move out of Poopieville that afternoon. Out of the one hundred guys, only about thirty-five guys escaped additional PT.

We would leave Poopieville behind us and move into Batt I. The first phase of our training was now complete. Thirty-two pilot officer candidates made up class 25-66. We called the move, the "Bataan Death March." At 1500, we took all our belongings, uniforms, shoes, towels, and bedding and put them in the middle of our flat sheets. We then tied a giant knot in the bundle and loaded it on our backs. It weighed over 50 pounds. We were in our Khaki uniforms, and we marched in formation about 800 yards down the Grinder toward Batt I. In the late afternoon, it was hot and humid. The load's weight added to the sweating and discomfort of walking. By the time we got to Batt I, we were exhausted and soaking wet.

BATTALION ONE (BATT I)

At Batt I, they assigned us rooms with double bunks in alphabetical order. They put me in room 2, in the northeast wing of building 623's southeast corner. Schools Command laid the room out with three sets of bunk beds viewed as we entered the room with one off to the right, one off to the left, and one straight ahead. They made the room's floor out of clean, polished concrete terrazzo. In the room's center, they placed two tables side by side and six chairs around them. They placed a Bible and an ashtray at the table's far end. A four-drawer dresser stood off the left and right of the center bunk opposite the room's entrance. Another four-drawer dresser stood near the end of the bunk bed off to the right. Two candidates would share a dresser. On the entrance wall was a sink and mirror off to the left and right. The entrance wall also had four lockers with padlocked doors.

They had designed the room for four people, but because of the influx of AVROC candidates, they changed it to accommodate six candidates. With four candidates in the room, each candidate would have his own locker. But with six candidates, two candidates would have to team up and share the three lockers. The fourth locker would remain unused.

There were five other candidates in the room. I would get to know Robert, Jim, Forest, Steve, and Paul very well in the next ten weeks. Robert and Forest would DOR after commissioning. If they had DORed prior to commissioning, they could spend two years as an enlisted sailor. A DOR, after receiving a commission, required a three-year military obligation as a commissioned officer. By waiting until after commissioning to DOR, they would enjoy an officer's pay and privileges.

I went to bed that night with a sense of satisfaction because I had made it through the AOCS Indoc Battalion's elimination phase. The NAMI Flight Physical, swimming qualification test, and academic placement testing were behind me. I was following in the giant's footsteps who had gone before me. Many trials and tribulations ahead would challenge me, but I was determined to make it. It became a transitional time of my life. I was becoming part of something bigger than myself. I was where I wanted to be. Fulfilling my childhood fantasy of becoming a Navy pilot. In the rush of training, I didn't consider how far I had come from a kid watching planes take off out of Willow Run Airport in Michigan, but that is where it all began. In the beginning, we're all probably a little selfish. Airplanes were a constant presence in my earliest days, even if I'm not sure how.

PART 1
Before the Active Navy

Chapter One
Growing Up 1943 to 1961

THE START

During the second world war, I, Ralph Andrew Hotton (Randy), came into the world on September 8, 1943, in Detroit, Michigan. I was named after my grandfather, who had named his son, my father Andy, after his grandfather. The alternating names of Ralph and Andrew have been a Hotton family tradition for seven generations. My dad, Andrew Hotton, a Ford Trade School graduate, was a Tool and Die Maker. For his skill, the draft board granted him a deferment for defense production during WWII. When I was born, he worked at Willow Run Airport, building B-24 Bombers.

Somehow Willow Run got in my blood, and I have never escaped my connection. Some consider it a curse. I consider it a blessing; my life has revolved around the Willow Run Airport and airplanes.

TROY TOWNSHIP

Mom, Elizabeth Meakin Hotton, graduated from Michigan State College in 1942 with a major in math. Mom wanted to be an engineer, but in the 1930s, universities did not allow women to enroll in the Engineering curriculum. She graduated with a degree in Math. Mom and dad met because the Hotton and Meakin families lived on the same street in Detroit. After my mom and dad married, she worked as a schoolteacher until she became pregnant with me. In the 1940s, if a schoolteacher was pregnant, they could not teach.

My Grandpa Meakin built a house in Troy Township, Michigan, about ten miles north of Detroit, near Birmingham. Mom and dad moved in with my grandpa after she lost her schoolteacher job. While expecting, she worked as a mail carrier, known in those days as a mailman. She delivered mail to Birmingham's U.S. Post Office RR#2 in Troy Township. So, someone might say I was in the mail delivery business before they delivered me.

In June 1945, in WWII's largest draft call up, the Army conscripted 440,000 men, including my father. Many men, like my father, lost their skilled trade draft deferments. After the war ended in Europe. America was building up for an invasion of Japan and needed a million-man army. In August 1945, my dad was at Ft. Lewis, Washington state, preparing to be one of the million. Then they dropped the atomic bombs and eliminated any need for the invasion. My father left the Army in 1946. My brother, Don, was born in 1946. After dad left the Army, he worked as a salesman for a steel tubing company. On the side, he developed and sold "Hot Rod" speed kits under the name of Hotton and Sullivan. He made and sold equipment for V-8 Fords, like hi-compression cylinder heads, dual carburetor manifolds, and dual exhaust kits.

AIRPLANES

In 1947, we moved to the city of Detroit, where my sister, Pat, was born. Mom wanted to live there because of Detroit's great schools. She had graduated from Cooley High school in Detroit. Dad attended Redford High School. Dad used his GI Bill benefits to buy a house for $7,400, with a $49.00 monthly payment. The GI bill filled our block with WWII Vets who also used their benefits to buy into the new homes being built. When I visited my friends' homes, I remember seeing pictures of the homeowners in their WWII uniforms: Navy, Army, Air Force, and Marine.

Sister Kathy came along in 1949, and sister Betsy in 1951. A family of seven lived in a two-bedroom, one bath, 800-square-foot house. I slept in a bedroom with my brother and two sisters. Three of us slept in the same bed. To save water, the kids would bathe three at a time in the same tub.

Until 1956, Willow Run Airport was Detroit's commercial airfield. We drove to Willow Run regularly to take people to and from the airport. I always wanted to go on these trips. I treasured standing on the airport observation deck and watching airplanes take off and land. Seeing the radial engines on the DC-3s, DC-4s, and other reciprocating engines, pop, and belch smoke while starting mesmerized me. The track home my parents bought in Detroit was close to 8-Mile Road, and Greenfield Road was near the National Guard Amory on 8-Mile Road. It had a small airport. I remember seeing airplanes fly in and out of the airport. It fascinated me. I would listen intently to hear a plane taking off or landing. They would fly over our house. I rushed out to see these airplanes and watched the Mustangs and T-6s buzz the airstrip. My brain raced. I wanted to be like those pilots.

In the 1940s, kids collected baseball cards that came in bubblegum packages. Not me, I collected airplane trading cards. We played a war game with airplane cards. Fighters could shoot down bombers. Bombers could destroy transport and patrol plane bases. Transport and patrol planes could cut fighter supplies. I built model airplanes. Plastic kits were rare in the 1940s, so I built balsa wood airplanes. I had to cut out the parts with an Exacto knife. Then I covered the model with tissue paper and brushed it with lacquer paint.

SCHOOL IN DETROIT

Nearly a dozen kids my age lived in the neighborhood. We played games, visited each other's houses, and were like an expanded family. Everyone knew everyone. I started kindergarten in 1948 at Bow Elementary school, a portable school with two classrooms. When I was only five years old, I walked two blocks to and from school by myself. My class went for a half day and had over 40 kids in the class. I would stay on the half-day routine with a class size of 45 students until 1951, when I started third grade. My grandpa Meakin purchased a TV for us in 1950. It had a 12-inch screen. Daytime programming didn't exist back then, and the TV played a test signal waiting for a program to start. We would sit around watching TV's test signal.

My Grandma Meakin died in 1951, and my grandpa gave his home on Beach Road in Troy to my mom and dad. The house was 4,000 square feet with three baths and four bedrooms on three acres of land. He knew our family with five children now needed the room. Our house was out in the country. I had no friends near our new home.

BACK TO TROY

In the fall of 1952, I started fourth grade in Troy, Michigan, at Poppleton Elementary school at the corner of 16-Mile Road and Crooks Road. I joined the Cub Scouts and went to the meetings. There, I met up with kids I knew from school and developed friendships. We spent summers in Lion's Head, Ontario, on Georgian Bay. My grandpa and grandma Hotton built a cottage there in the 1920s. Later my Grandpa Meakin would build a cottage right next door to my Hotton grandparents.

My dad's speed equipment hobby would turn into a full-time business when he formed his own company called Dearborn Steel Tubing. By 1952, the Ford flathead V-8 engines were not as powerful as the new Oldsmobile and Buick overhead valve V-8 engines. The speed disadvantage had caused Ford to lose police car sales to the more powerful GM products. Because of his Ford Trade School days, dad had many friends at Ford Motor Company. My dad told his buddies at Ford that if they put dual exhaust on their police cars, they would run 10 mph faster. To prove improved performance, they used Ecorse Road near Willow Run Airport as an unofficial test track. They marked off a standing mile between Denton and Beck Road. Then they ran the single exhaust 1952 Ford in the measured mile. It ran at 96 mph. Dad said he would take the car home that night and install dual exhaust so could test the same car tomorrow.

Dad did not only install dual exhaust, but he also replaced the 239 cubic inch Ford V-8 with a 254 cubic inch Mercury engine. My dad loved to build sleeper cars. They looked stock: unmodified on the outside, but under the hood, they had a powerful motor installed. The engines looked identical, but the bigger engine would ensure a higher speed. The "Cheater" Ford with the duals exhaust and Mercury engine ran at 110 mph. Ford ordered 100,000 sets of dual exhaust kits for their police carts. Dearborn Steel Tubing was now in business.

AIRPLANE RIDE

In February 1953, I went to Florida with my parents. At 9 years old, I was already an airplane nut. I couldn't wait to get on the airplane and fly. We were on an Eastern Airlines Lockheed Connie coming out of Willow Run Airport. I made sure I had the window seat so could look out. The "Connie" had the R-3350 Turbo Compound engines. I had a window seat and at about

12,000 feet, the captain made a Public Address announcement. He said they would shift to high blower. He told the passengers, "You will hear our engines come back to idle, then a clunk, followed by engines returning to normal power. There's nothing wrong. It is much like shifting your car into second gear to climb a hill. Don't be worried."

With my nose pressed against the window, I watched #3 engine out my window. The turbo charger went from bright orange to brown. Then I heard a "clunk" as the blower shifted. Then the turbocharger went from brown back to bright orange. *That was so cool.* The stewardess, as they were called in 1953, noticed my interest. She asked if I wanted to go to the cockpit. I looked at my mom and begged, "Mommy, mommy, can I go?"

"Of course," she said.

I remember the cockpit was cloudier inside, with everyone smoking, than the skies were outside. The captain pointed out his window to Columbus, Ohio. The Flight Engineers showed me all the engine instruments on his panel and what they did. I spent about 20 minutes in the cockpit. The cockpit was where I wanted to be. I wanted to be with pilots like those guys. But for a nine-year-old, it was a pipe dream. I did not know how someone became an airline pilot.

ELEMENTARY SCHOOL

I continued to build model airplanes. Now new plastic Monogram and Revell kits dominated my airplane collection. Revell brought out a new airplane kit about once a month. I would make sure I went to the hobby shop every week to see if any new airplane models had arrived. My bedroom ceiling had dozens of airplanes hanging on wires.

The NBC network played a TV series called *Victory at Sea* on Sunday afternoons. I focused my entire week around watching the show. One time, our family was going to pick out a new puppy and afterward go out to eat. Picking a new dog was a big deal. But if I went I would miss *Victory at Sea*. I said I wanted to stay home. The Navy stories captivated me. Particularly the Navy pilots. In my eyes, they were the coolest guys in the world. *Oh, how I longed to be like them. The shelves in my room had ships, primarily aircraft carriers. Aircraft carriers were Victory at Sea's stars.*

Dad set up an automotive workshop in the two-car garage at our house on Beach Road. He equipped it with machinery, lathe, bandsaw, drill press, welding equipment, tools, and a chain fall. At 10 years old, he allowed me to work in his shop. I loved working on cars. I would disassemble engines and transmissions to see how they worked. My hands-on mechanical knowledge would serve me well when I went through systems training on various airplanes. My sister, Peggy, was born in 1953.

JUNIOR HIGH SCHOOL

Mom and dad divorced in 1956. He had an affair with another woman, and they got married. I was now being raised by a single mom. Dad supported us and made regular visits. But he had moved out of our daily lives.

In 1956, for my 13th birthday, mom bought me a first edition book, *Samurai* by Saburo Sakai. It was a first-person memoir of Japan's greatest World War II surviving ace. I devoured his book. Couldn't put it down, I read it again and again. He put me in the cockpit of an airplane as a pilot and explained his connection to the aircraft. *I wanted to do what he had done and find that connection with an airplane.* I loved watching flying movies on TV and would beg mom to let me go to the movie theaters anytime there was a flying movie playing. Next to my bed, I always kept books with stories about pilots, air battles, and flying. I would read myself to sleep at night immersed in these flying stories. My Cub Scout buddies, and I became Boy Scouts.

We went on weekend camping trips and learned to do manly things like smoking and drinking. At 14, I was smoking a pack a day.

With dad's success at Dearborn Steel Tubing, he leased a Cessna-182, and he started taking flying lessons. I would tag along as often as I could when he took lessons. I never turned down a chance to get into an airplane and fly. He never got his license, but his brother, my uncle Bob, had his pilot's license. I got to fly with him occasionally. In 1958, I joined the Civil Air Patrol (CAP), hoping to get some flights with the CAP. It didn't turn out as I hoped, and I never got to fly. Too much politics were involved in who got to fly in the CAP. I attended airshows at Selfridge AFB. I either got my dad or a Boy Scout dad to take us to the shows.

For my 14th birthday, my dad bought me a Lambretta motor scooter. The scooter gave me the freedom to move around. However, the motor scooter almost cost me my life. I drove to a school to pick up my brother Don. On the way home, a car stopped in front of me, and I could not stop. I slammed into the car's rear end. We did not wear helmets back then, and I hit the station wagon's back. The crash resulted in a closed head injury, and I momentarily blacked out. They took me to the hospital and released me a short time later. Reporting my head injury would eliminate me from USAF Flight Training. My mom didn't want me riding the motor scooter anymore, and I was back to riding the bus to school. I met a girl on my bus route, and we became boyfriend and girlfriend.

HIGH SCHOOL

Perhaps driven by my dad's guilt over divorcing my mom, he built an in-ground swimming pool for us at the house on Beach Road. I became very popular with my friends in high school. Pools were a rarity in the 1950s. Having a bevy of young ladies strutting around the pool in their bathing suits ensured my buddies would drop by. I spent hours in the pool and became very comfortable in the water. Little did I know at the time that our pool would give me a big advantage in swimming, and water survival and training when I reported to Pensacola.

In 1959, on my sixteenth birthday, dad gave me a 1954 Red Ford convertible. It had a 361 cubic inch Edsel engine with a four-barrel carburetor under the hood. But he put a restrictor plate under the carburetor to limit the top speed. It would do 0-60 in around six seconds and speed up to 100 in a couple days. Now I could pick up my girlfriend and take her to school. Her name was Sharon, and she became my steady girlfriend throughout high school.

SLEEPER CAR

My dad still loved to build sleeper cars that looked as innocent as grandma's old coupe but were souped up. The first two 1960 model economy cars came out in the fall of 1959: the General Motors Corvair and the Ford Falcon. Detroit Dragway, the drag strip, was going to have a Falcon Convair introduction night. Here the two cars would run through a series of elimination races. Dad wanted to have some fun. Working with his buddies at Ford Motor Company, my dad got two identical 1960 Ford Falcons a few weeks before their introduction date. In one Falcon, he installed a 312 cubic inch Thunderbird engine with two four-barrel carburetors. Special leaf springs looked stock but were actually traction bars. He took the stock Falcon and registered it for the race. The drag strip painted the car's number on the window in Glass Wax. My dad had someone else drive the souped-up Falcon into the pits, but did not register it, instead calling it a support car. The support crew erased the Glass Wax number from the stock car and put it on the souped-up Falcon.

Now the elimination race started. The souped-up Falcon would always just barely beat a competing Falcon. The Convair was going through an identical elimination process. Then the night's final race pitted the fastest Falcon versus the fastest Convair. The souped-up Falcon turned the quarter mile at 107 mph in 14.3 seconds, about 15 car lengths in front of the Convair. The crowd went wild. The drag strip's owner went crazy. Dad had made a fool out of the drag strip owner with his sleeper car approach. Just a stock-looking car with a big engine under the hood. When the owner found out who had pulled off the stunt, he banned my father and Dearborn Steel Tubing from ever coming to his drag strip again.

I had just gotten my driver's license when it happened. In those days cruising Woodward Avenue north of Detroit looking for cars to drag race off of traffic lights was fun. My dad gave me the souped-up Falcon for the weekend. I cruised Woodward in the sleeper car. I looked like I was 14 with a couple of young-looking friends in the car. When I pulled next to a Corvette, I revved up my engine. The driver looked at me with a look of "What is this kid thinking?" and raised an eyebrow. After the light turned green, the sleeper was going 60 mph in six seconds. The souped-up Falcon blew away everyone on Woodward Avenue. The car soon earned a reputation: Don't mess with that Falcon. A Ford engineer, my dad knew, lived in Birmingham, and wanted to borrow the souped-up Falcon to cruise Woodward Avenue. Well, he got the car, and no one would race him. My dad didn't tell him I had been out there cruising the weekend before.

HIGH SCHOOL JOBS

Now I had a car, I looked at getting a job. One of my friends worked at a bowling alley in Birmingham. He said the owner was looking for pin setters. His bowling alley had manual pin setting machines. I got the job and had to manually load the pins and reset them for each game. I got paid 10 cents for a game. If I worked three alleys, I could make about $1.00/hr. Students could only work 10 hours per week. The pin-setting job did not last that long. The alley automated the pin setting with new machines. I was out of a job, replaced by a robot.

My girlfriend had a job at the new A&P store in town. She asked the manager if they needed help. He said they could use some bag boys on the weekends. It landed me a union job at $1.10/hr. The job gave me nearly $10/week take home pay. I could buy a carton of cigarettes at $2.00, fill my car up for $3.00 and have $5.00 left over dates with my girlfriend and lunch at school.

CARS

Because I had a well-equipped garage to use on Beach Road, my buddies would come by my house to work on their cars. One night, three of my car buddies and I converted my buddy's car from a stick shift to an automatic transmission. He wanted an automatic transmission so he could put his arm around his girl while cruising in his car. Another buddy wanted to get rid of his automatic to have a stick shift in his car. They were both 1950 Fords, so the parts easily moved between the cars. Using the equipment my dad had left in the garage on Beach Road, we pulled the engine out of each car. Then we swapped the transmissions and put the motors back into the cars. Then we swapped out the shifting mechanism and clutch attachments. We drove the cars out of the garage at three in the morning.

HIGH SCHOOL GRADUATION

I coasted through high school, and if I liked a course, I got good grades. math, physics, and chemistry were easy for me. In English, Latin, and composition, I extended little effort. They were boring subjects in my mind. Because of my interest in cars, I thought about becoming an engineer. I wanted to be a pilot but did not know how someone went about becoming a pilot. I took a drafting class in my senior year and enjoyed making drawings for machine parts. On my SAT, I tested at 1250, 700 Math 550 Verbal.

I applied to the University of Michigan and Michigan State University. Both schools offered me an opening for the fall 1961 class. The schools offered summer orientations. My mom graduated from MSU. I liked the open green campus along the Red Cedar River at MSU a lot better than U of M's city setting, so I accepted MSU's offer. I graduated from high school with a 2.9 GPA and ranked #24 out of 180 in my graduating class. Nearly in the top 10% with under 3.0 GPA. No one in my class had a 4.0 GPA. In 1961, Troy was still in a rural setting. Only about 10% of my classmates attended college. After I graduated, I drifted away from my girlfriend.

Chapter Two
Michigan State University 1961 to 1966

GOING TO COLLEGE

The big change in my life started on Sunday, September 24, 1961. I no longer lived where I had grown up. The nights in the garage where I hung out with my high school friends were now behind me. My mom drove me up to MSU to start my freshman year. We drove down Michigan Highway #59 (M-59) and stopped at a Gulf gas station on the northeast corner of M-59 and US-23. I remember it was the only building on the corner. M-59 had a stop sign at US-23. We didn't have I-96 or US-23 expressways in 1961. So, we drove down Grand River through the towns of Fowlerville, Weberville, and Williamston.

We arrived at East Shaw Hall on the edge of MSU's campus. She thought it would be a good idea to buy me a green MSU blanket with a white MSU block letter to put on my bed, and she found one at the Student Union Bookstore. I later found out that having a White Block Letter blanket was a violation of Jock Club rules, Jocks being athletes. Like a guy buying a varsity letter for his jacket when he had not earned one. Joe, one of my roommates, had been a high school jock, ribbed me about my unearned letter. I still have the blanket.

FRESHMAN YEAR

MSU assigned me to room 376 East Shaw Hall. The dorm was across the street from the Agriculture Students' cattle barn. When the wind blew out of the south, it filled our dorm with barnyard aromas. With the smell of the cows, we knew why Michigan State was called "Moo U." My formerly four-man room became a six-man room. With the rapidly growing influx of students, the number of people assigned to each room increased. I had five roommates. The six-man room concept would be a disaster.

Not really knowing what I wanted to do and at my dad's encouragement, I signed up to be a Mechanical Engineer. When I found out what engineering encompassed, I wasn't that interested in engineering. But not having any other ideas on what I wanted to do, I stuck with engineering. Because I was a freshman, the Engineering Department had a set curriculum for me, and I had little choice about the classes I would attend. They gave me a list of these classes. Now I needed to build a schedule.

Registration was an interesting manual process. It took place in the Jenison Field House gym. Based on the first letter of my last name, "H," MSU gave me a time to go to registration and pick out my classes. Then I walked around the crowded and noisy gym to find a station for that class. Nearly every station had long lines. Building my schedule took hours. I would go to a station and ask what class times were available. The person managing that class gave me the times and days available. If I found a class that fit my schedule, they would give me an IBM punch card for that class. Then I would go to the next station and try to fit my next class into a schedule. If a conflict developed, I would have to go back to one class I had already picked and turn in that card. Then draw another class to make my schedule work.

After I had built a complete schedule, I went to check out and gave my IBM punch cards to the registrar. They put them into a computer and printed out my schedule. Overall, it was a bewildering process for a new freshman. Over my years at MSU, if my name came up for early registration, it would be easy to build a schedule. However, if I got the last day, it would be impossible to get any good times or elective classes. Fortunately, the starting day and time for registration were rotated each term. I still wanted to be a military pilot and signed up for Air Force ROTC (AFROTC).

One class I had to take in the fall of 1961 was Natural Science (NatSci) 181. The class summarized biology. The class dealt with the biology of sperm and egg joining to conceive a baby, a tricky subject in a co-ed class that covered human reproduction. They paired us boy-girl as lab partners, and they showed us renderings with full-frontal views of a man and women. The class was a hot topic among the guys back at the dorm. Talking about sex in mixed company was a nearly taboo topic in 1961. Was it all *part of a multitude of experiences that expanded my mind beyond just going to college?*

GETTING DRUNK

In the fall quarter, I had a heavy load of 17 credits. High school had been a breeze for me. With little studying, I kept decent grades and graduated near the top of my High School class. MSU was different and would require a much more disciplined approach to studying. I did not have those skills. Skipping class was easy. Not doing my homework became the norm. I fell behind in my classes. I lacked discipline, a fact AOCS DIs would drill into me five years later. If I had better discipline, my grades would have been different. Mid-term grades came out. I was about to flunk out of MSU in my first quarter. Failure was a genuine possibility. I could end up being drafted into the Army, and it put me down in the dumps.

I needed company. When I went home, I got together with my buddy Jack Rector. Jack had a bottle of Scotch. It took us about 30 minutes to finish it and we drove to Woodward Ave. We picked up a hitchhiker at Maple Road. After a brief ride with a couple drunks, he wanted out. By the time we got to Ted's Restaurant at Woodward and Square Lake, the liquor had taken its effect. Sick to my stomach, I went to the bathroom and started throwing up. The restaurant called the cops, who came to pick up Jack and me. The ride in the cop car took a while. I had developed the "dry heaves" and told the cop I was going to throw up. The cop would have to stop the car, then get out, open my door, and watch me try to throw up. The rear doors had no door handles. I did it more than once.

We finally got to the Bloomfield Township Jail on Telegraph, just south of Long Lake. They put me in a cell and called my mom. She came and picked me up. My mother did not say a thing, nor did I. We drove home in silence. I was ashamed of what I had put her through. My hungover condition was no concern to mom when she rolled me out of bed early the next morning. I didn't complain. I still felt guilty about my behavior the night before. She took me to work at the church setting up chairs. I felt bad while experiencing my first hangover. However, I noticed how much better I felt as the day progressed.

The police never made an incident report and there was no official record. *Another lesson learned, and a bullet dodged. A drunk and disorderly charge could have been a showstopper a few years later, when I applied to become a Navy pilot. Little did I know the fickle finger of fate had favored me when it could have been a disaster in my career.*

I went back to MSU with a determination to save my first term. Math was a lost cause, and I just quit going to math class.

But I really hit the books in my other classes and got Cs. My GPA was 1.4 for the quarter. I was now on probation. MSU sent mom a letter telling her I would lose my student eligibility at MSU if my performance did not improve. After Christmas, in the winter quarter of 1962, I got serious about going to college. I stopped skipping classes, did my homework every night. A repeat of the math course I had flunked in fall earned me an A. Studying hard landed me a B in a four-credit chemistry class. My GPA for the winter quarter was over 3.0. I still wanted to be a military pilot and joined Air Force ROTC. In 1961, everyone had to have two years and six credits of ROTC. I enjoyed being in uniform and going to these AFROTC classes.

Then spring came and being outside with my buddies, going to parties and playing games became more important than my studies. We had to have one credit Physical Fitness class each term of our freshman year. When it was my turn to sign up, there were few classes left, and couples' figure skating fit my schedule. I elected to sign up. I met a girl named Marge in the skating class. We hit it off, and I spent a lot of time with her. My grades suffered, and I got a couple of Ds. But I ended my freshman year with a 2.3 GPA. I was off probation and would be back to start my sophomore year. I had no direction or focus and just did whatever I wanted to do at the moment.

SUMMER SCHOOL

To make up for incomplete courses in my first year, I elected to attend summer school in 1962. MSU compressed ten weeks of class into five weeks. A nine-credit load was like an 18-credit load, and the courses advanced rapidly. East Shaw Hall was closed for the summer. A girls' dorm, Abbott Hall, served as the men's dorm in the summer. My cousin, Jim Beall, would attend summer school and we roomed together on the third floor. The university made summer a laid-back setting. I took NatSci 183, a physical science course, something easy for me and Calc II to catch up on my math courses. My summer break came in August and not much happened before I was back at school. Marge was still my girlfriend, and I went to visit her at their family's cottage in Indiana. I said I would buy her a car because I liked her so much. I asked her what color she liked. So, I built a model car and painted it that color. She thought it was cute.

SOPHOMORE YEAR

In the fall of 1962, I moved back into 376 East Shaw Hall, because all my friends were returning to East Shaw. The room still housed six men, and my cousin, Jim Beall, moved in with us. Chaos followed, including more antics, more skipping classes. In fact, we started a nonstop bridge game that went on for two straight weeks. If someone had to do something like go to class, someone else just stepped in and started playing. We set up a slot car racetrack in our room. Shaving cream fights and other out-of-control pranks ruled the days.

One weekend, four of my roommates and I drove my 1957 Ford convertible down to my home in Troy. On the way back to MSU, my buddies bought some beer for the ride home. Sure enough, I got pulled over by the Bloomfield Township police. The same cop who had picked me up at Ted's Restaurant a year before. My buddies tried to hide the beer. But the cop found it and asked me what the can of beer was doing in my car? I had not been drinking, but I feared I would go to jail again, and it could go on my record. The cop confiscated the beer and told us not to do it again. He then let us go on our way. An arrest for open alcohol in the car could have killed my chances of getting into the Navy. *Another bullet dodged.*

Late October 1962, we gathered around the radio to listen to President Kennedy tell us about the Cuban Missile Crisis. We were worried a war would start. A sobering moment. They might pull us out of college and draft us into the Army. Again, I fell behind in my math class, Calculus III, and flunked it. My grade point was down to a 1.7 for the term. I dodged probation since my overall was still above 2.0. Grades were a disaster for our room. The room average was 0.9 GPA and four students, including Jim Beall, lost their student eligibility. I had the second highest GPA of six students with a 1.7. Only Steve Hayscar, a brilliant guy, was above me with a 2.7 GPA. I believe Fall '62 was the only time Steve had less than a 3.0 GPA. The other four roommates would not be returning for the winter quarter.

My former roommate, Joe, recruited me for his fraternity and I tried to pledge, but my low-grade point average prevented me from joining. In hindsight, the fraternity experience would have been good for me. But then I might have never met my future wife. Again, I was a hostage to fortune and fate. Perhaps not joining the fraternity was a good thing for me?

In the fall of 1962, one guy on the third floor of East Shaw Hall ran the "Turkey Trot," a 10K race. He won the race, and the university gave our precinct a live turkey. The dorm's kitchen would cook it for them on Thanksgiving. The third-floor guys decided executing the turkey was cruel and unusual punishment for a simple crime of being a turkey at Thanksgiving. To prevent the turkey's demise, we moved him into room 376. We built a cage out of a bunk bed. We laid the bunk bed on its side with a mattress over the top. Having a turkey in my room was noisy and smelly.

Our Precinct Monitor, read floor boss, said the turkey in our room violated so many rules he could not count them. He called the authorities; they were told to take our turkey away. We could not allow it to happen, so we snuck the turkey out of the dorm. We hid the turkey in the woods near campus, still using the bed as a cage. Saturday, November 24, MSU played Illinois. We carried our turkey onto the football field at halftime to protest killing turkeys at Thanksgiving. The university confiscated the turkey, and we never learned what happened to our temporary roommate.

After the fall disaster in room 376, MSU decided that the six-man room was not a good idea. In the winter term, 1963, 376 became a four-man room. Steve Hayscar and I were the only original members in the room from the fall of 1961. We had new roommates, two genuinely nice, down-to-earth guys. One of the new roommates was a neatness freak and our room always looked like it was ready for inspection. With my lack of interest in my engineering major's classes, I knew I did not want to be an engineer. USAF flight training is what I wanted, and that required a degree. Unsure of what I should pursue, I went to the student counseling center and told them of my disinterest in engineering. They gave me a test to figure out my career preferences. I rated high in the working alone career areas and exceptionally low in the group social settings. #1 one was a research physicist, #2 farmer, and #3 pilot. The test results confirmed I should follow my dreams of becoming a pilot.

I had a good winter term, with close to a 3.0 GPA. The four-man room made it easier to concentrate on my studies. Becoming an Air Force pilot became my goal. I planned to go into advanced AFROTC during my last two years of college. In the spring of '63, I took Air Force flight training aptitude tests. I scored high on the written tests. They scheduled me to go to Selfridge Air Force Base in Mt. Clemens, Michigan, for a USAF Fight Physical. I flunked the Fight Physical because of my motor scooter accident in 1958.

They felt I may have suffered a concussion which excluded me from any flying position, including navigator. The disqualification devastated me. The Air Force had shattered my childhood dream of flying in the military. Advanced AFROTC was now not a consideration. If I could not fly, a military career no longer appealed to me. With my changing attitude and uncertainty, my relationships changed. Marge and I stopped seeing each other in the spring.

CHANGE OF MAJOR

In the spring, I dropped out of engineering and elected to pursue a degree in Industrial Arts. Many of my engineering credits would transfer into the curriculum. It made for a logical change. I met with my academic advisor, Doctor McLane, a Navy Reservist, and a pilot. Though he had not flown for the Navy. A private pilot, he owned his own airplane and flew with the Civil Air Patrol. He filled me with stories of his adventures in the Navy during WWII. We hit it off. He looked over my transcript and said I should have a major in Industrial Arts and a minor in either math or physical science. I was not that excited about being a shop teacher, but it appeared to be a path for a job after I graduated. I was a hands-on guy and thought teaching auto shop classes might be a fit for me. In the summer, I worked for my dad at Dearborn Steel Tubing. He was getting ready to conduct 1964 Comet's 100,000-mile endurance test at Daytona International Speedway. They let me work on the cars being prepared for the test.

JUNIOR YEAR

In the fall of 1963, I returned to MSU and back to room 376 East Shaw Hall which still was a four-man room. Steve Hayscar and Bill Noch, my roommates from the fall of 1961, remained. I don't remember the fourth man. Switching majors was the right move. The classes were likeable, and my grades improved. The other students and I hit it off. Despite being turned down for Air Force flight training, my fascination with flying remained. I kept reading flying stories and looked up every time I heard an airplane fly over me.

JFK KILLED

Friday, November 22, I got out of class early and started driving down to Ann Arbor in my '63 Ford Falcon. Another cousin, Dave Beall, Jim's brother, who attended the University of Michigan, was having a party. I planned to join him. I tuned the radio to 760 AM, WJR. Pulling on to I-96 at Okemos Road, my program interrupted when an announcer broke in. He said someone had shot President Kennedy in Dallas, Texas. No further details came fourth, and they returned to the regularly scheduled programming. My mind raced.

What is happening? Why did it have to happen? A world gone mad.

The music continued for another ten minutes. Then the radio station interrupted the program again with continuous coverage of JFK's assassination. The county was in a state of shock and disbelief engulfed the county. I got to Dave's apartment in Ann Arbor, and we made a trip downtown to get drinks. We walked into the bars in downtown Ann Arbor. I was under the legal drinking age, but nobody asked for ID. We mourned the loss of a beloved president that night. At a newsstand, I picked up a Detroit News Extra Edition, it headlined KENNDY DEAD. It cost a dime. We drank until very late, and I don't know how I got back to the apartment. I woke up hungover the next day. No one else was up. I hopped in my car and drove back to MSU. The school called off Saturday's MSU football game against Illinois. MSU canceled classes on Monday November 25, for JFK's memorial service. The campus was in mourning.

NEW ROOMMATE

In the fall of 1963, 376 East Shaw remained an unruly room. My roommates would stay up all night playing cards and shooting the bull. I couldn't get any sleep. One night I had enough interrupted sleep. A buddy, Bob Sellers, had an empty bed in his two-man room down the hall. In the middle of the night, I moved into Bob's room, 379 East Shaw Hall. His room suited me, and I asked Bob if I could move in. He said sure. I moved all my belongings into Bob's room. The arrangement worked out until our Precinct Monitor found out. He ordered me back into 376 and said I could not live in 379 because they had not officially assigned me to that room. I asked him to give me time to make it official, but he said, "No, you must move out right now!"

What a jerk!

So, I packed up my stuff and took it back down to 376. I dumped a lump in the middle of room 376. Then I went down to the Dorm Master and explained why I wanted to move out of 376. He agreed with me and officially moved me to 379. A half hour after being kicked out of 379 by the "Floor Boss," I picked up my lump and officially moved back into 379. I would stay there until I left the dorm in spring 1964. Bob and I became lifelong friends.

I really enjoyed the Industrial Arts classes. The hands-on aspect was right up my alley. My grades improved. I enjoyed close to a 3.0 GPA. My dad gave me a car that had been used in the 100,000-mile reliability test: a 1963 Comet. It became the focus of my projects. I planned to make the dashboard look like an aircraft instrument panel. In my metals class, I fabricated a new dashboard. Colored lights, switches and gauges covered the new imitation instrument panel. I rewired the car to make the switches functional. In the Comet's trunk, I made room for an extra 12-gallon gas tank. The car could carry 25 gallons. The fuel transfer system was more complicated than most airplanes with multiple selector valves and fuel pumps.

In the spring of 1964, I elected to finish my minor in math by taking one more geometry class. Geometry had always come easy to me. But the course was a non-linear geometry class based on Einstein's theory of relativity. The class was beyond me, and I could not comprehend the material. After about three weeks, I failed an exam and tried to drop the course. But I could not drop the class because I had a failing grade. I quit going to class and got an F.

Drinking under the legal age in Ingham County, where MSU was located, was illegal for everyone under the legal age, but carried significant consequences for MSU students. Underage students found with alcohol in Ingham County, the home of MSU, could face disenrollment. We had to plan all our parties outside of Ingham County. One of our winter indoor hangouts was the Crest Motel, near M-59 on Grand River Avenue. The owner would rent us an empty room without furniture for about $50 for the night. If someone stayed the night with their date, he would put the bed back into the room for another $20. Because it was in Livingston County, we were safe from MSU oversight rules. The hotel became a regular hangout for the precinct nine crew.

Springtime meant outdoor parties and alcohol. We had found a good place to party in Shiawassee County: an out-of-the-way spot in the woods near a gravel pit. A former roommate set me on a blind date with his girlfriend's friend. He asked me because I had a car, and he did not. We went to Yankely Dorm on the MSU Campus to meet our dates. Two girls came down: one was very attractive; one was much bigger and maybe not so attractive. Yep, I easily guessed which one was my date. I got to the party spot. Not interested in my date, I drank a lot. I got so drunk I was close to passing out. Lying on the hood of my car, I watched the stars spin around in the night sky. My former roommate suggested we should go, and since I was smashed, he should drive. *Good idea,* I thought.

I got back to my room 379 and fell asleep. At four in the morning, I woke up. The lights were on. Bob wasn't back, nor were any other guys from Precinct Nine who were at the party. I didn't know what was going on and I was worried. About 0800, I got a call from Bob Sellers asking if I could come over to Owosso and pick him up. Shiawassee county jail was releasing him. The sheriff raided the party shortly after I left. He arrested 17 students and put them in jail. He was up for reelection and wanted to make a name for himself by getting tough on these student parties.

During the summer of 1964, I worked for my dad at Dearborn Steel Tubing. I teamed up with Clark Ward, a friend from high school. We hauled Jim Clark's Indy Race Car around to dealers as a promotion program for Ford.

SENIOR YEAR

Now twenty-one years old and eligible to live off campus, I returned to MSU in the fall of 1964. Renting a place was a novel experience of freedom for me as a student. I had girls over, had beer in the icebox, and no floor boss checking up on me. I could start living life as an adult. Ed, a party buddy from Precinct Nine, and I found and shared a one-bedroom apartment at 1022 Washtenaw, on the State Capital's west side. Ed and I worked out our responsibilities. I would cook, and he would clean up. I enjoyed cooking because I was building something with my hands. My Grandma Hotton sent me a receipt for pasties. I loved making them.

Three guys from Precinct Nine East Shaw Hall moved into a three-bedroom apartment at 2001 ½ East Michigan Avenue. It became the party hang out for the men who had been in East

Shaw Hall Precinct Nine since the fall of a 1961. We were our own small fraternity. I did not do as well in my classes as I had while living in the dorm. Maybe freedom was not such a good thing.

One night after too much partying, I was driving back from a 2001 ½ party while definitely under the influence of alcohol. My lights were off. I was so drunk I forgot to turn them on. On the way back to my apartment at 1:30 in the morning, I came across a police barricade. I knew I was in big trouble. The cop came up to my window and asked what I was doing. I told him I was going home. He said, "Well, turn your damn lights on and get the hell out of here. I got a murder on my hands and no time to deal with drunks like you."

I said, "Yes sir" and like he told me, I got the hell out of there. *Wow! Another big bullet dodged.* I had yet to learn from all these bullets dodged. I may have had a guardian angel watching over me and guiding events in my favor.

I was still building model airplanes and reading aviation history books. In our bedroom, I put up a map of WWII in the Pacific and hung my models over my desk. I read about the Navy's role in the Pacific War and thought those Navy pilots were tops in the flying business.

In the summer, the Gulf of Tonkin incident took place. Our new president, Lyndon B. Johnson, received congressional approval to build up our forces in Vietnam. He responded to what later turned out to be a fabricated North Vietnamese aggression. The election was coming up and there were concerns of we would become involved in another war. LBJ said his opponent, Barry Goldwater, would get us involved in a war. He ran as the Peace President. To reassure the American people he would not expand the war, he issued a statement two weeks before his election. "We are not about to send American boys 9 or 10,000 miles away from home to do what Asian boys ought to do for themselves" Because I was of draft age and could end up in a war, and because I preferred not being shot at, I voted for LBJ. By the end of 1964, draft numbers were increasing. Within the year, I would be in the military and on my way to Vietnam. I have not voted democrat since 1964.

In February 1965, I took a week-long break from MSU to fly down to Daytona Beach to visit my father. I flew down in my dad's Lockheed 12A, baby Electra. His pilot, Bill "Firecan" Haddock, was a WWII P-47 pilot. Bill let me sit in the right seat and talk on the radio. I loved it; I felt like a pilot. My role playing as Bill's co-pilot grabbed me and reinforced that I wanted to be a pilot. Flying became my focus for the rest of my life.

JOINING THE NAVY

LBJ was cranking up the war in Vietnam. I might have been eligible for the draft when my four years of college were up. If I had to go into the service, I would want to go as a pilot. In 1961, I joined AFROTC at Michigan State and tried to get into Air Force pilot training. I thought would be the easiest path because the Air Force had more pilots. However, due to my motor scooter accident, the Air Force had turned me down for pilot training. The USAF was not an option. But Navy flight training might be another possibility. I did not know how a person became a Navy pilot. I needed to find out more about Navy Flight Training. *In my mind, I was thinking, Naval Aviation was an elite competitive program. I was not sure they would select me even if I applied.*

After I got back from Florida, I was sitting in the Student Union reading the Michigan State University school paper. An ad in the paper caught my attention. It said the Naval Aviation Recruiter would be at the Student Union on Wednesday. They were recruiting candidates to become Navy pilots. *Again, the fickle finger of fate crossed my path when I saw that ad.*

On Wednesday, I went to the Student Union at Grand River and Abbott Road. The recruiter was upstairs in the second-floor ballroom. I took the stairs up to the second floor. The large ballroom was empty except for a table set up in a corner with some men standing around it. I walked up to the table covered with a blue felt cloth and embossed with gold Navy Wings. Navy brochures and posters covered the table. The recruiter was a Lieutenant Junior Grade "Plow Back" pilot, in his dress blues. "Plow Backs" were pilots who had just received their wings and came back to their hometowns on temporary duty to help with pilot recruiting. He acknowledged me while he was talking to some other men.

When he finished talking to other men, he extended his arm, shook my hand, and greeted me with, "How can I help you?"

I looked him straight in the eyes and said, "I would like to become a Navy pilot." He asked if I wanted information on the program. I said, "No, I just want to do whatever it takes to start the process."

The recruiter gave me an information sheet to fill out with, name, address, projected graduation date, major, etc. He then said there were a couple of tests I needed to take to determine if I was qualified for pilot training. He took me to a room on the third floor. Other candidates were there taking the tests. The first test was like a college entrance exam. It included math, English, mechanical comprehension, and figure/shape orientation. He timed the test for each section. My pre-engineering math and physics made these tests easy. Three years later, after I got my wings, I learned my score was the highest grade one could get. The test gave me a nine, four standards deviations above the mean of five.

A second test gathered biographical inventory. The questions asked about what I liked, things I had done, like riding a motorcycle, working on cars, sports, etc. I scored a seven, two standard deviations above the mean. The recruiter told me I had passed the tests and fit the profile for a Navy Pilot. *He was telling me I could become a Navy pilot. I could not believe it. They wanted little old me. Could it be a childhood fantasy coming true?*

Everything changed when I learned that Naval aviation was a top-level program I was qualified to pursue. Suddenly, my life focused on getting accepted into Navy Flight Training. Now I clearly knew what I wanted to do with my life. The recruiter said they would contact me to schedule a flight physical and interview for the Aviation Reserve Officer Candidate program. In the AVROC program, a candidate went to Aviation Officer Candidate School (AOCS) for six weeks one summer. Then, the next summer after graduating, they returned for another six weeks.

The recruiter gave me a booklet about Naval Aviation. It had the USS Enterprise's picture on the cover that turned out to be a connection to my future. Ten years later, I would get orders that sent me to the USS Enterprise in a ship's crew billet. Better known in Navy terms as "Sheep's Company," because you were part of the herd of 3,500 men. About three weeks later, recruiters notified me it was too late to get into the upcoming summer's AVROC program. They told me they would consider me for AOCS in June 1966 after graduation from MSU. The recruiters from NAS Grosse Ile, Michigan, would call me and set up a flight physical in the coming summer.

By May 1965, the Vietnam War's needs had affected the Pilot Training Rate and demanded a higher output than seen in the early 60s. When some colleges dropped NROTC, the Navy lost a source of Naval Officer pilot candidates. AOCS became the source to fill the pilot candidate shortage. AOCS would need to raise its output to meet the demand. To increase the number of candidates going through the program, they reduced the length of AOCS from 16 to 11 weeks.

SOLO FLIGHT

Since I was going to give learning to fly a shot, I figured I should see if I had any talent for flying. My dad leased a Cessna 182, N1971X. My first instructional flight was on February 22, 1965, with my dad's pilot, Bill Haddock, in the C-182. A high-performance airplane meant I started my training in a more advanced aircraft than normal.

On May 8, 1965, I soloed in a C-172, N7846U, at Willow Run Airport. I had 18.5 hours of instruction. Bill turned me loose for solo. He got out and left me in the pilot's seat after telling the tower he was letting me fly solo on runway 14. When he got out, he picked up some grass clippings and threw them up in the air. Watching them fall, he checked the winds. He told me to make three takeoffs and landings and make sure I came back to pick him up. Bill stood there in the grass at the side of runway 14 and watched me take off.

Willow Run was still a busy commercial airline airport. Airliners were using runway 23L, while I worked an opposite traffic pattern from the bigger airliner traffic. The tower cleared a United Airlines DC-8 for takeoff path that crossed my runway. The tower gave me a "Land and Hold Short" clearance on my second landing. A land and hold short only allows the landing airplane to use the landing runway up to the intersection with the next runway. After the DC-8 took off, they cleared me for takeoff. Back then, we knew little about wing tip vortices. Luckily, I encountered no problems.

After completing three solo landings, I picked up Bill Haddock from the runway's side and taxied back to the ramp. The FBO gave me a Cessna Solo Trophy, and I had my picture taken with it. Now there was no such thing as too much flying. Just in case the weather was good enough to fly, I would drive to the airport only to be told, no, the weather is too bad today. My total focus in life now was becoming a pilot.

GOODBYE TO SOME

In spring term in 1965, flying captivated me. One day, I walked by a bookstore on Grand River in East Lansing. I saw a book in the window with a picture of a B-24 with an engine on fire. The title was *Goodbye to Some,* and it looked like a first-class read, so I bought it. It was a fictional story of a WWII Navy patrol squadron flying PB4Y-1s. A PB4Y-1 was a Navy Patrol version of an Amry Air Force B-24 bomber. The squadron flew patrols out of the Philippines along the coast of what would later become Vietnam.

I had trouble putting it down and read it a couple times. During WWII, the author, Gordon Forbes, flew the PB4Y-1 missions in VPB-111. He gave me a first-person story of flying patrol airplanes and what it was like to be part of a crew. Forbes put me in the cockpit as a pilot of a patrol plane. Since I was trying to join the Navy to become a pilot, I decided I wanted to fly patrol planes and be part of a patrol plane crew. An irony was, four years later, I would fly patrol airplanes from the Philippines along the coast of Vietnam. The book ends with the book's main character crashing on a Pacific Island on his way home from the war.

MEETING LOU

Another major life event happened in the spring of 1965. One of my friends from East Shaw Hall, Tommy, was dating a freshman girl. One night, he brought her by my house in Lansing. I had a chin-up bar set in the door to my bedroom because I wanted to be in shape to meet Navy Physical Training (PT) minimums should the Navy select me for flight training. The girl Tommy brought over was on the MSU swimming and diving team. She grabbed the chin-up bar and started doing pulls ups. I thought "Wow! this is kind of neat!" She was cute, athletic, and had a big smile. However, she was dating a friend of mine, therefore off limits.

Her name was Luesta Strader. Six months later, we would have our first date, and the next year we would get married. *Life is strange how things come about. A random meeting with the woman who would become my lifelong partner. Is it divine guidance? A guardian angel. Is there a big plan? Or is it a random occurrence? I do not know, and I do not question it.*

MEET MR. LEE IACOCCA

Late in the spring, I was driving my Comet back to MSU. I drove by my dad's house in Belleville, Michigan. My wallet was getting empty. I wanted to hit him up for some money before returning to school. When I went into his house, I saw my dad was talking to a friend of his. The man wore a T-shirt, shorts, and shower shoes. They had been out water skiing on Belleville Lake. My dad introduced me to the man: "Meet Mr. Lee Iacocca."

I said "Hi" as he shook my hand.

Lee Iacocca was the Ford Mustang's father and a rising star at the Ford Motor Company. My dad had worked with him at Dearborn Steel Tubing to develop the Mustang.

Mr. Iacocca asked, "What are you doing?"

"Going to Michigan State University."

"What are you going to do after you graduate?"

"I am going to be a Navy pilot."

He looked at me and said, "That is the dumbest goddamn thing I have ever heard of." Then, Mr. Iacocca said, "Here's what you should do. Go back to MSU, get your degree in Mechanical Engineering, and there will be a job waiting for you at Ford

Motor Company. Ford will send you to the U of M to get your MBA. You will have a real future at Ford Motor."

I thanked him and said, "I'm pursuing my childhood dream of being a Navy pilot."

He looked at my dad and said, "Kids, what are you going to do?" He wished me luck, and that was my meeting with Lee Iacocca. In hindsight, maybe I missed an opportunity, but I doubt the Ford job would ever have been as fulfilling as my Navy experience.

NAS GROSSE ILE

In June 1965, the Navy notified me to go to NAS Grosse Ile, Michigan for an Aviation Candidate Flight Physical. Bill Haddock, my, dad's pilot and my flight instructor, said to me, "Don't tell them anything that they can't find out for themselves." Bill said he had fallen off his motorcycle on the way to his Army Air Force physical during WWII. Although he had laid in a ditch for a few hours, he did not tell the Army.

He gave me good advice, and I never told the Navy about my 1958 motor scooter accident. During the eye exam, I tested 20/25 on near vision in my right eye. I missed one too many letters. Failing the eye test would disqualify me from Navy pilot training. The recruiter, who escorted me through the physical exam, pulled the Corpsman aside. He said, "Let him try again. He is a pilot candidate, and we really need pilots." They gave me another try, and I passed. *A bullet dodged; I was still in the running. Fate had put me in the right place at the right time with the right outcome.*

After I finished the physical, the recruiter gave me a package of forms to fill out. He told me I would be called for an interview. In August, I went back to Grosse Ile and to be interviewed by a couple of Navy pilots. They talked to me about the Navy and asked me some questions. I fit the profile of most candidates coming into AOCS as a firstborn male child. In 1966 only men entered Navy Flight Training. The questions slip my mine, except one. They asked me "Do you prefer to ride on the back of a motorcycle or drive the motorcycle?" I answered, "I enjoy driving because I knew who is in charge." For a pilot's answer, they liked that.

The recruiters did not tell me about the challenges I would face at Aviation Officer Candidate School. They did not tell me how the Marine Drill Instructors would test my motivation with their unrelenting stress to perform at higher levels. I knew nothing about the physical training demands, and the unending threat of elimination. Instead, they told me how great the beaches and golf courses were in Pensacola. A massive surprise awaited me a year later when I reported to AOCS.

My Navy recruiter told me I should stop taking civilian flight lessons. He told me I could pick up bad habits that would have to be unlearned to become a Navy pilot. On September 13, 1965, I took my last civilian flight as a student pilot. My logbook showed I had about 40 hours total flight time of which 10 hours were solo. In Navy flight training, my civilian flying gave me a leg up. I had developed a landing sight picture and understood how an airplane responds to control inputs. Plus, flying in a complex aircraft, I had learned to use the prop RPM and Manifold Pressure for power.

If I did not get into the Navy, I would look at becoming an Auto Shop teacher. I wanted to improve my qualifications, so I got a job as an auto mechanic at Bob Borst Lincoln Mercury in Birmingham, Michigan. The job filled my summer vacation. I made good money, averaging $100 a week, or around $5,000/yr. It matched starting pay for a schoolteacher. Late in the summer, I quit my job and went back to school. The dealership tried talking me into staying on as an auto mechanic. It flattered me, but my focus was Navy Flight Training. My college roommate

Bob Sellars got married that summer and honored me by asking me to be his best man. He married a girl named Linda from the 2000½ party gang.

SENIOR YEAR PART II

When I started MSU, I was in the 1965's class. But I since had changed majors, I wouldn't have enough credits to graduate with my class. That fall I returned to MSU. Although being a Navy pilot became my primary focus, it was not a sure thing. There was still a demanding selection process to complete. In the fall of 1965, I returned to Michigan State. They only offered one of the two required courses I needed to complete my Industrial Arts degree requirements. I took a three-credit photo shop class, ED 441D ADV PRINT GRAPHICS. I would not be a full-time student. So, I elected to repeat first year ATL 103 where I got a D in the spring of 62, and School and Society where I had also received a D in the winter of 65. Repeating these courses would improve my grade point average. It also made me a full-time student and I would be eligible to live in the dorm again. I returned to East Shaw Hall on the third floor, room 378, a two-man room. Many of my friends from previous years still lived there. I was looking forward to going back. It would be a fun way to end my time on campus at MSU.

ACCEPTANCE TO NAVY FLIGHT TRAINING

Returning to school, I received no additional updates from the Navy. In reality, I felt the chances of me getting selected were low. I was an average guy. Unaware of events in early September, I did not know; the Navy had considered me fully qualified and selected me as highly recommended. In early

October, I came home one weekend. Mom and I planned to attend a football game in Ann Arbor to watch U of M play MSU. I remember it vividly. While driving down Pontiac Trail to Ann Arbor, near where highway US 23 was under construction, mom surprised me with the news, "Oh, the Navy called last week and informed me they have selected you for Navy Flight Training." *The Navy wants me to become a Navy pilot?*

I could not believe it. I always regarded Naval Aviation as an elite program, probably out of my reach. Now they have invited me to become a member of an exclusive club. Becoming a military pilot would no longer be a childhood fantasy, with selection being uncertain. Now they offered me the opportunity of a lifetime. The knowledge of my acceptance brought me some apprehension. No longer chasing selection. I was now thinking, *I'd better watch out. What I ask for, I might get it. I would now have to prove myself. There were doubts. Was I good enough to make it through the program?*

First thing Monday morning I called my recruiter. When I called, he congratulated me and confirmed my selection. They assigned me to a class starting in June 1966. The recruiter asked me to schedule a date to visit Grosse Ile and take my Navy Enlistment oath. I set up Wednesday, October 27.

FIRST DATE WITH LOU

Since Tommy was no longer dating "Lou" Strader, I asked him would mind if I asked her out.

"You ought to take Lou out, she's just like you," he said.

"Give me her number," I said. I called her on Tuesday, October 13, and Lou said yes. The next weekend, Saturday, October 16, I had my first date with Lou. We went to the football game and saw MSU destroy the Ohio State University football team. Michigan State was #1 in the nation. They beat Ohio State

35-10. MSU held OSU to negative rushing yards. Woody Haynes, the Ohio State coach, was livid on the sidelines. Sitting in the student section with Lou, cheering on the Michigan State Spartans was fun. We hit it off, and I felt flattered by her interest in me.

After the game, we went to 2000 ½ Michigan Avenue for a post-game party. We experienced a connection that was almost love at first sight. In 1965, women had to be back in their dorms by 11:00 p.m. on weeknights, 1:00 a.m. on weekends. I had to sign a note promising I would have my date back to her dorm by the curfew. If I failed to get her back on time, the school could ground her. For women, college was *"in loco parentis,"* Latin for "in the place of a parent," in the mid-1960s.

From our first date, I wanted to spend every minute I could with her. I was afraid she would get away. Many of these dates ended up with the gang in 2000 ½ which was still the party house for the former residents from Precinct Nine East Shaw Hall. We were together all the time. I worked on selling myself to Lou and told her I was going to be a Navy pilot. The Navy had selected me for an elite program. Navy pilots were successful people, and I had a bright future. In early November, I took the serious step of meeting her parents. They seemed to size me up as someone who might be a good match for their daughter.

On October 27, 1965, Captain R. K. Brown, the Commanding Officer of NAS Grosse Ile, administered the oath of office and swore me into the Navy. My swearing in date was important because it established my Pay Base Entry Date (PBED). It would determine the date of all my future pay raises. They slated me for a June 29, 1966, class date at AOCS and assigned me to class 25-66. They made a clerical error in my report date. It would make me a day late reporting to Pensacola, but I did not discover the error until I showed up in Pensacola. With a war going on, suddenly things seemed a little more serious.

In the photo shop class, we learned how to develop photo negatives. In a dark room illuminated by a red light, I placed some photos in the photo press. I was about to flatten them, and the lid was open. Someone bumped into the lid, and it slammed shut on my hand. The pain was terrible. Expletives that would make a sailor blush flowed from my mouth. The instructor came in and reprimanded me for using such foul language. He said, "You cannot talk like that in front of students."

He looked at my hand. It seemed fine because the red light did not show the blood on my hand. Then we left the dark room, into white light. He saw a large gash in my finger, and it had covered my hand with blood. Blood was running down my arm and dripping onto the floor. He said, "Holy shit, we better get you to the clinic." *So much for controlling one's language.* The instructor quickly drove me to the campus clinic. They put three stitches in my finger and bandaged my hand. Luckily, the injury would not impact my Naval aviation candidacy.

ONE MORE CLASS

In early December, the Navy sent mom a letter reassuring her. They told her they would take care of me and give me the best training available. Lou and I spent time together over Christmas going to gatherings with both families. On New Year's Eve, we went to a party at the Rooster Tail on the Detroit River with my father and his second wife, Joyce. To test how interested Lou might be in me, I bought her a fake engagement ring. I gave it to her to wear to the party. She gladly accepted wearing the fake ring and gave me a big kiss. Wow! She enjoyed wearing the fake ring, and it was a sign she might want to marry me. I was madly in love with Lou. Little did we know New Year's Eve would be our wedding date a year later. I was crazy about this woman and ready to spend the rest of my life with her.

I returned to Michigan State in January 1966. I needed one more three-credit Industrial Arts class, only offered in winter quarter, to complete my on-campus class work. Because I was not a full-time student, living on campus was not an option. I shared a room in an off-campus house in East Lansing with another student whose name I do not remember. Staying in East Lansing to be around Lou was important to me. Lou was busy with school as a full-time student. Many nights we didn't see each other.

With my free time, I got a part-time job as a cab driver at Varsity Cab Company. They paid me 50 percent of the fare, and I got to keep tips. But I had to buy my gas. I ended up making about $1.00 an hour, barely minimum wage. We did not have radios in the cars in 1966. The company had a cab stand at the corner of Mac Avenue and Grand River, with a telephone at window height. I waited there for calls to pick up fares. The job was fun, but students were the worst tippers on the planet. Once, an older gentleman asked me where he could find some girly action. I did not know where to go, but I took him to the hotel near the Capitol Building in downtown Lansing for an excellent fare, and he gave me a nice tip. I wonder if he got lucky?

June was on the horizon with my upcoming departure to Pensacola. I knew I wanted to marry Lou. I felt she wanted to marry me. In February, we went engagement ring shopping at Fox's Jeweler in Frandor Shopping Center and picked out a wedding/engagement ring set. She thought we were just looking, but I was serious. I started saving my taxicab driver pay and bought the ring set with plans to ask her to marry me before I left for Pensacola.

On March 20, 1966, we were shopping at Hudson's in the Northland Shopping Center. In the parking lot, I slipped the engagement ring on to her finger and asked her to marry me. She accepted. It thrilled me beyond belief that she wanted to marry me. We planned on getting married in June 1968 after she graduated from Michigan State. We went to my house and announced our engagement. My sisters were excited. They really liked Lou. That night, we went to her house and told her parents. They were happy for us, but I did not think they were ready to lose their daughter.

STUDENT TEACHING

During the spring quarter of 1966, I was a student teacher at Barnum Junior High School in Birmingham. As a student shop teacher, I taught drafting, woodworking, and metals. To graduate from MSU, I needed to finish student teaching. I lived at home. My time with my mom and sisters was a return to the life I had known over the years growing up in Troy. My heart was not into my student teaching. I did everything I was supposed to do and received good grades. My student teacher mentor told me I would be an excellent teacher, but I was ready to move on. Becoming a Navy pilot was my goal. To get in shape for AOCS, I started running up and down Beach Road after school, along with push-ups and sit-ups. By June, I was running two miles in 14 minutes.

To monitor our progress as teachers, we had weekly meetings with Mrs. Reed, our student teacher supervisor. We had to give reports on what we were learning and how the students were reacting to our roles as teachers. After I had given my report, another student teachers, a girl teaching English at Seaholm High School, commented on my presentation.

She said shop teachers were not teachers, because they worked with students who were not college material that only worked with their hands and not their heads. I was speechless; she was so full of herself. The student teacher supervisor said we all had our teaching roles in different areas. We no longer have shop classes in most schools and the reason could be many teachers see no value in students not going to college.

In May, I received orders to report to NAS Grosse Ile to take my entrance flight physical and ensure I was still qualified to enter flight training. Because of my eye problem at the previous year's exam, I was sweating the eye test. But I encountered no troubles, and they cleared me to go to AOCS. Two weeks later, I got my airlines tickets and travel orders to proceed to Pensacola on June 29.

In the spring of 1966, shop teachers were in high demand. I received inquiries from many schools, which I gracefully declined. But the Owosso High School's Principal got me on the phone. I remember talking on the old rotary dial phone on the kitchen wall at 4853 Beach. He told me he had a brand-new shop facility at his high school. It would be a great opportunity for a teacher such as myself. I thanked him and told him I was going into the Navy. He told me I could get a draft deferment as a schoolteacher and would not have to join the military. Again, I told him I appreciated the offer, but I was fulfilling a childhood dream of being a Navy pilot. His voice became a little louder and more concerned. He told me I could end up going to Vietnam when I could safely teach shop in his high school. I said I understood that but becoming a Navy pilot was what I really wanted. He came back saying my dream was the dumbest thing he had ever heard of and, if I was that stupid, he did not want me in his classroom.

SAYING GOODBYE

In early June, I skipped the graduation ceremonies. I knew few people in the class of 1966 because most of my friends had already graduated. I had three weeks left before I reported to Pensacola, and I wanted to spend time with Lou. We went to

Lion's Head, Ontario, Canada and spent a week with Grandpa Meakin and Grandma Lou. Grandpa made sure we were in separate bedrooms. We fished with grandpa. Lou and I hiked the trails in the woods and learned to play card games with grandpa. On the way home, we were driving a Ford Cortina and stopped on the shore road to take pictures on the flat rocks. Lou was standing on the flat rocks on the road to Lion's Head. Both grandparents' cottages were in the background. I spent many summers there while growing up. But that life was behind me now.

Lou started summer school the next week. I drove her back to MSU for our final weekend together before I left for Pensacola. We spent one last night together at the Crest Motel on Grand River Avenue near Fowlerville. The former party hangout for the Precinct Nine gang, staying there was a closing trace of my college days. *Those party days at the Crest Motel that we thought would never end were behind us now. Life had moved on, and I moved on with it.*

I dropped her off the next day at her dorm and would not see her again for three months. The drive home seemed long, again as a part of my life was ending. College was behind me. Soon, I'd no longer live in Michigan. I'd no longer spend time with Lou. I'd soon move from the comfortable to the unknown.

I had to put the '63 Comet into mothballs before I left for Pensacola. I started the car and warmed the engine up. With the engine running, I poured oil down the carburetor until the engine quit. An oil coating on all the interior parts would prevent corrosion while the car was in storage. I removed the valve covers to release all the rocker arms and take the tension off the valve springs. The Comet would stay in moth balls for over three years in the Beach Road garage.

Tuesday, June 28, 1966, was the last night of my life at home before I reported to Pensacola. The war in Vietnam was cranking up. Daily, the news told stories of shot down pilots becoming

POWs. The next day would be the first day of the rest of my life. To do something my last night at home, I went out for a beer with my college roommate, Bob, and Jack, a high school buddy. Bob worked for General Motors (GM) and was at a conference down at the GM headquarters in Detroit. We chatted over a couple of beers.

On the way home, Jack and I stopped for one more beer at a bar on Woodward Avenue south of 14-Mile Road. We had spent many nights cruising Woodward Avenue over the years. A last night on Woodward Avenue would be a way to say goodbye to cruising. The end of another connection to the life I knew. Thinking about the next day and the unknowns distracted me while reminiscing about our adventures on Woodward Avenue. Jack dropped me off at 4853 Beach Road about 10:00 p.m. Mom and I chatted a while before I went to bed.

PENSACOLA

Wednesday June 29, 1966, was one of most memorable days of my life. The Navy sent me my airline tickets and travel orders to Pensacola. I got up early that morning and put on some casual clothes, a popular Indian cotton Madras shirt, green chino pants, and brown penny loafers. Mom and my sisters, Pat, Betsy, and Peg, drove me to Detroit Metro Airport. A vivid memory seared into my mind, like a snapshot, as we drove down the driveway at 4853 Beach Road. At 6 a.m. the light was just coming over the horizon on a cloudless, sunny day. The dew reflected the morning light, and the sun cast the tree's shadows across the driveway.

Turning onto Beach Road, I looked over my shoulder and captured the house's image. I pressed the image into my mind. I knew I would never experience the same attachment again. Except for a brief time in Detroit, during my childhood, 4853

Beach had been my whole life up to this day. That life was over now, and I was going away to face different challenges.

The Delta Airlines DC-8 was leaving at around 8:30 a.m. We said goodbye at the gate; I lingered, not wanting to get on the airplane. As soon as I boarded, I felt alone. I was so close to tears.

Before we taxied, the captain discovered a problem with the aircraft. He announced there would be a delay before we could take off. He said if we wanted to, we could get off. I got off and found mom and the girls still waiting at the gate. We said goodbye again, which was much easier the second time. I had already experienced that feeling of loss.

One thing I knew would happen in Pensacola was a Math/Physics qualification test. The test would determine if my basic knowledge was adequate to complete Navy pilot ground school. I took my college physics textbook with me and studied on the way down to Pensacola.

My travels orders required me to change airlines in Atlanta. The connecting flight put me on an Eastern Airlines Lockheed Electra that would take me to Pensacola. Atlanta's terminal was under construction, a maze of tunnels, dead ends, and walkways. I wasn't sure I could find my gate, but I made the flight. We made a stop at Montgomery, Alabama. I got off the airplane, found a postcard, and mailed it to Lou. I wanted her to know I was thinking of her and did not know what would happen next. She might not hear from me for a while.

En route to Pensacola, we flew over the Navy training airfields in southern Alabama, and I saw T-28's in the landing pattern. In a few months, that flyer could be me. *In my mind, I knew it was a challenge to be met. I was lucky to be heading toward Pensacola.* When I stepped off the airplane onto the open ramp, the heat and humidity of Pensacola's southern summer struck me. I had experienced nothing like a southern summer before, and it took my breath away. The climate change from the cool dry summers in Michigan would challenge me in ways I did not yet know.

I wondered how I would get from Pensacola's airport to the Navy Base. Two other AOCS candidates from Detroit, Larry, and Bruce, were also looking for a ride to NAS Pensacola. We found a van. The driver had made the run many times before and knew exactly where to go. It seemed like a long ride down a series of side roads and detours. Going down one of streets, I remember seeing a junkyard with a scraped WWII Catalina patrol airplane. We were in a Navy town. The driver took us to the main gate at NAS Pensacola.

A Navy guard asked to see our orders and told the driver to take us some place on base. An orderly, peaceful setting permeated NAS Pensacola. We drove through a golf course, dotted with palm trees swaying in a soft breeze and sand traps filled with the pure white sand of Pensacola Beach. Officer housing, a collection of classic buildings with colorful shutters, surrounded by trees dripping Spanish moss, suggested another world of tradition and privilege. Next came a collection of sturdy two-story brick buildings lining the streets. These buildings housed the AOCS Battalions. My upcoming experiences in the Battalions would be anything except peaceful and orderly.

The airport van driver dropped us off at the Schools Command Duty Building, a little wooden shack off the Parade Ground's side. We went inside where man stamped our orders with our arrival time and date. It showed we reported to AOCS at 1412 on Wednesday, June 29. The sailors in the shack talked amongst themselves, snickering, laughing, and looking our way. They knew how unprepared we were for what awaited us. NAS Grosse Ile had made a mistake on our orders.

We were a day late.

The three of us were supposed to arrive No Later Than (NLT) 2400 on June 28, 1966. A Navy duty driver told us to get into the back of a beat up old gray Navy pickup truck. He had a smile on his face. He knew what we were about to encounter. We had no idea what would come next. In the pickup truck's bed, I squatted on my haunches and held on to the truck's side, careful not to get my clothes dirty. When I checked in, I wanted to make a good impression. The duty driver drove us a short distance to Building 699. He dropped us at the front door, pointed up the stairs, and told us to go inside. I climbed the steps into Bldg. 699, and my life was about to change. We met Sgt. Sanders, who screamed at us to get off his quarterdeck, and the change started. I passed my physical and academic tests and did more push-ups than I ever believed was possible. I finally made it through Indoc Battalion and with my class 25-66. Our class marched done the Grinder with our heavy loads to AOCS Battalion One, or "Batt I" as we called it.

PART 2
Navy Flight Training

Chapter One
Aviation Officer Candidate School (AOCS)

BATT I

We had made it through Indoc Battalion and were now living in Battalion One (Batt 1). The three separate buildings were known as Batt I, Batt II, and Batt III where AOCS candidates lived. The class experienced a more relaxed atmosphere than Indoc. When we went to chow, we could take our time, stand at ease in line and talk while eating. That weekend, the class officers taught us how to set up our rooms and prepare for inspections. The candidate officers were there to help us get ready for the next nine weeks. They shared their experiences on how they coped with the constant pressure.

My class met our Drill Instructor (DI), who would guide 25-66 through the AOCS obstacles for the next nine weeks. Schools Command assigned Gunny Weirling as our DI. Gunny was a Marine nickname for a Gunnery Sergeant. He was a WWII veteran who had invaded Tarawa. He wore the Purple Heart for wounds received there. Occasionally, over the weekend, the DIs would visit to check on our progress. We marched to church in our whites. The class had to march everywhere as a group. They had not secured us yet, which meant we were not free to come and go as we liked. Preparing for an upcoming inspection, PT sessions, and getting ready for the next nine weeks. AOCS academics consumed most of our time. Until they secured my class, life revolved around a small area made up of Batt I, the chow hall, the academic building, and the parade grounds.

CLASSROOM

For the next nine weeks, AOCS started with the typical Monday through Friday schedule, 0530 Reveille and 2200 Taps. The 0530 get up was easy, the sun came up early, and it gave us time to get our room organized, get dressed, and be outside ready for morning PT. We would run about two miles in about 15 minutes and then do exercises for another 15 minutes before getting back to our room. The shade behind Batt I was a great place to cool off after our morning run. We returned to our rooms to prepare for the day. Before going to breakfast, we would shower, get our uniforms ready for the day, and clean the room. After breakfast, we marched back to Batt I to pick up our bookbags and then marched in formation to Bldg. 633 for classroom instruction.

They issued us our books and a Navigator Flight bag to hold our books. The navigator's bag became our bookbags. The way we moved these bags was a military ritual. We carried the bookbags in our left hand. Doing so allowed our right hand free to render salutes if necessary. We followed the commands of "Up bookbags, up" and "Down bookbags, down" to lift and drop the bookbags in unison. All these rituals were part of molding us into a military unit.

On our first day of academics, we went to classroom Bldg. 633, for a couple of lectures from the higher ups in the chain of command. The classes were much the same as going to college. Classes included Naval History and World Affairs, Naval

Justice, and Naval Orientation. They showed us the schedules for the first five weeks, from Monday, July 11 to Friday, August 12. The schedule became our guide at AOCS. We were going through training with around 70 AVROCs who also lived in Batt I. The combination of AOCS and AVROC classes running simultaneously resulted in something unusual for class 25-66. We had bunk beds with six people in a room. They also customized our schedule to accommodate the AVROC students going through the same training as class 25-66. The AVROCs departed after their six-week summer orientation, and we experienced less joggling of our schedule.

All the classroom work was in Bldg. 633 where an instructor would take us through the subject. After exercising and getting a little sleep at night, staying awake while sitting in a cool classroom would challenge anyone. My eyes would slam shut. The instructor would come to me and tell me to stand up in the room's rear. Then, if I fell asleep again, I would fall and wake up. It was brutal. The worst class to fight off sleep was the Study Habits class, a reading improvement course. They shut the lights in the room off and they projected a controlled reader on the screen. Everyone slept in Study Habits class, and I doubt anyone became a better reader.

The classroom work required rote memorization in areas new to me. With little time to study, I struggled in ground school. A particular incident comes to mind. In Naval Orientation, a Boatswain's Mate Chief was teaching shipboard terms, like deck, bulkhead, head, hatch, etc. He explained the port and starboard terms by saying, "When standing looking at the bow, port is on the left, and starboard is on the right." On the daily quiz, I answered just the opposite. I got a razing from the Chief about being an ill-informed "landlubber." The Navy slang for someone who had never been to sea and had little knowledge of ships. In correction, he showed me the layout of a ship. He had given me directions from the bridge. Since I had never been on a ship, my orientation when he said looking at the bow was from the pier.

Every day was different. Sometimes we had classroom lessons, swimming, PT, drills, or inspectors. The ritual I used to show myself what was behind me was that I marked off each day on the schedule with an X, then at the weeks end, I put lines through the entire week. Now another week was behind me, and I could see progress by looking at the Xs and lines through the weeks.

PHYSICAL FITNESS

The first week in Batt I, they introduced us to the Obstacle Course, better known as the "O" Course. The "O" Course was a series of obstacles to test our upper body strength and our legs with short distance sprinting. A major difficulty in running the course was the sand. I could not get any traction. I would push off and the sand just pushed backwards, which slowed everyone down. The "O" Course started with a tire run leading to the climbing bulkheads, one with a rope and one without. We had to meet a minimum "O" Course time to graduate from AOCS.

I had never been a jock and found myself at a real disadvantage. My times did not match my classmates. We needed to complete the course in four minutes to qualify. I was doing over four minutes at first, well above the time needed to qualify. The last obstacle was a maze of iron pipes we had to weave through. The "O" Course took every bit of my energy and wiped me out. But I found if I used my arms to pull myself around the corners, it would speed me up and cut down my time. Running the "O" Course increased my strength, and I became smarter navigating the course and my times came down.

The Cross-Country Course was another physical fitness requirement for AOCS graduation. We ran through a shade-covered path near Officer Housing. The path was level until a turnaround point where we reached a steep sand covered hill. Again, as with the "O" Course, pushing off in the sand was a wasted effort trying to go uphill. I took two steps forward and I would be one step back. Out in the open with the bright sun boiling down on me, the course really tested my endurance. Then we ran back down a parallel trail to the starting point. I continued to improve my completion times.

They issued me my M-1 rifle on Thursday, July 14. It would be my nemesis for the next nine weeks. I learned to take it apart and put it back together. Old drill rifles rust, but mine was the worst in my class. My rifle was an old, beat up, neglected, and abused AOCS rifle that cursed everyone who touched it. Someone had scrubbed my rifle so many times with steel wool that they had rubbed the bluing off. It would rust within an hour of being prepared for inspection.

MAKING PLANS

At the end of our first week in Batt I, the class had a meeting with Captain Cody. He told us they would commission us on Friday, September 16. Because of the pilot demand, there would be little time off in the next 18 months while in flight training. He said most of us would go to fly in Vietnam. We were told not to make plans very far in the future. He said, "When you get your wings, plan on being gone." Captain Cody told us the only time we could count on having off was the two weeks at Christmas of 1966 while we were still in the Training Command. He clarified that the Navy's needs came first, and my personal life would not interfere with Navy plans for me.

I thought about my marriage plans with Lou. If we delayed our wedding until June 1968, I might not even be in the states or have a little time with her before they sent me overseas. Being married to her was something I wanted to do sooner rather than later. We could spend time together before I deployed overseas. With the probability of flying combat in Vietnam, there was the possibility there might not be a later. I loved her madly and wanted to start our life together.

On Friday night, July 15, I was allowed to use the phone for the first time, and I called Lou. I heard the phone ring on a long-distance call. Hearing her voice after four weeks was thrilling. I told her what Captain Cody had said and asked her to think about moving our wedding date up to December 31, 1966. She thought that was a good idea and told me she liked the idea of getting married sooner. We decided there was no reason to wait. We were in love and committed to each other. But it would mean moving to Florida, and she would have to drop out of school. She said that would be OK. We wouldn't tell anyone about it right away. She told me she would talk to her parents.

SECURED

While we were out of our rooms, they were subject to spot inspections. A candidate officer or DI could drop by to see if our room and personal equipment were up to inspection standards. Something as simple as pointing the discharge nozzle over the dot of the "i" on the Rise shaving cream can and keeping the head clear of all residual shaving cream foam required attention to detail. Which meant I had to take the can's top off and wash it out after every use. Attention-to-detail issues ate up our free time. Our solution was to have another shaving cream can in our laundry bag, because the laundry bag was off limits for inspection. The Rise can in our cabinet remained unused and would become what we knew as a "static display."

On Saturday, July 16, we passed our inspection. The DIs secured us for the first time. Now we could come and go from

Batt I by ourselves and go on liberty, meaning we were no longer confined to Batt I. After morning PT and Schools Command intramural completion, we had lunch and changed into our "Liberty" uniform: the summer Tropical White Long. Schools Command confined us to the base, and we couldn't use our cars. No problem for me since I did not have a car.

Instead, I became a tourist in my new, chosen career. The USS Lexington was the Navy's training aircraft carrier used for carrier landing qualification. The Navy tied the carrier up at the NAS Pensacola pier. On the weekends, it was open to visitors. I had never seen an aircraft carrier and was eager to see one up close.

First, I went to the Navy Post Exchange (PX) and bought some postcards so I could tell Lou about my aircraft carrier visit. Then I walked down to the pier and boarded the ship. I wandered around the hangar deck and flight deck. It surprised me how small the ship looked. Landing on the ship was going to be a challenge, but one I looked forward to attempting as part of a rite of passage in becoming a Navy pilot. A year later, I would make my first carrier landings on the Lexington.

In the evening after dinner, a bunch of us from my class went to the Aviation Cadet Recreation and Athletic Club (ACRAC) to have some drinks. Saturday night just hanging out with buddies was a welcome change from the constant pressure of the DIs and Candidate Officers at Batt I. Even though I still had to wear my Liberty uniform, the relaxed ACRAC atmosphere let me connect with my classmates.

GYMNASTICS

Gymnastics loomed as another challenge as we approached graduation. Schools Command assigned a small German gentleman as our instructor. The instructor was a short, wiry, middle-aged former gymnast. He was very directive, and he talked in sharp commands with his strong German accent. We bet he had been in the German Army in WWII. For one graduation exercise, we had to climb up a rope hanging 20 feet above the floor in a certain amount of time. With the climbing skill, we could rescue ourselves from a burning ship or similar situation. I had no trouble going up. Climbing the rope was something I could have never done six weeks prior. However, going down was a different story. My body would pick up momentum, which I didn't want while going down the rope. Also, I did not want to look down, because it was like being on the roof of a house and the fear of falling entered my mind.

Another one of our graduation tests was the shuttle run. We had to run six sprints of fifty yards each, up and back on a marked course. I really had to put out maximum effort to make the timing minimums. When my turn came, I kept up with my group and finished. I relished having the run behind me. Then I went to the German instructor for my time, but he said he did not have one on me. He had reset his stopwatch while timing. He wanted me to do my sprints again. WTF? Here I had done what they asked of me, but because of someone else's mistake, I had to do it again. Pure BS! I protested, to no avail. My legs burned, but I had no choice and had to do the shuttle run again. I passed and moved on.

SWIMMING

The swimming schedule consumed much of our time. We marched to swimming as a class with our swimming suits rolled up in our towels. The first three weeks in Batt I, we went to the pool every day for two hours. The first sessions were at the Enlisted Pool near Poopieville. Later we went to the Training Tank pool by the "O" Course. for classes on treading water and drownproofing. The instructors taught drownproofing as a technique to stay afloat in water for an extended period with minimum effort by using one's natural buoyancy. The "Dilbert Dunker," dominated the end of the pool. Later it would test our ability to escape from a submerged airplane.

To pass the swimming test, we had to tread water for one minute with our hands in the air, then tread water for another four minutes using our hands. They trained us to jump off a 12-foot-high platform into the water. We had to touch the pool bottom and swim 50 feet underwater. All these drills increased our chances of survival, as Navy pilots, should we ever go into the water.

I was a better swimmer than many of my class, having spent so much time in the water at the beach and my mom's pool. My comfort level in the water landed me a spot on the intramural swim team and I swam in the medley relay during the Saturday inter-Battalion Competition. We had our swim test, and I passed with no problems, another hurdle behind me. I had really sweated the treading water and the underwater swim test, but I had no problem with these events. My training efforts were paying off. I was getting better and stronger as time went by.

INSPECTIONS

The DIs gave us our first rifle inspection on July 20. The DI would come by, and I would hand him my rifle. He would do his fancy "swing it around" routine and look in the rifle, then wipe his white glove across the rifle. If the glove showed brown, it revealed rust. His gloves showed brown. I received my first demerits. He gave me a Weapon Not Clean (WNC), and it resulted in an automatic 5-1. In simple terms, that punishment meant 5 demerits and one hour of Extra Military Instruction (EMI) which meant one hour of marching on the Grinder.

The DI made us march around the Grinder on Saturday afternoon, while everyone else in our class was secured. Candidate officers drilled us. Someone else from class 25-66 marched with me the two times I had to march off demerits. The ACRAC was adjacent to the "Grinder." In a scorching afternoon summer Pensacola sun, I became soaking wet while marching my hours. My classmates were going in and out of the ACRAC. They saw me marching and would say "Hi," while laughing and telling me about the cold beer found at the ACRAC.

The DIs must have taken pity on me because of my rusty rifle. My rifle earned me no more demerits. The next day, a candidate officer found my locker open. I was not in the room. The laundry truck was there, and I went to pick up my uniforms. He was going to confiscate my rifle and give it to the DI. I begged him not to take it, because the DI would take my rifle apart and hide the parts all over the place for me to find. He told me if I wrote a 500-word essay titled "Why I love my rifle," he would let me keep my rifle. I also had to sleep with my 10-pound M-1 rifle in my bed. The candidate officer's punishment was still better than the DI's treasure hunt.

No one scheduled us for Graduation Parade practice yet, so we did not take part in the Graduation Parade our first week in Batt I. They drilled us on Graduation Parade procedures the second week. During the second week on Friday, the 22nd of July, we started taking part in the graduation parades on Friday mornings. We would form up after breakfast in our khaki uniforms, bridge covers, and rifles. Our class would go down the street again to the parade grounds. During our first week of parade, we were the newest class. We would have to stand at attention longer than any other class. The graduating class would be in their Choker Whites. All the other classes would stand at attention while the graduating class went through the graduation ceremony.

After the graduation ceremony, they marched the classes off the parade ground with the senior class going first. Standing at attention with our rifles in the Florida sun for what seemed like hours would cause candidates to fall over if they locked their knees and cut off the blood flow to their head. Fortunately, I avoided locked knees and never suffered an embarrassing fall forward onto my face.

ACRAC ANNIE

AOCS's Regimental Ball was scheduled for July 23. The ball was a formal event where all candidates had to have a date and go through a reception line and greet the officers from AOCS Schools Command. For those candidates without a date to accompany them, the social director arranged dates with local girls. They referred to the girls as "ACRAC Annies." We had to wear our Choker Whites. They set me up with a girl, but she didn't show up and I escaped the blind date.

One of my classmates fell in love with his date and they got married over Labor Day weekend. After having sex with her, he said it was fantastic and the only reason to get married. I don't remember how that marriage worked out. We went to the ACRAC after the Regimental Ball. After having about five gin and tonics, I had a grin on my face. The grin reflected how I felt about what I was doing. School Command restricted us to only using the ACRAC as our sole "watering hole." If we wanted a drink when secured and on liberty, we went to the ACRAC.

The next day Larry, a good buddy from high school, and his wife came over from Panama City, where he served in the US Air Force (USAF). They took me off base where I had been confined since I showed up in June, and we went to town for dinner. Larry, who was married to his high school sweetheart, kidded me about getting married. He said misery loves company.

THE ROUTINE

Lou sent me a pin up photo of herself in a bikini which provoked much kidding from my roommates. I think they were jealous. Her picture also brought comments from the candidate officers and DIs during our inspections: "What the hell does she see in you?" She looked unbelievably hot.

They showed free movies on weekends in Bldg. 633. I planned on seeing them with my buddies as often as possible for a pleasant escape from the burden of AOCS. After the movie, we visited the ACRAC for a couple of cold ones.

One assignment that rotated through the class was Regimental Messenger. While carrying out the RM duties, we did not have to go to classes, except specific ones deemed mandatory. The most dreaded messenger stop was Batt III, the Marine Batt. Staff Sgt. Montemayor, a legendary DI, hung out in Batt III. Just entering his office reminded me of my check in at Poopieville with Sgt. Sanders.

I would bang the door jamb to enter the office and then stand at attention. The staff sergeant looked me over with a fine-tooth comb until he discovered a discrepancy. I couldn't adequately prepare to make it through his inspection. A dirty fingernail, an "Irish Pennant" on a belt loop, nose hair or dust on a shoe sole seam, anything would bring his wrath. Any discrepancy would bring mandatory PT, but just enough to have me break a sweat. Often, if there were other DIs present, they would play tag team in their RM harassment. I could not get out of Batt III soon enough.

We were always subject to inspection. One thing they checked was the number showing under the index on our combination padlock that secured our locker (closet). Our class was 25-66, so we had to put the number 25 under the index. On one of these surprise inspections, they found my lock not to be on number 25. I shared the locker with Steve Gillis. When we came back to the room, we met a class officer, who confronted us and lectured Steve and me on "Teamwork." He said before dinner we had to draft a 500-word essay on teamwork. I had read a lot of Naval history, so I used the story of a WWII Navy pilot, Jimmy Thach, and his "Thach Weave" as an example of teamwork. The "Thach Weave" was where pilots weaved behind each other to use the team concept to defeat the Japanese Zeros. The class officer liked it, and we received no further punishment, such as demerits and marching.

On Friday, July 29, after the morning parade, we went back to NAMI for our shots. We got them all: Thyroid, Cholera, Yellow Fever, Dengue Fever, (whatever that was) etc. An assembly line moved us through the shots. They gave them in the upper arm with a high-pressure injection gun. I walked to the station. Then a corpsman on each side of me would grab my arms and grip them. Wham, wham. On to the next station, for more shots. My arms really ached, but our DI had a fix for that: physical training in the late afternoon.

Classes were over at 1630, and we had free time until dinner at 1700. We were always tired. We had no time to rest or catch a nap. The DIs forbade sleeping between 0530 and 2200. If we wanted to "rest our eyes," we would climb under the bottom bunk and hook our hands in the bedsprings to hold them up. If they caught us, we could say we were checking for "Irish pennants." Funny how so many of my classmates were checking for "Irish pennants."

Going to Chapel on Sunday morning for the church services continued to be an escape from AOCS. After breakfast, we would put on our summer whites and march to church. They formed us up by Batt I and marched us down the street past

Bldg. 633 to the chapel, junior class first. The junior class were the candidates in the "poopiesuits" who came from the Indoc Battalion. Marching candidates to church was a tourist event. People would line up on the street to take pictures and watch us march. Each week, we would move closer to the Church's back. As in "Poopieville," I remember almost nothing about the services, except they were air-conditioned, and we escaped harassment.

August 8, 1966, we lucked out. They canceled the Graduation Parade because it rained. Things were getting better, with about four weeks to graduation. The routine became familiar and the pressure from the Candidate Officers and the DIs became predictable. Our hair was growing longer, even though we got a haircut every week, the barbers allowed the top and front to grow back toward normal length. If our hair was longer, it signaled we'd been here longer, and it gave our class a certain status. Every Friday morning in Parade Formation, we moved closer to the graduating class and didn't have to stand at attention as long. Morning PT on the seawall, though still demanding, became much easier as I gained strength, endurance, and learned to pace myself.

While we were in class, we got another one of those candidate officer surprise inspections. In our room, the candidate officer found two pillows backwards on the beds and he put our room on report. We were now unsecured, which meant they confined us to Batt I unless marching in formation to chow, class, or scheduled function. All I could think was, *what a jerk and it was pure BS*. I was getting used to the harassment. I had trouble keeping a straight face while being yelled at by these candidate officers. They were so full of themselves. Arrogance was not my style. Our class DI secured us again after dinner, so it was not that big of a deal.

In another one of those surprise inspections by a candidate officer, he found two fingernail clippings in a wastebasket. He put our entire room on report and gave us each one demerit, which would mean a Saturday afternoon marching off our deficiency. Again, pure BS, and our DI, told us we didn't need to march for just one demerit. Power just seemed to go to the heads of some of these candidate officers. I was determined that, when I became a candidate officer, I would not follow their example.

SWORD DRILLS

One skill we had to develop was sword movement skills. We needed to do salutes, shoulder swords, parade rest, etc. Our DI drilled us in sword movement. I was terrible and way behind the learning curve. My athletic coordination skills were virtually non-existent. Added to my sword handling difficulties, I was doing it with my right hand when I was left-handed. While we were out on the Grinder practicing the DI's sword drill commands, my sword got stuck in my bridge cover. There I was, standing in formation with my hat hanging on the end of my sword. Everyone laughed.

Later, Gunny Weirling ordered us to go from swords at Parade Rest, where the sword rested next to your foot, to attention. I flipped up the sword with my right wrist to bring it from my toes to my shoulder. It slipped out of my hand, flew backwards and almost hit a guy behind me. Gunny Weirling went nuts and dressed me down for trying to kill one of my classmates. He then had me march five places to the left of our formation to drill by myself and protect my class.

In my mind, I knew my sword attack on a fellow class member added to my reputation as a "Cluster Fuck." I feared a reputation as someone who couldn't do anything right and screwed up everything he touched. A shortcoming that most likely reduced my Officer Like Qualities (OLQ) rating. We were approaching the end of our 11 weeks as candidates in AOCS but were still subject to the unceasing pressure to meet all the expectations set before us.

RLP INSPECTION

On Monday, August 15, we had an RLP, Room Locker and Personal Inspection. We stood at Parade Rest waiting for the inspection team to enter our room. Progressing through the rooms of class 25-66, we heard the inspection team making calls of "DEAD BRASSO" and the sounds of dresser drawers being dumped on the deck. The term "Dead Brasso" referred to residual brass cleaner found in the crevices of our belt buckles.

As the team entered our room, we were called to "Attention" and the inspection started. We could have one picture on our dresser. I had a picture of Lou because I missed her so much. Her picture brought the inspecting DI's attention. He kidded me on how a hot chick like her could see anything in me. During the inspection I got hit with a Room Violation (RV), probably something like my undershorts not folded exactly 3 1/4 inches by 3 1/4 inches, placed a quarter inch from the top drawer's front and left side and stacked three high. The inspector gave me ten demerits for the violation. I would spend two hours marching on the Grinder on the coming Saturday, August 20. These demerits were the last I got at AOCS.

We were approaching the end of AOCS and had many requirements for graduation, classroom, swimming, PT, and "O" Course, behind us. I met the qualifying times and only needed to pass the qualification runs in pre-flight. We were moving closer to the graduation position on the parade ground. The end was in sight. Only three graduating classes were in front of us now. We were becoming a bit "Salty," and we started coasting because it was almost over.

MICKEY MOUSE

On Thursday evening, August 25, while we were in study hours, a Marine DI came by and said our area was a shit hole, particularly the deck. He wanted the deck stripped and re-waxed before the lights went out at 2200. He had us get down on our hands and knees using razor blades to scrape the old wax off the floor and the splash joint where the floor and wall met. The demands were pure Mickey Mouse, and one of my classmates started singing the M-I-C-K-E-Y M-O-U-S-E song. We all knew the song from watching the Disney TV program while growing up. All of us joined him. The feeling of taking charge while being oppressed by the DI unified us.

A sign our morale was sky high. A camaraderie now bound us together. We would stand up as a team. Nothing could stop us now. The DI knew what we were doing. We had transitioned from a collection of civilians living together to a military unit with a mindset of teamwork to rise to challenges facing us. Our class would answer any call to duty. I think it pleased him, and he even had a little smile on his face while he addressed our shortcomings. But there were no DOR calls like we had experienced earlier at AOCS. Although he threatened us with canceling our liberty the coming weekend, it did not happen, and we were free for the weekend.

LABOR DAY WEEKEND

Labor Day Weekend was approaching. With three days off, they allowed us to go out into town and wear civilian clothes. I thought about flying home for the weekend, but they restricted us to 600 miles from Pensacola. My mom came down instead. She drove with my sisters and Lou, who drove my 1966 English

Ford Cortina to give me wheels. Mom rented a motel on Pensacola Beach. Back in 1966, the beach still had the basic cheap late-1940s-style motels for $25 a night. She rented a couple of rooms. Lou and mom stayed in one and I slept on the couch, while my sisters stayed in the other room.

I was off from Friday evening until I had to be back at Batt I by 2200 on Monday, September 5. We played on the beach and enjoyed our time away from the pressure of AOCS. On Sunday, September 4, of course, we went to the Episcopal Church on Pensacola Beach for the 0800 service. Mom still made us go to church on Sunday, no matter where we were.

Seeing Lou thrilled me because we had not been together since we moved our wedding to December. I could not believe she wanted to spend the rest of her life married to me. Not to mention I could not wait to get my hands all over her. Lou loved Pensacola, the beach, the water, and the warm weather. She would make a great navy wife. When mom and the girls drove home, Lou stayed in Pensacola.

One of my AOCS classmates, Bert Chalona, was married and his wife lived alone while he lived in Batt I with me. Lou stayed with her. I only had short afternoon periods between the end of class and dinner, when I could see her. I made sure we got together every day. Lou and I would go to the ACRAC and enjoy each other's company.

NO ONE CAN BE THIS STUPID

We took our final exams in week ten. My overall academic performance was not that good. We just had no time to study, and the classes were almost all rote memorizations. Like in Naval Justice, "What article in the UCMJ applies to a sailor for missing muster?" Hell, I didn't even know what encompassed missing muster, let alone which UCMJ article would apply. In areas where I had some knowledge, like navigation or Naval History, I did well. I was not a talented speaker in front of a crowd nor a topnotch writer, so my communications score was low. And as I have mentioned before, I struggled with PT but got better as the time passed and got passing scores. The multiplier for the Officer Like Qualities (OLQ) was the heaviest weight, 6 times the score. My OLQ was the real downer in my score.

I flunked the Naval Orientation final exam on September 7 in week ten. *Fear of not graduating with my class struck me.* The instructor took me aside after the class and gave me the "gouge," to retake the final exam. The "gouge" involved reading the questions and giving me answers. I took the test again. The instructor graded it. I got an even lower score. Now I was really worried. The instructor said something like "No one can be this stupid." Then the instructor realized he had used the wrong answer key. He got another answer key and graded the test again. The second time I passed with a good score. His wrong answer sheet use scared the daylights out of me.

Relief swept over me, I ran out and caught up with my classmates. By now, we were a confident bunch, and we knew we were going to graduate. Our class went down to a building near NAMI, the place where we took our entrance flight physicals. The visit to NAMI ten weeks ago seemed more like ten years ago. So much had happened since the third day at the Indoc Battalion. We had to take our electroencephalography test. The test would establish a baseline for brain activity in case of a head injury or concussion. They stuck about 25 electrodes into the skin over my skull. Then they put me in a room by myself with no windows and no pictures on the wall. A single light was in the ceiling, and I sat on a three-legged stool with no back in the room's center. I could not rest my head on anything and had to hold it still. The test took about 25 minutes; it seemed to go on forever.

CANDIDATE OFFICER

Thursday, September 8, was my birthday. I turned 23. It would be my last night in Batt I. No more RLP inspections, no more candidate officer or DI surprise inspections. In eight days, on Friday September 16, I would graduate from AOCS and receive my commission as an Ensign in the United States Naval Reserve (USNR). That day, my old rusty M-1 rifle had one last inspection. It had been my nemesis and caused me to fail an inspection and pickup demerits. To get it ready for its last inspection, I scrubbed it with steel wool. Then I rubbed it with aluminum foil to make it shine and oiled it. The beat-up old M-1 rifle was so shiny it almost glowed that day.

The inspection was a low-key event in the alley behind Batt I. The DI marched up to me called "Present Arms." I thrust out my rifle and he grabbed it, did his flipping maneuver with the rifle, and snapped it back at me. He said nothing and moved to the next candidate; I was relieved that my piece of crap rifle would not bring me any more special attention. After the rifle inspection, we broke out of formation and turned them in. It was a happy AOCS moment to see my rifle move out of my life.

We went to parade formation on Friday, September 9, and stood next to the graduating class 24-66. They commissioned 24-66 after the parade was over. After lunch, class 25-66 moved out of our rooms in Batt I. We moved to various candidate officer assignments at AOCS. Nine weeks of challenging AOCS Candidates in Batt I, following my week in "Poopieville," were now behind me. With the transition from a civilian mindset to the military mindset, I had reached another milestone in pursuit of my Navy Wings.

We spent our eleventh and last week in AOCS as candidate officers. We filled leadership roles throughout the AOCS

Battalions and classes. USMC Captain Cody, our class officer, would assign everyone in class 25-66 candidate officer ranks. The OLQ rating determined a candidate officer's rank. With each rank came a specific responsibility within AOCS's command structure. They gave me my candidate officer rank. I got to wear a gold two bar insignia on my collar. Captain Cody assigned me to be the candidate officer in charge of AOCS class 27-66 who lived in Batt II.

When I moved into Batt II as class candidate officer, I had a room to myself. The DIs told me to keep my room in an orderly fashion, bed made, towels properly hung by the washbasin, chairs properly set around the table and nothing adrift in my room. Adrift means just lying around. The DIs would not inspect my closet, dresser drawers, and medicine cabinet. I could use these areas as I wished. They only wanted my room to look "Squared away" if someone looked in the door. I would be busy over the weekend as the class leader. My responsibilities included marching them to chow, inspecting their rooms and ensuring they followed the AOCS rules in Batt II. That evening, class 36-66, 59 AOCS candidates, would now move from "Poopieville" into our former rooms at Batt I, as class 25-66 had done nine weeks before.

On the weekend of September 10, Lou and I got a room at the famous San Carlos Hotel in downtown Pensacola where all the pilots from the 1930s, 40s, and early 50s gathered. It cost me $7.50. The San Carlos Hotel was part of Pensacola's Naval Aviation History, and I wanted to be part of it.

One of my duties was to get up at the sound of reveille and take my class out for their morning run and PT. We would go out on a two-mile run. Like the DIs at Poopieville, I would run beside them. Two miles of running at about a seven minute per mile pace was easy for me. I was in the best shape of my life. Then back at Batt II, we did 15 minutes of jumping jacks, pushups, sit-ups, and leg lifts. One morning we were running down the sea wall towards the USS Lexington's pier. I was about to turn back toward Batt II, when a candidate named, if I remember, Brent called out, "What are you getting tired?" Brent joined me later at Naval Recruiting District (NRD) Detroit. His challenge could not go unanswered. I went easy on them not running as far as other classes, so I said, "Not at all. Let's go for more time." And we ran on for another mile. One of Brent's classmates yelled, "Jeez Brent, keep your mouth shut."

Thursday, September 15, 1966, our Candidate Officer week was ending. All of us were going to graduate the next day, and the Navy would award us our commissions. All AOCS graduates receive reserve commissions, with a five-year active-duty obligation. Those people wanting to make the Navy a career could request augmentation to a regular commission during their first assignment.

We were called into an assembly room in Batt II shortly before lunch. We sat down and Captain Cody, our class officer, came in to address us. I remember what he said: "The fun and games are over." *What I just went through was fun and games?* "It gets serious from here on out. We are in a war. They will train you to fight in that war. Look at the man to your right and the man to your left. Five years from now, one you three will either be KIA, a POW, MIA, or a dropout from this program." *I felt sorry for the guys on my right and left because nothing was going to happen to me. I was 23 and indestructible.*

Captain Cody made a good guess. About one-third of class 25-66 would drop out of flight training. Tommy was the only guy in my class to get killed. On takeoff from the aircraft carrier, he got a cold cat shot in an A-3. A cold cat shot is when the catapult malfunctions and the end speed isn't adequate to make the airplane fly, and it falls into the ocean. Such are the dangers of Navy flying. Captain Cody told us the only time we could count on having off for the next three to four years was the coming Christmas. I cannot remember what else he said, because

I was thinking about not being with Lou. It confirmed the decision we made in July to move up our wedding date to Christmas time 1966 was exactly the right thing to do. I wanted to have time with her before I became an active Navy pilot and faced the possibility of flying in combat in Vietnam.

We learned our grades on our Officer-Like Qualities (OLQ) that afternoon. My grade was low at 46. The Navy scoring system was based on a mean score of 50. They assigned us grades in terms of standard deviation from the mean. A 60 was one Standard Deviation above the mean or the upper 85% of those candidates being evaluated. Captain Cody asked us to fill out our "Peer Rating" score sheet. The "Peer Rating" is where we graded the top three candidates in our class in terms of leadership, personality, level of being squared away, academic knowledge, and Navy Officer potential. We also graded the bottom three.

We nicknamed the score sheet the "Spear Rating." The rating process did not go well for me; My peers rated me as 27 out of 32. I had shown my short temper. I could not keep my mouth shut and had performed at levels below many of my classmates. Early on, athletics had been a struggle for me. My preparation for inspection left something to be desired. I was almost downright dangerous with a sword. I also lost points because of my demerits, and I had not been a standout in any area. But my grades were average except for the "Spear Rating."

Our Class officer, Captain Cody, counseled me on my rating. He said my potential as a Naval Officer was below my peers. Captain Cody said the bottom three normally cannot make the Navy a career. He added I was not in the bottom three and he thought my performance had improved steadily during my time in Batt I and he rated me as average. He thought I should build upon improving performance to reach my potential.

My class ranking disappointed me, and I wished I had done better. But I had made it through. Even though they rated me average, I competed with the best in the nation. I thought being average in an elite collection like the guys in my class would be above average just about anywhere else. The first stage of Navy Flight Training was complete, and I was on my way to becoming a Navy pilot. I could not get the smile off my face.

COMMISSION

Finally, Friday, September 16 arrived. For the parade, we wore our Choker Dress Whites. Class 25-66 would be the head class and pass in review in front of all the other classes, who were standing at attention in their khakis. Then we marched to a building behind the chow hall, where Captain John Haynie USN, head of U.S. Naval School Pre-Flight, administered our Oath of Office. We were now Ensigns in the USNR. I had an official Navy photograph taken of me receiving my commission as an ensign in the United States Navy Reserve. Lou placed my ensign shoulder boards on my uniform.

I made it and was now an officer in the United States Navy. When I left the building as an officer, Gunny Weirling, greeted us. He saluted me and said, "Good Moring Sir." After I returned his salute, I handed him a silver dollar as part of a graduation ritual. He went from our class DI, who ruthlessly drilled military discipline into class 25-66 to respecting us as officers he helped shape. Handing Gunny, the silver dollar represented the first moment I realized my childhood dream had come true. After the commissioning, we moved out of our various Batts where we had been Candidate Officers and went over to the Bachelor Officers' Quarters (BOQ) to be given rooms as officers.

I was off until Monday morning when I would start preflight school academics. An officer now, I had no curfew and no room inspections. I was free to come and go as I wanted. That evening, I had dinner with dad, Lou, and Betsy, my second youngest sister. Lou and Betsy really hit it off and were good friends. Dad and Betsy flew back to Detroit on Saturday morning. Lou stayed with me in Pensacola, and we drove over to Panama City to visit Larry Huff, a Troy High classmate. On Sunday, we drove back to Pensacola and Lou flew to Detroit to start her fall quarter at Michigan State. I watched her airplane until it was out of sight and did the lonely drive back to the BOQ. Boy, I missed her. I had so much fun with her during our two weeks together, I could not wait for us to be married.

The impact of AOCS on my life is easy to define. I had a time in my life before I stepped on the quarterdeck at the Indoc Battalion on June 29. Then there was a time after hearing those words, "GET THE FUCK OFF MY QUARTER DECK." In AOCS, they tested me as I had never been tested before. The pressure was unrelenting. No matter how hard I worked, it was never good enough. They pushed me to give more.

What I discovered was that before AOCS, I was a coaster. If something interested me and I wanted to do it, I approached it enthusiastically. But if it did not interest me, I blew it off. In AOCS, skating by was not acceptable. I had to give my max no matter what the task was. With discipline drilled into me, I found I could do so much more than I ever thought possible. These skills would have served me well in high school and college. My grades would have been entirely different. I now had direction and the self-imposed control to meet any challenge. The ability to focus on tasks served me well in Navy Flight training and resulted in me being near the top of my class in every phase. I badly wanted to be a Navy pilot, and I would put up with anything to reach that goal.

Ed McMahon made a comment on the Johnny Carson show when he talked about his experience going through the V-5 program during WWII. The V-5 program was the precursor of AOCS. He said, "I would not go through the program again for a million dollars, but I would not give it up for ten million dollars." Like Ed McMahon, I cannot imagine my life without the AOCS experience.

PREFLIGHT

The history of Preflight began with the Aviation Cadet Program. In 1935, the Navy instituted the cadet program to give the Navy a civilian source for flight training to augment traditional pilot sources. The Aviation Cadet Program carried forward into WWII as the V-5 program. Later, it became known as the Flying Midshipmen. Then it transitioned to the Naval Aviation Cadet (NavCad) program in the early 1950s. Finally, in 1955, the Cadet Program became AOCS. Pre-flight covered Navigation, Aerodynamic, Aviation Physiology, General airplane engines and systems, and Naval Operations. Throughout these assorted programs, Preflight remained the core of basic aviation knowledge for prospective Navy flight students.

Classes started on Monday, September 19, in the same academic building where, a week ago, I had been an AOCS candidate. Preflight classes included graduates from the Naval Academy (USNA), Officer Candidate School at Newport, RI and (OCS) and the college Naval Reserve Officer Training Programs (NROTC). Foreign students, to include Vietnamese and Australian pilots, were also in these classes. During the tests, the Vietnamese students would talk to each other in Vietnamese. They chatted throughout the test, and nobody said anything about it.

Preflight split class 25-66 into different sections. Class 25-66 would no longer attend classes together. But some of my 25-66 AOCS classmates remained in my preflight section. As we moved through training, class 25-66 drifted further apart. Our fragmentation diluted the closeness we experienced in Batt I. However, I formed a few lifelong friendships with my AOCS classmates. We had four weeks of academics, Preflight was like college, classroom presentation with nothing else to do except study. We now relaxed as commissioned officers in a college-like atmosphere.

I only had one roommate in my BOQ room. My roommate, a guy on medical hold, enjoyed the partying aspect of being in Pensacola. He was rarely in the room, and his absence made it a perfect setting to study. I spent each evening alone in my room, going over the day's ground school and rewriting my notes to clarify my understanding. Unlike AOCS, where the subject put me to sleep, the subjects in Preflight commanded my attention. Schools Command posted test results for every class. The scores showed how well I was doing, particularly in Aerodynamics. I did exceptionally well in Pre-Fight and was near the top of my class in every subject. I now had the willpower to follow through and excel.

We went back to the AOCS Training Tank the first week for a swimming test. The swim test covered treading water, jumping off the platform and swimming under water, the same as we had done at AOCS. The test was a piece of cake, and I passed, as did all the AOCS students. They released us from swimming classes, and we got time off while others in my Preflight class were still going to the pool.

We went to the altitude chamber as part of our Aviation Physiology training. The pressure chamber climbed to an altitude of 30,000 feet. We removed our oxygen masks and experienced hypoxia. A person encounters hypoxia when there is not sufficient oxygen in the air to maintain their mental capacity. To experience, firsthand, the effects of hypoxia and the degradation of mental functions, I took my mask off and played a game of putting pegs in holes. After about a minute and a half, I could not match the peg's shape with the matching hole and put my mask back on. One of my preflight classmates, a highly rated lacrosse player from the Naval Academy, was in the altitude chamber with me. He went for almost five minutes without his mask. Then he refused to put his mask on. He became violent and had to be subdued to force his mask forced back on his face. The instant he took a breath, he was fine again. A real lesson in oxygen deprivation.

The same day as the altitude chamber, we went to the night vision laboratory. They turned the lights off, and the room was dark. The instructor illuminated the display of ships and buildings with only red lights, and I could see nothing. After fifteen minutes, I could see objects as my eyes adjusted to the darkness. The instructor told us to close one eye, and they turned the white lights on. They darkened the room again, and I could see out of one eye and not see with my eye exposed to the white light. I learned that once my eyes adapted to the dark, any white light could destroy my night vision.

EVERGREEN, ALABAMA

A 25-66 roommate, Mark Ernst, had been a varsity football player at Wake Forest, and they were playing a game on Saturday, October 8, in Auburn, Alabama. He did not have wheels. I had my 1966 English Ford, and he asked if I would drive him and his buddy up to Auburn for the game. It sounded like a plan, so I said, "Let's go." The drive up was fine, and the game was fun. Then the post-game party started at the fraternity house with lots of drinking. I had not planned on the party and only had one beer since I had to drive back to Pensacola. Finally, late in the night, around 2300, we started the drive back to Pensacola. My two passengers were drunk, nearly passed out. No expressways back then, so I had to take the two-lane road, US-31 route, back to Pensacola.

At 0130 in the morning, I came down a hill into Evergreen, Alabama. I was doing about 60 mph. At the hill's bottom, there was a speed limit of 35 mph. I took my foot off the gas and started slowing down. Oh no! An unmarked car appeared with a portable red flashing light on the roof. The local sheriff pulled me over. My car had a Michigan license plate. The sheriff walked up to the car's driver's side. He had on blue jeans, a khaki shirt with a badge that looked like it came out of a Cracker Jack box, and a gun stuck in his belt.

He said to his buddy, "Hey Leroy, looks like we got one of them Yankee Speeders here." Leroy was a guy on the car's other side in civilian clothes. "Y'all know you were doing 45 in a 35 zone?"

I said, "Yes, I was speeding, but I was slowing down,"

The cop said that slowing down was no excuse, and we would have to see the Justice of the Peace. *I was thinking it was 0130 and there was a Justice of the Peace nearby?* The cop said, "Follow me and don't y'all try to get away now, ya hear," so back down the road I went.

We went to a garage, and I got out of my car. In the back of the garage, a man was performing electric welding. Blue electric arc light silhouetted his body on the corrugated metal wall at the garage's back. The cops yelled "Hey Norm, we got one of dem Yankee Speeders here."

The mechanic stopped welding and removed his welding gear. He went into an office, pushed papers aside on his desk and pulled out a Justice of the Peace Conecuh County name tag. I was thinking, *What a farce. When do I see the Kangaroos associated with his court hop in?* He read the charges "Doing 45 mph in a 35-mph zone" and asked, "How do you plead?"

"What are my options?"

The Justice of the Peace said, "Plead 'guilty,' pay a fine and be on your way, or plead 'not guilty' and go to jail. Then wait for the judge to come by on Tuesday."

Some options. I plead guilty.

He said, "That will be $15.00 fine and $10.00 court costs, cash only."

I told the JP, "I only have $12.42 on me. I am in the Navy and must be back in Pensacola tomorrow."

He said, "See how much your buddies have in their pockets?" I shook down my buddies and collected another $5.50. I now had $17.92.

"Well, I was a vet," he said, "And I am going reduce my charge to $2.97. The case is closed."

We didn't carry credit cards back in the 1960s. The cops had taken all my cash, and I could not buy gas. Running on empty, I found an open gas station near Brewton, Alabama, and the owner agreed to give me $1.00 gas for my spare tire. Not such a good deal, but what other options did I have? Gas was only $.25 a gallon, and a dollar's worth would get me back to Pensacola. A night not to be forgotten.

We got back to Pensacola at 0430, just as the sun was coming up. When I had my background check for a Secret Clearance in 1968, I reported the kangaroo court ticket, but it never showed up on my record. I bet they split the cash and bought beer.

We all had to run the "O" Course and Cross County courses again as part of Pre-Flight, because everyone had to qualify, including Naval Academy, NROTC and OCS graduates. I ran my best "O" Course time of 3:34 and would have done better if there had not been a slower person in front of me. Since AOCS students had been running the "O" Course for the last 12 weeks, it was a breeze for us and all AOCS graduates qualified on their first attempt. Again, it meant more time off. Fortunately, they scheduled the Cross-Country course to run at 0700. The lower morning fall temperatures would make the run much easier than the AOCS experiences in the sultry afternoon summer sun. Like all AOCS graduates, I qualified on my first attempt.

One more time to the pool for the one-mile swim in my flight suit. I slowly drownproofed around the pool. It took me a while before I finished, but I was not the last to finish. Then, in mid-October, they issued us flight gear. We got two orange flight suits, a helmet, and our neat Naval Aviator leather flight jacket. I really felt like a pilot wearing government-issued gear.

SURVIVAL TRAINING

After four weeks of academic training, we went into sea survival training. We didn't need to study for preflight anymore with no more written tests. Nights of drinking, visiting Trader Jon's strip tease bar, a famous Naval Aviator hangout, and playing bridge became the norm. Navy pilots fly over the ocean and face the distinct possibility of finding themselves in the water after bailing out or ditching their airplane.

The ultimate graduation exercise in sea survival was escaping from the "Dilbert Dunker." The dunker rig was intimidating. They strapped me into the steel cage, a simulated T-28 cockpit mounted on a track, which would send me to the pool's bottom upside down. I hadn't even been in an airplane cockpit yet, and now I faced the possibility of drowning at bottom of the swimming pool. Not that I had much choice, so I climbed up Dilbert Dunker's ladder and strapped in for a ride into the pool. The instructor released the rig, and I rode it into the pool.

When the dunker hit the water, it flipped upside down. It stopped close to the bottom of the pool. I now hung upside down in the cockpit and had to wait for the bubbles to disappear. They taught us to wait so we could organize our thoughts, plan for the escape, and not go into an unorganized panic exit. I saw a diver in scuba gear observing my cockpit exit progress. After the bubbles disappeared, I undid my seat belt, threw my shoulder harness straps over my shoulders, went out cockpit's right side, and swam toward the surface. The scuba diver gave me a thumbs up, showing I had met the escape requirements. The exercise was over and wasn't a big deal. I completed it on my first try.

When parachuting out of an airplane over the ocean, response to the initial entry into the water would be a key to surviving. To prepare us, we had a week of sea survival. During one event, they dropped us into Pensacola Bay off a 12-foot platform on the back of a boat going through the water at 5 kt. They put a parachute harness on me and pushed me off the boat's back. I landed face first in the water. The boat's speed through the water forced water up my nose and gave me a drowning sensation. A key to survival in the water was getting rid of my parachute because a water-laden parachute could drag a pilot under and drown the pilot. I reached up over my head and crossed my arms on the straps. Then I flipped over on to my back and got rid of my harness by releasing attachment clips. With the harness gone, I activated my life vest.

Now floating upright in my life vest, I had to deploy my life raft and get out of the cold water. The one-man raft in my seat kit needed to be inflated. I gave a jerk on the inflation lanyard and the raft blew up. I struggled as I climbed in, but then sat in my raft. From the drop off the boat until I climbed into the raft, I doubt the whole evolution was more than a minute. A critical minute in sea survival. I sat in my raft for two hours with my signaling mirror, waiting to be rescued. The cold air and water chilled me, and the sea water chafed my skin. They picked me up and I was happy to get out of that raft.

Paul Good, my bunkmate from Batt I, was in my section going through Pre-Flight. We often studied together. When ground school ended, we went to the bars for drinks. Over beers one night at some beer joint, Paul told me I was lucky to find a girl like Lou. He said, "You are doing the right thing getting married to her. If you let Lou get away, you would never forgive yourself." He hoped he could be as lucky as me in his search for a wife. From Paul, it meant a lot and, of course, I felt the same way about Lou.

The last week of Preflight was Land Survival. A survival guide accompanied the class, and we went overnight in the woods at Eglin AFB to practice our classroom lessons. We dressed up in flight suits, carried survival knives, salt tablets, and a half a parachute. We foraged for edible food, such as bugs, palmetto hearts, and bay leaves. The guide found a skunk walking down a trail, killed it with a slingshot, and skinned it. He said we could eat it that night. That evening, we made skunk stew with palmetto hearts, bay leaves, and salt tablets. It tasted like a skunk smelled, YUK!, but I ate it anyway. After not eating all day, it amazed me how the stew renewed my energy.

I built fish traps in a nearby stream and foraged for food. That night I made my bed out of pine boughs and counted on eating some skunk stew in the morning. But when I woke up, the stew was gone. I figured, Oh, someone must have eaten it. Upon going to the latrine, I noticed skunk stew in the trench. Someone disliked it so much they tossed it in the latrine. I thought it was better than nothing, which is what I now had.

I excelled in Pre-Flight; most courses were science and math based, and my college pre-engineering classes really paid off. I did extremely well in Aerodynamics, Air Navigation, and Engines. A final score of 62 put me better than one standard deviation above the mean. My Physical Fitness score was below average, but better than my AOCS PT score. In swimming, I achieved a top score at AAA, two deviations above average, the highest achievable swimming score. My test score placed me 6 out of 83 who finished with me. I had the highest grades of all AOCS candidates.

Paul commented it looked like I had found my "groove," a Navy term for the final approach to an aircraft carrier. I competed with the nation's best and excelled. It gave me great satisfaction. The grades would be critical, as I went through flight training, when I received an unsatisfactory flight grade. I finished on Friday, October 28, and received orders to report to Naval Auxiliary Air Station (NAAS) Saufley Field just outside of Pensacola to train in the T-34B Mentor. Finally, I was going to fly planes.

Chapter Two
Training Squadron One VT-1

NAAS SAUFLEY FIELD

At VT-1, (V being the Navy identifier for a fixed-wing, heavier-than-air aircraft, T the Navy identifier for training) I checked in and found there were no rooms available at the BOQ. Building up for Vietnam resulted in an increase in flight training. With the surge came a shortage of BOQ rooms at Saufley Field. The Navy offered us an off-base housing allowance. Four of us got together, two of my 25-66 classmates, Chuck Bagley, and Chuck Johnstone, plus a week later a 26-66 guy, joined us in temporary housing. We rented an 800 square foot, three-bedroom furnished house on a slab at 29 Norwood Drive. The three 25-66 guys got bedrooms and the 26-66 guy slept on the living room couch. We spent limited time there. Tiny cockroaches filled the house. We could not get rid of them. We frequented the nearby bar and Whataburger. The house is now gone.

GROUND SCHOOL

At VT-1, they flew the 100-octane-powered T-34B models. Even then, at VT-1, I knew why the T-34 was called the "Teeny Weenie." At Saufley Field, we were based with VT-5's T-28Cs, the carrier qualification birds. We flew the T-34 with no radio communication. When T-28s taxied, they talked to the tower. All the T-34s had to stop and let them pass. They ruled the field. The T-28s idling R-1820 nine-cylinder radial engine sounded mean, powerful, and manly. They would rumble by me in my idling IO-435 that sounded like a kitten purring. I looked up at these birds as they passed, and I saw the old oil- and grease-stained flight suits on these T-28 student pilots. Then I looked at my fresh-off-the-rack, spotless flight suit and I knew I was a complete rookie in the Navy flying business.

A thing we had to do at VT-1 was get a "First Solo Flight" Public Relations (PR) photo. Navy PR would send a press release to our hometown newspapers to help with recruiting. They made it a pure production line event. I wore my spotless brand-new orange flight suit. They had me print my name on a piece of masking tape and put it on the flight helmet's bottom. When my turn came up for the picture, I put on a parachute harness, the top half only. Then I walked in front of a picture of a T-34, placed the flight helmet on a post, and stood still. I was done, took less than 30 seconds. Thousands of these pictures were taken at VT-1 in the 1960s.

During the first week, we had to do a bailout drill. We started by sitting in a T-34 cockpit with the engine running. Then we dove out toward the right wing's rear edge into a net. Being young and indestructible, jumping headfirst into a net was almost fun. We also had to complete a blind cockpit test. We put on blindfolds, and as directed by an instructor touched the various controls and instruments in the cockpit. I had studied for the evaluation. The instructor gave me an Above Average grade for my Cockpit Familiarization.

Our life at VT-1 revolved around the Academic building, the student Ready Rooms, and the hangar, where we checked out airplanes. After the first week, we started going to ground school in the morning and flying in the afternoon. The schedule alternated each week with afternoon flying and morning ground school. The ground school comprised T-34 Aerodynamics, T-34 engine, constant-speed propeller, and electrical system plus Morse Code. I enjoyed the training, conducted by a person, normally a pilot, called a platform instructor.

We took notes like in college. Then I studied those notes to ensure I knew the subject. By the spring of 1967, the Navy started going to program learning with self-study textbooks. I did not like the loss of face-to-face time with the platform instructor. The instructor's colorful stories of flying in the Navy added to the classroom experience. Of all the subjects, Morse Code drove me nuts. They had us sit in a booth facing a wall with headsets on to hear dots and dashes. Then we turned the noise into letters. I needed to read 25 letters a minute. I passed and must admit I can still identify about half the alphabet by Morse code.

FLYING THE T-34

Student Control accounted for every minute of our time at Saufley. After or before ground school, depending upon my schedule, I showed up in the ready room. I checked the schedule board to see if my name was there. If I found my name on the board, I would see it paired with an instructor and a posted a brief time. Then I waited and studied to prepare for my flight.

I took my first flight on November 7, 1966, a 1.2-hour ungraded intro flight with Lt. Robert Weibly. He was a 1958 Naval Academy graduate and a classmate of John McCain. He later went to work for Trans World Airlines in 1967. Lt. Weibly had flown carrier-based airplanes. After our flight, while walking back to the ready room, he asked me what I wanted to fly in the Navy. I told him I wanted to fly P-3s. They were land-based patrol airplanes that flew in Patrol Squadrons (VP). He looked at me, then looked at his shoes while shaking his head and said, "Randy, I would rather have VD in my health record than VP in my logbook." Carrier-based pilots looked down on land-based patrol plane pilots. My first seven flights were with him. I took four ungraded flights, then he graded the remaining flights. He was an excellent instructor and gave me good grades. Because of my progress, he waived warmups when we had extended no-fly periods caused by the weather.

At Cannel Field, an outlining practice field in Southern Alabama, I had my first flight into the landing pattern. Since I had soloed in a C-172, Lt. Weibly said he would let me make the first landing in the T-34. Wow! he must have had a lot of confidence in me. I relished the moment. I set the airplane up for what I thought was a good landing, and left on a little power, held it off into a flare, touching down softly. A smooth landing like mine should impress my instructor.

On the downwind, he banged the stick on my knees. A technique used by an instructor to get a student's attention. Then he said, "If I ever see a pussy landing like that again, I am going to recommend you join the Air Force." He laughed and said, "Now let me show you how it is done." LT Weibly held a constant attitude and used power to hold the airplane on a glide path. Then, over the landing area, he cut the power, held a constant attitude into the flare and the airplane settled with a firm landing onto the runway. On all future landings in the T-34 , he taught me to do a carrier touchdown technique. I did not perform a traditional landing flare in an airplane until I flew the P-3 a year and a half later.

One challenge facing a new pilot at Saufley Field was to learn the home field pattern entry. We did it without radios. Pattern entry at Saufley Field was a complicated, detail-filled procedure. At our house, I laid a piece of paper with a runway on the floor. To hone my skills, I walked through the pattern, reciting the call outs, power setting, configurations, and checkpoints. We had explicit calls out at certain points in the pattern. For example, when going into the downwind break, I had to say, *"Gear down and locked, brakes firm, parking brake in, temperature and pressure normal."* Failure to say it exactly as written in the procedures would cause a below average grade. The practice drilled the procedures into my brain and allowed me to be ahead of the airplane while I mastered landing procedures at Saufley Field.

At Saufley, the runways were 6,000 feet long and 150 feet wide. The Navy divided the runway into four quadrants, each 3,000 feet by 75 feet. Dividing the runway this way meant, when landing, I would use the runway's opposite side the airplane in front of me. If no airplane was on the right side, I would land on the right side. While I was landing, airplanes were taking off on the left and right sides of the runway's last 3,000 feet. The pattern was busy and gave me a feeling of accomplishment, having mastered the traffic pattern as a pilot with 10 hours of Navy flight time.

A three-day break was coming up over Veterans' Day weekend. It would be a chance to go home. Friday was Veterans' Day and Thursday night I got a flight on a National Airlines Lockheed Electra out of Pensacola. My friend, Larry Traskos, who had come down with me in June, was going home to get married. We sat in the seats by the window. Both of us marveled at the huge blade angle changes we saw as they added power for takeoff. The Electra was the same airplane as the P-3 I wanted to fly for the Navy. The visit home was a whirlwind of seeing Lou and visiting friends and family. I remember little other than that it allowed a momentary escape from the self-imposed pressure of flying in VT-1.

STRUGGLES

Monday morning, it was back to Saufley Field to work toward the solo flight. I became a master of both high and low-altitude emergencies, pattern entry, and landings. I knew my procedures, but I had trouble staying in front of the airplane. My instructor yelled at me, following every one of my "goof ups." It took some fun out of flying. I still liked it, but it was more of a chore. I was getting above average grades, but I had room for improvement.

Thanksgiving was coming up and it would be my first Thanksgiving away from home in my life. Being away from family was strange. My 25-66 classmate, Bert Chalona, and his wife, Sonia, were kind enough to invite me and some of my 25-66 bachelor classmates over to their house for Thanksgiving dinner. I stuffed myself. That weekend, the guys from my house and I went down to Trader Jon's for a couple of beers and watched the strippers do their routine.

My flying picked up the week following Thanksgiving. They scheduled me for more flights, and everything started coming together. I was now ahead of the airplane, and I foresaw the next event. Flying was fun again.

CAPTAIN'S LIST

The combination of preparing for ground school and flight at the same time was a demanding workload. But the discipline drilled into me at AOCS gave me a solid foundation for doing well in ground school. I had top scores on all my quizzes and exams. Ground school would continue through Friday, December 9. I found out I finished ground school at the top of my class. It placed me on the Captain's List for Academic Excellence. On December 14 in a brief ceremony, the Commanding Officer of NAAS Saufley Field awarded me a certificate. My high ground school scores were important in keeping me at the top of my class standing. I was living a dream, and I could not get enough of being a pilot in the Navy.

I had to look for an apartment or house for Lou and me. We needed a place to live when we returned to training in January.

My flight and ground school scores guaranteed I would get my first choice of training pipelines. The path to the P-3 and multi-engine training in Corpus Christi, Texas, would go through NAS Whiting Field in Milton, Florida. After NAS Whiting, I would return to Saufley Field for Carrier Landing training. Choosing a place close to the middle was logical. The buildup of Navy Training caused a housing shortage in the Pensacola area. I found a converted two-car garage in Pace. At only 400 square feet, it had two rooms: one room had a bathroom off to the side, and the other room had the kitchen.

The place was in the backyard of another house. To find the house, we would count 63 stripes on the road and turn left onto a dirt road. It cost us $70 a month, furnished with utilities. We couldn't figure out how to set up the house and we moved the furniture between the rooms. Finally, we decided we preferred having a living room with a bathroom as opposed to a living room in the kitchen. We lived there for eight months until we moved to NAS Corpus Christi.

SOLO FLIGHT

On Thursday, December 15, 1966, I soloed in the T-34. Unlike civilian training, where the solo day is an unknown, in the Navy they scheduled my solo on flight PS-12 at 14 hours total time. I went to Faircloth Field in Alabama and made seven landings with the instructor. Then we pulled over to the taxiway, the instructor got out and said, "Go make three takeoffs and landings, and don't forget to come back and pick me up." I joined a line of first solos waiting to take off. Flying by myself didn't scare me, but I knew my instructor was watching me, and I did not want to screw up. I did well and received good grades.

After picking up my instructor, I flew back to Saufley. I felt like a pro now, I had soloed. During pre-solo training, I looked up to those pilots who had soloed as being the real pros at VT-1. Now had joined their ranks. They immediately sent me out on my first solo flight, PS-13. The thirteenth flight of T-34 flight training. On my solo flight, I went to the practice area in southern Alabama and back to Saufley. That afternoon, all the pilots who had soloed that week went to a tie-cutting ceremony at the O'Club. Cutting the tie was a symbolic tradition to show the pilot had cut his ties to his instructor. Amidst beers and celebrating, Lt. Weibly cut my tie. The next morning, I bummed a ride to Detroit with a couple of other flight students who were driving home. I was going home to spend Christmas in Detroit and get married to Lou.

GETTING MARRIED

Lou and I got married on New Year's Eve 1966 on the only Saturday I knew I would have off for the next five years. My father gave us a brand new 1967 Ford Fairlane for our wedding present. Mom gave us a 19-inch black-and-white TV. We needed both. On January 1, 1967, we loaded the car with our wedding gifts and started our drive to Pensacola. Our honeymoon was a three-day drive to Pensacola. We got to Pensacola at midday on Tuesday, January 3 and went to our new home. I carried Lou across the threshold. Getting married during flight training was absolutely the right thing to do if I wanted to build a life with Lou. We would have 16 months together to grow as a couple, followed by three years of constant separation. Had we waited, we would not have had the time together and could have grown apart.

VT-1 was still in post-holiday stand down with no training scheduled. The next day we drove over the Saufley so I could check in from leave. One thing I had to do was get Lou listed as a military dependent and get her a military dependent ID card so she could use the medical facilities, exchange, and commissary. The Personnel Chief Petty Officer (PNC) who processed her paperwork said to me, "Sir, it is not my position to offer advice to an officer, but if you don't mind, I would like to do so." The thought of me refusing advice from someone so knowledgeable with my limited experience in the Navy would be stupid.

I said, "Sure I would appreciate it."

"You should join the Navy Federal Credit Union (NFCU)."

He told me how NFCU worked and gave me an application. I filled it out and mailed it to NFCU. I was still a beginner in understanding how the Navy functioned. My focus was flight training. With his advice, I became a lifelong Navy Credit Union member. We had joined a single financial institution that had offices at all the Navy bases. We could set up savings and have a financing source when we needed to buy our home. The credit union was a good fit and reduced some stress associated with banking while going through flight training and moving every six to eight months. Mentors like the Chief Petty Officer filled the Navy at all levels. They were quick to share their knowledge and ensure a smooth transition into your Navy life. It would instill in me a mentor role I followed my entire life.

ACROBATIC STAGE

I reported back to Saufley on Monday morning, January 9, and resumed flight training at VT-1. They scheduled me for my first dual acrobatic flight. During acrobatics training, I learned to perform advanced maneuvers such as the loop, Immelmann turns and ½ Cuban Eights. What a blast! I mastered these maneuvers as a 20-hour pilot. It boosted my confidence to handle anything that might happen to me.

The next day put my training to the test. On my solo takeoff, my airplane would not climb, the oil and cylinder temperatures were rising. I was climbing slowly and had only climbed to 500 feet AGL. Something was wrong. My airplane was not flying as it had in the past. I was alone, there was no instructor to help with my dilemma. I was thinking: *"Oh Crap I going to crash on my second solo."* But I had the confidence I could handle a potential emergency. I looked around the cockpit, trying to figure out what was wrong.

I discovered, even though the landing gear was up, the wheels were still showing down and limiting my climb performance. They had taught us in ground school the gear was electrical. So, I looked at the circuit breaker (CB) panel behind my right elbow. The landing gear CB caught my attention. It had popped out, exposing its white shaft, making it stand out. I pushed the CB back in and the gear came up. Things returned to normal, and I continued my flight.

I was double scheduled again on Friday: a dual flight followed by a solo flight. Then on Monday January 16th, I took my last flight and graduation check ride from VT-1. My above average flight training grades, combined with my performance in ground school, got me off to a good start in Navy Flight Training. The following day I checked out of VT-1 with orders to VT-2 at Whiting Field. Another hurdle behind me on my path to becoming a Navy pilot.

Chapter Three
Training Squadron Two VT-2

NAS WHITING FIELD NORTH

On Wednesday January 18, I reported to Whiting Field, and they told me to come back the tomorrow to join a class they were putting together. At Whiting I would fly the North American T-28 Trojan. Student pilots called it the "beast." It had a powerful engine and performed like a WWII fighter. When I checked, I found the VT-2 Training Officer assigned me to Class 1D, the fourth class of 1967, STB (Starboard).

GROUND SCHOOL

That afternoon, they gave us a lecture on how training functioned at VT-2, how the scheduling board worked, and our responsibilities while at VT-2. Our Port or Starboard designation determined when we would go to ground school and when we would fly. Ground school in the morning and flying in the afternoon swapped each week between the groups. Same as at VT-1, we would check the pilot assignment board in the schedule's room each day to see if we were going to fly. They gave me a locker for my flight gear. In 1967, because flight suits were working uniforms, we couldn't wear them off base. We did not fly for the first two weeks.

Flight training was more than becoming proficient in flying. Those of us going through at the same time came to know each other. We became friends and our families became friends. Our little house shared a driveway with the larger, ranch-style home. We got to know the couple who lived there. His name was Brian Mathison. His wife was pregnant. He was a flight student in VT-3 at Whiting Field who had temporarily rented the house. He was about three months ahead of me. We would barbecue with them, watch TV sometimes, and talk about the Navy. He moved out in mid-March and my AOCS roommate, Steve Gillis, and his wife, Sara, moved into the house. We were great *Star Trek* fans, and we made our date night watching *Star Trek* at Gillis's house.

A STAGE INTRODUCTION AND ACROBATICS.

I looked forward to flying the T-28 and, in the third week, they scheduled me to fly for the first time. But they canceled the flight because of poor weather. My flight showed up on the schedule board as an HC (Hop). I had to wait another day to get my first T-28 flight. My first instructor was Lt. John Hamilton, who was great. He gave me good grades, and I really enjoyed working with him. I remember on flight T-2, I showed him a T-28 preflight. At the engine's bottom were three drains, and he asked me to tell him what they did. I had all the right answers. He gave me above average grades on my preflight. I was off to a good start with him. After three flights, they called me into Student Control. The Student Control Officer told me I was not having any problems in training. He said LT Hamilton was one of their best instructors and there was a weak student who could benefit from his instruction. They would give me a new instructor. Those were the breaks of Naval Air.

I met my new instructor, 1st Lt. John Tyc: a poster-perfect Marine, stocky with an almost shaved head. He had a Doctor Jekyll/Mr. Hyde attitude and could swing between the two personalities on short notice. He told me he did not want to be an instructor, and he wanted to go back to Vietnam and fly the OV-10. He wasn't exactly what I was looking for in an instructor, but I had little to say about the matter. Later, I learned after leaving VT-2, 1st Lt. Tyc died in an OV-10 accident at Yuma. Arizona while he was preparing to return to Vietnam. I was sorry to hear about his passing. He had been my instructor and helped me progress through training. But such are the risks associated with preparing to fly in combat.

READY ROOM GOUGE

One of things we picked up on while sitting around waiting for our flights was "Ready Room Gouge." The "Gouge" was tips from other students that helped us master the T-28. Such "Gouge" as, on takeoff, push the right rudder all the way to the floor before releasing the brakes, and never touch the left rudder. That tip was good and earned me Above Average grades with Lt. Hamilton. Another tip was using the Pensacola VOR radio to guide our return from the practice area into the east break at Whiting Field. If we tuned in to the Pensacola VOR, then centered the VOR needle, it would guide us to the turn point where we set up to enter the break for the active runway.

One day, coming back from the practice area, I flew over Fomation Corners, the initial entry point north of Whiting Field. Fomation Corners was a distinctive crossroads with a white building in southern Alabama. I tuned in the Pensacola VOR, 108.2. The centered needle showed me on course. I patted myself on the back and started flying toward the VOR. Things didn't look familiar, and I wasn't sure where I was. Suddenly, something was banging off my helmet.

1st Lt. Tyc screamed, "What the hell are you doing?"

"I am going into the east break point, sir."

"Look back to your 8 o'clock."

"Oh!" Whiting Field was right there. I turned back to make my landing.

During the debrief, he asked, "I don't understand what you were doing? You haven't had pattern entry problems before?"

I explained the "Ready Room Gouge" to him.

He laughed, saying, "You have to turn on the VOR for that to work." I hadn't gone through Radio Instruments yet, so I was not familiar with VOR procedures.

I started getting a lot of flights in a row and was progressing normally. Then, in mid-February, my grandma, Petra Hotton, passed away. Lou and I took three days of emergency leave to attend her funeral. When I came back, I pulled Runway Duty Officer (RDO) duties. Working as RDO, I stood at the runway's end with a flare gun and watched the T-28s line up for takeoff and landing. If I saw something unsafe, like landing gear retracted during an approach to a landing, I would shoot off a flare. The RDO duties, combined with emergency leave, meant I didn't fly for 10 days.

After my RDO duties, I went out on my F-7 flight with 1st Lt. Tyc, who would determine if I was ready to take my "safe for flying solo" check ride. He said I was ready, did not need a warmup hop, and should take the check ride. The next day was my F-8 "safe for solo" check ride with Lt. Lucci. He gave me a down, an unsatisfactory performance. His comments mentioned my time not flying and recommended two extra hops. I had to go to a Jacket Review.

At the Jacket Review, the instructor and Training Officer would determine how to address my unsat grade. The student control officer called me in and told me they had a recommendation to continue my training. The next week I flew one warm up and did a satisfactory job. My instructor told me I did not need another warmup flight, and they would count the next warmup flight as my "safe for solo" check ride. I received good grades on my T-8 recheck and ended up with an average grade in the Transition Stage. Another bullet dodged.

They now scheduled me to start the acrobatic phase of Basic Flight Training. After taking over six weeks to move through nine flights in the Fam phase, I jumped into the Precision Acrobatic phase and completed 14 flights in 10 days. Seven flights were solo flights. I would double hop almost every day. They scheduled me for ground school in the morning and then two afternoon hops: a dual and a solo. I mastered acrobatic maneuvers like wingovers, 1/2 Cuban Eights, Loops, Barrel Rolls, and Immelmann turns. I progressed from barely hanging onto the "beast's" tail, to becoming its master. I could make that airplane talk.

On one flight, the instructor asked me to show him a barrel roll. I had barrel rolls wired and went right into the maneuver. With the power set, I moved the stick to the right and pulled it back. The T-28 rolled right and reached a 90-degree turn fully inverted. The turn continued until I put the airplane back on its original heading with level wings at the starting altitude. I pulled off a near perfect barrel roll. However, I did not do clearing turns. The instructor gave me an Above Average for my barrel roll, but a Below Average for headwork because I skipped the clearing turns. Constant flying with the hops close together helped my progress, and I did very well in Acrobatic training. I got above average grades and finished Acrobatic stage on Tuesday, March 28, 1967.

BI STAGE: BASIC INSTRUMENTS

On April 3, 1967, I started the Basic Instrument training phase with my first simulator training session. The WWII Link Trainer, known as the Blue Box, was still in use. My class was among the last to use these old Link trainers. These outdated boxes were pneumatic actuated devices where the stick moved a valve that ported air to the bellows to give the box bank and pitch. An instructor sat at a table that traced my imaginary path through the air. The panel was as primitive as a WWII airplane.

We practiced instrument patterns like the Alpha pattern and the Charlie pattern we would display when flying the T-28. Making minor heading changes with the bellows system, particularly in the old, worn-out Blue Boxes. By the time I moved the stick to make a correction, the simulator would overshoot. The same with minor airspeed changes. Again, "Ready Room Gouge" came in handy to help me master the Blue Box. Flight students who had completed their Blue Box training gave me the "Gouge." We learned a great trick for minor heading changes. We just had to lift our butts up and plop down on the seat's side in the direction we wanted to turn. The Blue Box would change heading about five degrees. The same with airspeed to make minor airspeed reduction, we could deploy a variable speed brake on the throttle quadrant and pull it out to lose a little speed.

An embarrassing moment would be when I was having trouble with a maneuver. The enlisted simulator technician would stick his hand inside the blue box and fly a near perfect pattern. He flew; while standing outside, the blue box was better than I did inside the trainer. The new T-28 simulators were being installed in the same building, but they were still in the set-up phase. They looked just like the T-28 cockpit. I would not use these new cockpit trainers. I would use the Blue Box for both basic and radio instrument training.

Lou found a job at the Milton Hospital. She worked as a nurse's aide, making only $1.00 an hour. There, she met a nurse named Helen, who was Jerry Kevitt's wife. Jerry and I met at the Indoc Battalion nine months before. He was a candidate officer when I was an AOCS poopie. Jerry and Helen became our bridge table buddies and lifelong friends. Playing bridge was something everyone did in the Navy, and we regularly got together.

I did eleven Basic Instrument flights between Wednesday April 11, 1967, and Thursday April 26, 1967. I did the training in the T-28's back seat. At 400 feet, I placed a view limiting device, called "The Bag," over my head. It extended to the instrument panel and blocked out all outside visibility. I struggled with vertigo. Another challenge was the hot Florida sun beating down on the bag was difficult, making the rear cockpit uncomfortable. I did well in Basic Instruments phase and received above average grades for the stage. I finished Basic Instrument stage and was ready to start Radio Instrument training phase.

RI STAGE: RADIO INSTRUMENTS

I went into a pool, Navy term for a log jam in training, where flight students awaited instructor assignment and scheduling. Radio Instrument flight training had a backup. I went without flying for six weeks. My flight records show a lot of P for Pool, IS for Instructor Shortage, and NS for Not scheduled. I had five flights in the Blue Boxes again, doing instrument approaches. But I showed up every day, at either 0600 for morning schedule or 1200 for afternoon schedule, to see if I was on the scheduling board, only to find out I would not be flying that day. I completed Ground School on May 3 and finished with high grades. Since I was not flying or attending ground school, I had a lot of free time. Playing golf with my buddies, going to the beach with Lou, or hanging out at the Whiting Field pool became the routine while waiting for an instructor assignment. My flying skills were getting rusty during the extended lay off.

On Wednesday, May 24, I went over to the formation flight and asked if I could catch a ride in the back seat of a T-28. I would go into the formation phase when I finished the Radio instrument phase and wanted to see formation flight. They assigned me to fly in the T-28 with a chase instructor. I sat in the back seat. A chase instructor followed solo formation students to observe their formation flying skills. I loved the thrill of being close to another airplane in flight. The instructor allowed me to handle the controls and showed me the minor corrections needed to maintain formation. I couldn't wait to fly formation flights.

Finally, on June 1, I flew my first Radio Instrument flight. The extended periods of no flying were catching up with me. I had a terrible flight on my instrument cross country to NAS New Orleans. My holding pattern entry at the NAS New Orleans TACAN was a disaster. My instructor, Capt. Wyrick USMC, said if we were back at Whiting Field, he would have given me a down. But he said since we were in New Orleans, it would waste the flight back to Pensacola. With the pressure to keep the training flow moving, he elected to use his instructor's discretion and graded me as below average and not give me an unsat. On the way back to Pensacola, I got ahead of the airplane and had a good flight. Approaching Whiting, they gave me a holding clearance at the Pensacola VOR. My holding was a near textbook performance. He said, "I knew you could do better, and I could continue in training as planned." Whew! another bullet dodged, and I avoided the dreaded Jacket Review.

As luck would have it, scheduling paired me with Capt. Wyrick for my Radio Instrument check ride. He wrote how my hop was outstanding and said I showed real improvement. I got above average grades and ended up with a 3.04. While going through the radio instrument, I got some good grades and some not so good grades. Again, the flight training completion without big breaks was the key to doing well. I was becoming a Navy pilot, still working on my dream, almost pinching myself to see if each day was real.

F STAGE: FORMATION

My last training phase at VT-2 would be Formation Flight. The training would include formation flights in two- and four-plane formations. In formation, I would master running rendezvous, two-plane join and break up, four-plane join and break, plus cruise formation. It also included nighttime flights, as well as cross-country flights in the day and at night.

On Thursday, June 15, 1967, I took my first formation flight. I got off to a good start. I got good grades on my first couple of hops, and they were fun. Running rendezvous was challenging. I approached the airplane in front of me at a good closure rate. I wanted to pull back the throttle to slow down, but the instructor would keep me charging into another airplane until the last moment. Then my world of formation flying fell apart. On my next three formation flights, I got 13 below average grades. My F-4 instructor gave me seven below averages and said, "Good luck on F-5." But I only got three below averages on F-5. I got the hang of formation flying, and my grades steadily improved.

DN STAGE: DAY NAVIGATION

Part of formation training was a day formation cross country flight. Two students would fly formation with an instructor who flew chase during the flight. We planned a flight to Meridian, Mississippi. Clear skies were everywhere making it a great day for flying. Right after taking off, our instructor said we must go to our alternate location, McCoy AFB, in Orlando, Florida, because of the weather. I am thinking, *What weather?* McCoy was off limits because McCoy's B-52s were flying in Vietnam. Reportedly, some wives were, shall we say, "lonely." Our instructor had some reason for going there and, as students, we did not ask questions. We had a blast just cruising cross country in formation. I didn't care where we went.

The flight to McCoy was easy, good weather, early morning with no thunderstorms along the coast. Just following the coast made the cross-country navigation easy. The instructor was goofing around, did a barrel roll in front of us, and ragged on us about our cruise formation being too wide. Approaching McCoy, we formed up into a three-plane parade formation, with the instructor in trail and flew into a Navy break. We taxied to base ops. Since McCoy was off limits, the instructor told us to get off base as soon as possible. We rented a car and drove to Daytona Beach for dinner.

The next afternoon, we took off to return to Pensacola. Since it was afternoon, thunderstorms started to build up along the coast. I had the lead and while dodging clouds, I flew into a blind canyon. I could not turn left or right, nor could I go straight ahead or turnaround because I had an airplane behind me. The instructor screams on the radio, "Break Up, Break Up." I flipped over on my back and made a split "S" out of the canyon.

We got down below the clouds and the instructor asked where we were. We formed a back up and finished our flight to Whiting Field. I feared I would get a below average grade for going into the blind canyon, but to my surprise, he gave me three above averages and no below averages. I always thought my grades had to do with his diversion to McCoy and his desire not to have anything said about it.

When we got back, we went into a three-day Fourth of July holiday weekend. To keep getting to know our fellow flight students better, Lou and I got together with some friends of ours. We had a picnic at the Black River Recreation Area, where we rented boats and cruised the river with Bob and his wife, Alice. The break was a pleasant escape from the constant pressure to perform.

NF STAGE: NIGHT FAMILIARIZATION

After the holiday, I got three formation flights in three days and my first two-night flights into the landing pattern. I remember taxiing back to the ramp after my night solo NF-2. The taxi directors were exceptional, with the flashlights whirling around and handing me off to the next director. In the dark, it was like I was part of a rehearsed dance. It pumped me up. I really felt like I was now a member of an exclusive club. I was getting good at flying and was close to finishing VT-2. Then I went into a week with no flights.

On Monday, July 17, I had my first solo Night Nav in the T-28 in VT-2, (NN-1). We flew over a closed pattern, southern Alabama, and northern Florida. About an hour and a half into my flight, just north of Whiting Field, my engine quit for about 15 seconds. Dead silence! I had to descend. Then the engine started again all by itself. I called the escort instructor and asked him if I should divert to Whiting.

He asked, "How is it running now?"

"Fine."

"Finish the hop."

They were really pushing the graduation rate in 1967. If I remember right, we were at a low altitude, around 2,500 feet. We had little time to get out of if the engine quit. We flew 2.5 hours at nighttime, and I got home about 0030. I had two morning formation flights the next morning and had to report at 0800. So much for crew rest, the eight hours we were supposed to rest before we flew again. But maybe the lack of sleep was good training for being on deployment.

On Tuesday, July 18, I flew my last four-plane solo formation flight with a chase instructor. We could not return to Whiting because of thunderstorms in the area. We had to divert to Brewton Airport in Alabama. Approaching the airport, we joined up in a five-plane parade formation and flew into the formation break up for our landings. We taxied in formation and made a turn into parking like we were the Blue Angels. Other flights diverted to Brewton also, many of them in the initial stages of training. We sat around the line shack in our dirty flight suits, waiting for the weather to break. Those other students were fresh to the T-28 in their sparkling new flight suits, and we were the old pros. Yakking it up with our instructor, we were talking with our hands, and joking about who flew the best "form," slang for formation flight. We wore an air of confidence and bravado not yet developed in the students still in the early stages. Everyone hammed it up with the instructor. We ruled the roost at the Brewton Airport diversion. I did flights F-14 and F-15, formation flights #14 and #15. I got good write-ups. What a great way to finish formation after a rough start.

I finished the Formation Stage with above average grades. The instructors assigned the grades in a subjective manner. But I always felt the grades reflected my actual performance, and I received fair grades. It took time to master these formation skills.

I finished my time at VT-2 on Thursday, July 19, and checked out the following day. I had made good progress through some demanding training. Except for the Transition phase where I got an average grade, I had above average grades in every phase of flight training. I sometimes wonder how it was possible with my colorful writeups my instructors gave me. One below average might generate a couple of sentences on my shortcomings.

The pilot demand in the fleet was driven by the Vietnam War. I have heard of pilots in later years being dropped from training for minor errors. During my time at VT-1 and VT-2, I do not recall any candidates being removed from training for a failure. Everyone I knew who dropped from training was a voluntary withdrawal.

Now it was off to the next training squadron, a Training Squadron Five known as VT-5. They flew the T-28 with tail hooks. VT-5 was the pinnacle of Basic Flight Training.

Chapter Four
Training Squadron Five VT-5

BACK TO NAAS SAUFLEY FIELD

When I checked into VT-5, I had progressed to the ultimate challenge of Basic Flight Training, learning to land on an aircraft carrier. Unlike my experiences at VT-1 and VT-2, at VT-5, ground school ran only one day. It gave us a Field Carrier Landing Practice (FCLP) overview and carrier aircraft operations. Taxiing out in my T-28, the T-34s had to give way to my flight. Six months ago, while at VT-1, I looked up to those pilots in the T-28s. Now I was back at Saufley in VT-5 wearing a dirty flight suit. I taxied by those same T-34s in my VT-5 T-28C with the tail hook. While I taxied, I knew what the T-34 pilots were thinking.

CARRIER QUALIFICATION

VT-5 scheduled my first Carrier Qualification (CQ-1) flight on Lou's 21st birthday. We didn't go out to have a drink to celebrate her 21st birthday. I wanted to study and focus on my upcoming Carrier Qualification flight the next morning. In hindsight, I was a jerk, and Lou also thought I was a jerk. Lou's life as a Navy wife would demand we would miss doing many things together. Over the next four years, we would have to endure missing anniversaries, birthdays, holidays, and being separated for months. Fortunately, my sister Betsy was visiting us for a few weeks. Lou and Betsy went out for her 21st birthday. The first two of my CQ flights went smoothly. Then I went into a pool for a week.

STUDENT PILOT DISPOSITION BOARD

The next week I flew my CQ-4 check ride, the safe for solo, into the FCLP pattern. On a windy, gusty day, I struggled to make the airplane perform. My poor performance resulted in a down, an Unsatisfactory Performance grade (UNSAT). The squadron directed me to the Student Pilot Disposition Board (SPDB). Student pilots took the acronym letters and called it the "Speedie Board," because you could quickly find yourself booted out of Navy Flight Training. I sweated being called to the SPDB; it was another challenge on my path to becoming a Navy pilot, but one I faced with confidence. No way would I quit. The SPDB did a Jacket Review after my down. I know I did not attend the Jacket Review. Four days later, the Commanding Officer of VT-5 called me into his office. I took a seat in front of the CO seated at his desk and two other officers seated at a table to his right side. The event was formal, and I had to wear my Tropical White Long uniform. They were all also wearing Tropical White Long uniforms. The CO called me to attention and asked,

"Do you want to continue in flight training?"

"Absolutely, sir, I want to be a Navy pilot!"

The CO motioned in my direction to take a seat. He then turned toward the other officers and commented I had above average flight grades plus excellent ground school records. He said I had a high probability of being successful in Navy flight training. Here is where the Captain's List appointment at VT-1, and VT-2 ground school grades may have come to my rescue. He said I had a break in my training, and he recommended I have two warmups and a recheck on CQ-4. The board concurred with the CO's recommendation, and I was back into Navy Flight Training. Another bullet dodged. My path to becoming a Navy pilot was a road with many potholes. Training developed a backup, and they scheduled my warmups for the coming weekend. The squadron gave me two warmups and a successful recheck on CQ-4. After the weekend training, I again I went into a pool for four days waiting for my next flight.

FIELD CARRIER LANDING PRACTICE (FCLPs)

Going to the "boat" solo in a T-28C would complete Basic Flight Training. Navy pilots nicknamed the aircraft carrier the "boat," a jab at our surface Navy brothers, who called it a ship. I moved to the solo Field Carrier Landing Practice pattern at NAAS Barin Field in Foley, Alabama, to prepare for my carrier landings. On FCLP flights, the T-28 flew to an imaginary aircraft carrier landing area painted on the runway. On the touchdown zone's left, they placed a mirror. Mirror reflected an orange ball; Navy pilots called the orange light the "meatball." Students worked the aircraft to keep the ball aligned with green light bars called "Datum Bars."

Naval Aviators called Barin Field "Bloody Barin" because the accidents and deaths that occurred there over the years. The Navy closed the base in 1958, but they kept the airfield open for FCLPs. They designated a space in the old WWII aircraft hangar's rear as a ready room. We referred to the ready room as the "Officer's Club." A beat-up old sign over hung the door, identifying the space as the Officer's Club. It added to the unique glamor of Barin Field and carrier qualification. The vibe at "Bloody Barin" was relaxed, resembling a squadron setting. The instructors were like squadron buddies. I felt like a Navy pilot.

In April 1967, in keeping with Bloody Barin's marque, there had been a fatal T-28 crash in the FCLP pattern. The aircraft rolled into the ground while turning base. It turned out the T-28s had made so many arrested carrier landings that the outer wing panels were flexing. While turning to base, the aileron was bound to the flaps and started an uncontrolled roll. The pilot could not stop the airplane's roll and crashed. In a post-accident autopsy, it turned out he had tuberculosis (TB). Since many of us had trained with him, we all had to go through TB testing protocol. They tested me four times in the next year to ensure I did not have TB. The accident grounded all T-28s going to the aircraft carrier while they were making wing attachment inspections. These inspections caused a backup at VT-5 and resultant pools.

Once I started flying FCLPs, training moved forward in a hurry and constant flying was the key to my success. I started doing two FCLP patterns a day. I did my first FCLP on Tuesday, August 22, 1967. The carrier work up was about one week of doing daily FCLPs until we had at least 75 passes. A week later, on Tuesday, August 29, 1967, I would make my first aircraft carrier landing. An LSO (Landing Signal Officer) guided us through our FCLPs. I would make 4-7 passes as the LSO graded my passes. I flew, following a "meatball" projected on a mirror simulating the "meatball" found on the aircraft carrier's Fresnel Lenses. These flights were short: 0.5 hours. The LSO would talk me through my approach while I sang my aircraft carrier landing song "Meatball, Line-up, Airspeed." The song kept my scan going to stay in ahead of the airplane. During my approaches, the LSO made calls such as "Power, Attitude, going low, etc." I made corrections in response to his calls. In one week, I made 78 FCLP landings. My records don't show how many

Wave Offs I received. Maybe that explains the difference in how many FCLP landings I made in each FCLP period.

LANDING ON THE "BOAT

I mastered making FCLP passes and had mastered precision flying in the T-28. The LSO signed me off as field qualified for carrier landings. Now assigned to flight 57D with three other pilots. We would go to the aircraft carrier together. Flight 57D stood by in the ready room, waiting for our turn to launch out to the boat. I waited three days for my call to go to the boat. While waiting, we did one FCLP pass on the second day to maintain currency.

We did not have hard times for our launch to the boat. The T-28 could deck launch without the help of a catapult. Therefore, we were on a loose schedule around the jet Carrier Qualification (CQ) schedule. While waiting, we just sat around the ready room killing time in our flight suits, playing bridge, Acey Ducey, etc. Our airplanes had been pre-flighted, and we left our helmets and survival gear in the cockpit. It would be a solo flight going to the boat. When doing something as dangerous as a student's first aircraft carrier landing, no instructor would want to ride with a rookie and not touch the controls. So, we went solo.

On Tuesday morning around 1100, the instructor came in and said, "Flight 57D launching 30 minutes, let's brief."

The instructor briefed us to fly heading 180 degrees at 1,500 feet toward the USS Lexington, CVS-16 a WWII aircraft carrier. The carrier was operating in the Gulf of Mexico about 60 nm south of Barin Field. We would take off and fly south from Barin Field until we picked channel 67, Lexington's TACAN (homing radio for the Lexington). When we picked up the Lexington's TACAN, we would establish our flight on the 350 Radial and hold at 10 nm. In the hold, we would wait for our call to go into the break. The instructor doing the briefings told us we would make two touch and go landings followed by six arrested landings and deck launches. He explained further about our duties on the carrier, including roles like LSO and launch officer, communication on radios, and navigating traffic patterns.

Then it was time to launch solo into a four-plane formation flight. We took off, and I flew to the lead's left. Which meant when we flew into break, I would be the last airplane to go into the break. The break occurs when the pilot makes a hard turn from the course on the carrier's starboard side (right side) into the downwind leg on the carrier's port side (left side). It was "Walter Mitty" fantasy moment. Imagined I was in a flight of Hellcats in WWII, flying back to our aircraft carrier. My face split into a big grin. I was about to join an elite brotherhood of Navy pilots who had landed on aircraft carriers. We arrived at our hold point and started our hold procedures.

Our flight was called into the break, and I turned into the downwind leg. I started following the instructions they had taught me. Flying at 325 feet, 82 knots, gear down, full flaps and airbrake extended, I put left wing's tip along the aircraft carrier's waterline. When abeam the fantail, I made a 20-degree left bank until the boat was in front of the airplane. When I rolled out, I saw the ball on the mirror near the center. I made the "334 Ball" call and set my power to 22 inches of Manifold Pressure to start my descent.

The LSO responded with "Roger Ball."

I started playing "Meatball. Line-up. Airspeed" game. The LSO would not talk to me again unless I was late on making a correction. I just looked out the window, kept the meatball in the center with power, worked hard to stay on centerline and worked airspeed with nose attitude. All the while singing "Meatball. Line-up. Airspeed" song. I never looked at the ship or the landing area because it was moving away from me and created an optical illusion. My focus was on the ball and the centerline. I never looked at anything else on the ship. The visual glide slope would vary with the ship's speed through the water to make 25 kts of wind across the deck. The T-28's approach speed was 82 kts, so with 25 kts of wind across the deck, the closure rate was not that fast. When the green Datum Bar lights next to the "meatball" flashed on, I cut the power and flew onto the ship. I did not flare. After slamming into the carrier's deck I applied full power, retracted the airbrake, flew off the carrier's angled deck to complete my touch and go landing. Back into the landing pattern, the next pass was also a touch and go with my tail hook up.

On my third pass, I lowered my tail hook for my first arrested landing. I established myself in the pattern and flew the ball. Crossing the fantail, the green Datum lights on the Fresnel Lense flashed. I cut the power and caught an arresting wire. The deceleration after catching the wire was gentler than I imagined. It surprised me how simple the first arrested landing had been. A yellow shirt (aircraft carrier flight deck handler) gave me a pushback signal with his open palms motioning backwards. I released the brakes; the arresting wire pulled the airplane back and my yellow shirt director gave me a hook up signal.

Following that, the yellow shirt handed me over to the launch officer. We would deck launch without catapult support. The launch officer stood directly ahead of my right wing and looked around to ensure the deck remained clear. He pointed at me with his left hand clenched, signaling me to hold my brakes. Next, he waved his right hand in a circle above his head with his finger pointing up, showing I should go to full power. He listened to the engine for the right sound. When the engine sounded right, he nodded toward me. I lowered my head towards him to show I was ready. He dropped to one knee, slapped the deck with his hand, and pointed toward the starboard bow. When he dropped to the deck, I knew it was my signal to release the brakes and take off.

On takeoff, we were told during our briefing, when the end of the ship disappears in front of us, pull the stick back as far as possible. It will fly. Do not look at the airspeed indicator, it will read nothing. Told not to look at it, of course I looked at it. They were right. It read below 50 kts indicated airspeed (IAS).

SURPRISE LANDING

In the briefing, we were told if we crossed the ship's centerline on takeoff; we would receive an automatic down (failure), because of possible interference with the bolter pattern. Since I had already received a down on CQ-4, if I got another down, they might wash me out. To make sure the airplane was still on the centerline's starboard side, I unlocked my shoulder harness and looked over my left shoulder. I was in good shape on the right side of the centerline. In the middle of checking my position, the Air Boss, who ran the carrier landing pattern, called me to make my turn into the break. The distraction made me forget to reset my shoulder harness.

On my second trapped landing, my shoulder harness remained unlocked. I got the green cut lights and pulled back on the throttle hard with my left hand. The wire caught and Bam! My right shoulder and head slammed into the glare shield. Thank goodness for helmets. The shock of my landing reminded me of walking into a glass door I didn't see. I was stunned. I had a mindset *of WTF (What the Fuck) just happened?* My left hand had gone full forward on the throttle. I was looking over my left shoulder, with the right side of my helmet slammed against the glare shield. On the carrier's left side, the blue water and ocean's white foam were rushing by in the background under my left wing.

While collecting my thoughts, I saw the launch officer run over from the right wing to the left wing. He shook his fist at me while pulling back his thumb. A signal to pull off the power. The fog in my brain cleared, and I pulled the throttle back. They pulled the plane back and gave me the up-tail hook signal to release the arresting wire. After a quick pull back, the hook went up. My mistake had broken the carrier landing flow and came close to fouling the deck. A fouled deck would have prevented the next airplane behind me from landing. The launch officer hurried to get me off the carrier. He skipped waving his hand waving routine, and in an instant dropped to his knee and pointed me toward the starboard bow. Off I went again.

My next five traps were routine, with no wave offs or bolters. My confidence built with each landing. On the sixth trap, the yellow shirt taxi director held up a sign that read "DELTA." I nodded my head and took off from the carrier for the last time in the T-28 and climbed into the overhead DELTA pattern. I was the first person in my flight to complete carrier qualifications. The other planes in my flight finished their landings and climbed to the Delta pattern. We joined a formation. On the flight back to Barin Field, I knew I would make my last landing in the T-28.

Over the past six months, I had struggled to master the T-28. But now I felt like a horseback rider who had mastered taking charge of the horse. I could make the T-28 perform. It is a good thing they took it away from me before I became adventurous and hurt myself. When I went to the boat on Tuesday August 29, 1967, in the T-28C. I had 142.2 hours total time and 116.8 in the T-28. I knew by completing carrier landings, I would now make it through training and become a Navy pilot.

Few pilots ever get the chance to join the elite club of those flyers who have landed on an aircraft carrier. I had mastered landing on an aircraft carrier and joined them. That experience was a high point of my life, and I was still living a childhood dream. Even though I had not yet received my wings, I knew I was now a Navy pilot.

ADVANCED TRAINING

On Wednesday, August 30, I checked out of VT-5. Earlier, we had filled out our preference sheets for our desired advanced pipelines. But the Navy would not assign me a training pipeline until I finished my VT-5 training. Out of 16 pilots finishing that week, I finished with #2 overall grades, # 5 in flight grades, and #1 in ground training grades. Multi Engine training was my #1 choice. The training pipeline needed to request my fleet assignment to a P-3 Squadron. I got what I wanted: orders to NAS Corpus Christi for Advanced Multi-Engine Training. What a fantastic adventure! I felt incredibly lucky.

One guy I went to the boat with, Butch, invited Lou and me to look at a mobile home. It impressed us. A mobile home was a luxury compared to our 400-square-foot, converted two-car garage. We saw a Frontier two-bedroom, one-bathroom, 70-foot by 14-foot mobile home. We liked it and bought it for about $10,000, which took care of our housing at Corpus Christi. After Corpus Christi, we could either sell it or move it to our squadron duty station. Lou and I prepared to move out of our first home in Pace, Florida. The Navy would move our trailer from Pensacola to Corpus Christi, and we packed all our household goods in it. We had little besides a TV, some dishes, pots, and pans. We had two cars, our new 1967 Ford Fairlane and the 1966 Ford Cortina. We put a hitch on the Fairlane and towed the Cortina to Corpus Christi.

Butch got orders to advanced jet training and went into A-7's after he got his wings. About a year later, an accident killed him while he was flying in the night FCLP pattern. Routine Navy flying was never routine.

I didn't need to be in Corpus Christi until September 7. With the Navy's four days of travel en route to Corpus Christi; I took another 3 days' leave and flew back to Detroit. One of our college friends, Dave Demerest from the 2000 ½ gang, was getting married to Marcia. They invited us to their wedding. His family held the reception at the Oakland Country Club, which was, of course, very fancy. Dave joined the Navy the next year.

We flew back to Pensacola and our next-door neighbor, my former 25-66 classmate Steve Gillis, picked us up at the airport. He took us out to our old home site where we had left our cars. We said goodbye to our good friends, Steve and Sara Gillis, and our first home. Then we hopped into the Fairlane, with the Cortina hooked up behind, and we started our trip to Corpus Christi. I drove down the familiar driveway for the last time, looking in the rear-view mirror at Gillis's house as it faded away. We drove down Highway 90 toward Pensacola, which was like I was going to Saufley, as I had done so many times while at VT-1 and VT-5. It was a typical drive until we changed course for Mobile, Alabama. Pensacola had been my entire life for the past 15 months and was now in the rearview mirror. Endings always tug at my heart. I knew it was a phase of my life that was now behind me and something I would never experience again. New adventures and challenges awaited me in Corpus Christi. The dreams of a child were coming true. When I finished Advanced Multi-Engine Training, I would become a Navy pilot.

Chapter Five
Training Squadron Thirty-One VT-31

NAS CORPUS CHRISTI

Lou and I showed up at NAS Corpus Christi on Thursday, September 7, 1967. Three multi-engine training squadrons flew out of NAS Corpus: VT-27, VT-28, and VT-31. They all flew the Grumman TS-2A. The TS-2A was a multiengine trainer version of a carrier-based S-2 anti-submarine warfare airplane. It had two R-1820 engines, the same used on the T-28, and weighed over 25,000 pounds. It had folding wings, and we had to spread and fold on almost every flight. I did not know which squadron they would send me to.

When I checked in with Student Control, I found out I was in another pool. The Student Control Officer told me to report every morning at 0800. After mustering every morning, we had the rest of the day off. Lou and I would go sightseeing around the Corpus Christi area. The daily muster routine continued until they assigned me to a training squadron.

We looked for a mobile home park while waiting for our brand-new mobile home to show up in Texas. Our friends from Pensacola, Jerry, and Helen Kevitt, allowed us to live with them while awaiting our trailer. In flight training, everyone became instant friends with other flight students. We had little time for growing friendships. Jerry and Helen reflected that camaraderie. Flight students, without a second thought, let friends move in, use their car, and even let other flight students use their house. After looking around, we found a trailer park. The Gulfway Trailer Park, at 7436 South Padre Island Drive, met our needs. Near NAS Corpus Christi, the trailer park housed quite a few other flight students. It is long gone now. We moved into our mobile home on September 17.

THE HURRICANE

A couple of days later, Lou and I experienced our first hurricane warning as Hurricane Beulah approached south Texas. The TV news people were giving disaster warnings. The reporters said Beulah could be the worst hurricane in Southern Texas's history. News reports warned that thousands of people could die, there could be a twenty-foot flood tide, and heavy rains would destroy the infrastructure. The stations were trying to outdo each other on projected disaster levels to get those TV ratings. Then on the evening of September 19, they issued a Hurricane Warning that Corpus Christi Beach and parts of Flower Bluff were being evacuated. We lived just across the bridge from Flower Bluff. In the middle of the night, our trailer was rocking and rolling like a bucking bronco. The wind and rain made it sound like the trailer was coming apart.

We had friends in San Antonio where we could stay if we evacuated Corpus Christi. At 0200, we jumped in the car and drove to San Antonio. The storm peaked about the time we left. The hurricane missed Corpus Christi and passed between Corpus and San Antonio. Now the bad news, the storm flooded the roads between Corpus and San Antonio, and we couldn't return right away. I missed muster on Wednesday and

Thursday. The Navy sent someone to our trailer to see if we were OK. He saw the trailer door wide open, and one car parked there. But they could not find me. They thought I might be a storm's victim.

We drove back on Thursday. When I showed up for muster on Friday morning, I was told I had been UA, Unauthorized Absence, a UCMJ violation and I could be in trouble. However, I thought the Student Control Officer was more pleased to see me alive and in one piece. He would not have to claim a body. He asked what happened. I explained, and he asked why I did not call in and explain. I said I did not have the number. He said he would charge me with two days' leave and let the matter drop. Good thing I came back on Friday, September 22, 1967. I found out they had assigned me to VT-31, and I had to check in on Monday morning.

VT-31 FLIGHT TRAINING

I checked into VT-31 and found out the squadron had assigned me an instructor. His name was LT Bobby D. Mansfield. He had flown S-2's in the fleet. Not only would he be my primary instructor, but also my mentor. When we're not flying, I'd meet him for squadron tips. We even paid social visits to each other's houses. I would meet with him each week to review my training progress and standing in VT-31. Similar to other training squadrons, we began with half-day ground school and half-day flying. I do not have a daily record of activities like VT-1, VT-2, and VT-5. On Monday, October 2, 1967, I took a hop in the TS-2A riding in the back. Unsure if it was an orientation flight or just curiosity.

When we started training, VT-31 paired me with a flying partner, Rob Strayhorn. The flights were about three hours long. We would spend 1.5 hours in the left front seat and 1.5 in the crew station behind the cockpit. I took my first instructional flight on Friday Oct 20 with Bobby; he gave me good grades for my landings. After my first flight, I came down with an ear infection and had to go on antibiotics. The infection grounded me for two weeks. I still attended ground school. But instead of flying, I picked up Squadron Duty Officer (SDO) watches. Working as SDO, I was a central contact person for the squadron. I manned an office with an assistant and a telephone. SDO watches would become part of my life in my fleet squadron, so my SDO watch at VT-31 was an indoctrination session for SDO watches in my squadron.

In mid-November, before I finished A stage, the familiarization phase, I moved into the B stage, which was the instrument phase. Instrument training was supposed to be the most challenging part of advanced training. On the day before Thanksgiving, I took my first Basic Instrument flight, B-01. The B phase, instrument training, comprised 26 flights. Unlike VT-2, where I completed one stage before going into another stage. At VT-31, I found myself scheduled for almost any flight at any stage. The random scheduling continued until I completed a stage. Not only was incoherent scheduling different, but there was also no sequence to the flights in the stage. They might schedule a D-02 flight and the next day a D-14 flight, and a month later a D-11. Weather, aircraft, and instructor availability drove the schedule. The demand for pilots to fly in Vietnam drove the training command's maximum effort to complete training as rapidly as possible.

The Navy scheduled a Thanksgiving stand down to give everyone a break. No flying took place. Jerry and Helen invited us over for Thanksgiving dinner with them. Lou had her mother's recipe for dinner rolls and made some for our visit. We played bridge after dinner and enjoyed a wonderful holiday. Jerry and Helen became our family while we were away from family.

In December, while in ground school, the squadron administration briefed us on how to go about requesting our fleet assignments. Everyone filled out the Fleet Assignment Preference Request form known as a "Dream Sheet." On the "Dream Sheet," we listed our top three choices for our fleet aircraft assignment and three choices for home base. Although I wanted to be sent to a P-3 Squadron, it was not a sure thing yet. For aircraft, I listed P-3s, then P-2s, and as a final choice S-2s. For locations, I listed NAS Jacksonville, Florida, NAS Brunswick, Maine, and NAS Pax River, Maryland. Our assignment to a fleet squadron was based on the Navy's needs, our class standing, and, last of all, our desires.

THE TRIP FROM HELL

The Training Command shut down for fifteen days at Christmas. We took leave and made the stupid decision to drive to Detroit via Phoenix. But I am glad we did it. We planned to visit my Grandpa Meakin in Phoenix. Plus, our best man from our wedding, high school buddy, Jack, attended the University of Arizona in Tucson, so we could give him a ride home.

We took off on Wednesday morning, driving our 1967 Ford Fairlane to El Paso. With only a few freeways back then, the drive was slow. We ran into freezing rain. The wet road glared in the reflected lights and slowed us down. It took forever to get to El Paso. Once there, we found an iced over hill we could not climb. A motel was our only option.

The next day was a simple drive to Tucson. We spent the night there with Jack and then he drove with us up to Sun City to visit Grandpa Meakin. I didn't know it would be my grandpa's final time. On Friday, we took off for Detroit. We figured with two drivers we could drive it non-stop in about 36 hours. We drove up to Flagstaff. The weather was bad. The roads were snow and ice covered. We had to buy chains. At Flagstaff, we found the State Police had blocked I-10 and would not allow cars to continue. Ten hours later, we were back in Phoenix where we had started. Our alternate route took us back through El Paso.

We drove through the night and into the following day. Around 2 a.m. the following night, we hit an object on the road, causing tire damage. We limped into an open gas station near St. Louis with our damaged tire. Under the station attendant's recommendation, we bought two new tires. An hour later, we were back in the car and reached Detroit by noon on the twenty-third. I think about if the damaged tire incident happened in 2024. Different times. With service stations almost non-existent today, how would someone get a new tire at 2 a.m.?

The trip was pure hell. For the long hours, tire changes, and all-night driving, we not only had Jack with us, but we brought our cat, Scratch. The vet gave Lou tranquilizers and, after listening to the cat's constant crying, we upped the dose. The cat dropped off the planet. We thought maybe it was dead. It had collapsed in my Navy hat and took a crap in its sleep. Our cat's poorly placed defecations were the icing on the cake for the trip from hell. I will never be foolish to take a cat on a long trip again. We dropped Jack off at his house in Michigan and he flew back to Arizona after the holidays.

We had an enjoyable time at home and celebrated our first wedding anniversary with a dinner at the Northland Inn, where we also spent our honeymoon night. Then we went to a New Year's Eve party at Larry Huff's home, one of my buddies from high school, who was now released from the Air Force. He lived near St Joe's Hospital, in Pontiac. We enjoyed the vacation with the intensity of a newlywed couple who knew there was a very good chance they wouldn't be together on their next anniversary. The Navy would deploy me soon, possibly to Vietnam. We would go three years before we celebrated our anniversary together again. My sister Kathy rode back to Corpus Christi with us.

Scratch, our cat, enjoyed the quick trip to Corpus Christi compared to the extensive journey through Texas, Arizona, Texas, and Michigan. After stopping in Little Rock for the night, we had a leisurely drive back home the next day. The first Super Bowl was broadcasted on the radio for entertainment. I remember rooting for Bart Star and the Green Bay Packers. Once we arrived back in Corpus Christi, I would finish up pilot training and get my wings.

On Monday, January 16, I had an Instrument Flight #12, B-12, warm up to get me back into the saddle. The instructor gave me a couple of above averages and said to continue in the program with no further warmup flights. The long break over the holidays hadn't affected me like the layoffs in the past.

Early the next morning on January 17, 1968, I had my 13th instrument flight, B-13, dual night actual IFR training flight. Coming out of Corpus Christi, I was riding alone in the seat behind the cockpit, waiting for my turn to fly. During the first power reduction at 400 feet, the right engine made a noise like someone dropped a cast-iron kettle on a concrete floor. The RPM on the right engine went through the red line. All kinds of weird noises. I leaned forward in my seat, intensely watching my flying partner lumber his way through the 15-step memory items checklist. At step three, the IP punched the feather button and cut out the right engine, bypassing many steps. He acted without confirming or verifying with the student, as we had been taught. They ran the shut-down checklist, followed by an uneventful single engine ground-controlled radar approach back into NAS Corpus Christi.

I asked the instructor in the de-brief why he skipped ahead to step 8 by pressing the feather button, even though the student pilot was only at step 3. He looked me in the eye, took the cigar out of his mouth and said, "Listen, sonny, if hadn't feathered that son of a bitch we might be in the Gulf of Mexico right now. Sometimes you just gotta do what you gotta do."

I heard those words again later. The master rod had failed, and it could have affected the propeller's ability to feather. Our instructor had real-world experiences we did not yet possess and used his knowledge to address our engine failure. In the training world, they drilled us on steps needed to handle potential emergencies. Memorizing these steps would increase our chances of correctly handling an emergency. "So much for the training world vs. the real world." I finished ground school on January 22, 1967. I did well in ground school and scored a 59, one standard deviation above the mean or in the upper two-thirds of my class. We had been attending ground school for half a day and flying for half a day. Once ground school ended, I started flying all day, every day.

FLEET ORDERS

On Tuesday, January 30, I received my orders to my fleet squadron. I got my first choice of airplane and first choice of home base, the P-3, at NAS Jacksonville. I would fly the P-3 Orion in Patrol Squadron 45, VP-45. Lou and I could not have been happier. Our friends Jerry and Helen Kevitt, who left Corpus Christi ahead of us, lived in Jacksonville. We looked forward to seeing them again.

A couple of weeks later, a P-3 from VP-45 visited NAS Corpus Christi, bringing the news that the squadron would start flying patrols around Vietnam in December. Because the Navy planned to send me to Vietnam, as I expected, I would not spend my second wedding anniversary with Lou. The squadron was building up to a combat staffing of 15 crews and had a lot of pilots coming in.

Later, I found out I had the highest grades of anyone requesting fleet assignment the week I submitted my Dream Sheet. The Training Officer at VP-45 informed me the Navy selected pilots who performed well in training to join squadrons flying combat missions.

B-26 INSTRUMENT CHECKRIDE

On January 31, during the nineteenth Instrument Stage flight (B-19), we observed the cylinder head temperature of the left engine was increasing beyond the safe range shortly after takeoff. I recommended we shut it down. The instructor agreed with me. Since I was flying, he told me to go ahead, shut the engine down, and shoot an approach back into Corpus. The weather was good with clear skies and the instructor said we could do a visual approach. The visual approach would not provide glide slope information. A stabilized approach with a single engine would be easier if we had glide slope information to ensure a successful outcome. I asked for a ground-controlled radar approach (GCA) because I wanted glide slope information available. My instructor and I discussed it during the de-brief. He gave me a couple of AAs for headwork and the GCA.

I took my Instrument Check Ride (B-26) on February 2, 1968, my last flight in the B stage of training. If I passed my B-26 flight, it would qualify me as a Navy instrument pilot. The Navy would issue me a White Instrument Ticket that designated me as an instrument-rated pilot who could file instrument flight plans and fly when the weather was below visual conditions. With a high failure rate, everyone sweated the B-26 check. The instructor doing my check, Lt. Cmdr. Conrad, was a seasoned WWII pilot and a senior instructor at my training squadron, VT-31. He had a reputation of being a demanding check airman who had given many failures. My buddies said, "It is too bad you drew Lt. Cmdr. Conrad." Such are the breaks of Naval Air.

Lieutenant Commander Conrad told me new pilots had it so easy these days with all these fancy new radios like TACAN, a navigation radio that gave both bearing and distance from a station. Plus, we had instruments like Radio Magnetic Indicators (RMI) and the course deviation indicator (ID-249). I found him a good natured, if crusty, old WWII vet. Things were going well, and I knew had a good ride going. He tested my limits. For the fliers, my final approach looked like this: He had me shoot a Single Engine Localizer Back Course (LOC BC) into Corpus Christi International to the published missed approach. Our missed approach had a holding pattern on the LOC BC course and a crossing radial off the Corpus Christi VOR. A single VOR radio receiver found in the TS-2A came with a coffee grinder tuner, like hand tuning an AM radio in a 1950 car. The VOR radio was behind my right elbow on the console. When flying instruments, it was completely out of my normal field of view. Tuning the VOR, I had to stop and listen to the Morse code to ID the station. The Morse Code training at VT-1 made the manual tuning possible.

I was busier than a "cat on a hot tin roof" as I flipped the radio frequency and set the proper radial, held a steady heading while flying on a single engine until I identified the intersection. Then I made my turn into the hold. I started my turn back to the outbound course and reestablished on the LOC BC, which I successfully intercepted. Once I established myself outbound, Lt. Cmdr. Conrad pulled my other engine. Now I was under the IFR hood, a view limiting device, with both engines simulated shut down. He asked,

"What are you going to do?"

"Crash straight ahead, sir."

He laughed.

"Take off your hood and take me home. This ride is over."

I knew I had aced an all-important milestone in training. I finished the B stage with great grades and got my Navy Standard Instrument rating.

Now the flying really took off. I flew every day and many times I flew two hops. Most of the time, I was jumping between phases. I would do an F stage flight #1, Field Carrier Landing Practice (FCLP) in the morning, then in the evening do a C stage #4-night flight. I would log over 100 hours in the next five weeks. Now I was exactly where I wanted to be, flying my butt off.

FOUR UNSAT GRADES

Until the last two weeks of February, things were going great. Then I received four unsats. The first down was on a student solo F stage flight 6 with another student in the FCLP pattern at Naval Auxiliary Air Station (NAAS) Cabaniss. After completing my FCLP passes, there was a mid-period break scheduled. During the mid-period break, the other student moved to the left seat to make FCLP passes. We were supposed to pull off the runway to swap seats. I stepped on the brakes to pull off the runway. The airplane pulled to the left. I had no right brake. As we rolled toward the runway's end, someone came up on the Guard frequency, emergency radio, and called out, "305, your right brake is on fire."

A brake fire was an emergency procedure. Memory items were: Cut Mixtures, Mags off, and Master switch off. The brake could explode into the fuel tank right above the brake and start a fire. We evacuated through the cockpit overhead exits, ran to the end of the left wing opposite the potential fire. Then we jumped to the ground and ran away from a possible explosion and fire. The normal shutdown checklist was not completed.

The instructor, LSO, running the FCLP pattern saw us shut down and were running away from the airplane. He experiences a "WTF" moment: "What are these students doing?" While we were standing there, a gray Navy truck showed up and offered us a ride back to NAS Corpus. We figured, *What the heck, guess that is what we should do.* The LSO, not knowing what happened, gave us unsats for parking the airplane and not completing the FCLP lesson. We got back to NAS Corpus and checked in with VT-31 student control. They wondered what we were doing there. We explained what happened. They told us to go home.

The squadron fixed it and sent a maintenance pilot over to NAAS Cabaniss Field to pick it up. There had been no brake fire. The smoke resulted from a brake line that leaked on the brake and caused the smoke. In keeping with the emergency procedures, we had not completed the Shutdown Checklist. Checklist items like radio, inverters, and lights were still ON. The maintenance pilot did not know the brake fire story. So, he gave us an unsat for checklist use. I received two unsats from two different instructors on the same flight. I had to file an incident report. The Training Officer read my report and said to continue in phase but didn't remove the unsats. Now I have two unsats on an almost nearly spotless training record.

In the mid-1960s, because of the Vietnam buildup, the Training Command experienced an instructor shortage. The Navy had to ensure that these instructor positions got filled. So, when a pilot resigned, the Navy extended their service for one year and issued orders to the Training Command as instructors. A lot of instructors were just putting in their time until they could get out. We liked how laid back they were and enjoyed flying with these easy-going instructors. They also enjoyed passing their Navy flying experience along to their students.

A fun D stage flight was a Low-Level Cross Country. On our dual low-level training flight, we flew with an instructor who had a job waiting for him at Delta Airlines. He had about 30 days left in the Navy. To prepare for our dual Low-Level Cross Country, our instructor did not do any preflight briefing, no flight planning, no flight log, no fuel log. He just had us hop in and go. We took off and roared across south Texas at 500 feet above the ground. Sometimes we were down to 50 feet chasing jackrabbits and coyotes. What a great flight. It pumped me up to do my student solo low-level cross country where two students would fly their own low-level cross country.

They scheduled another student pilot and me for a low-level cross country, D stage 15, the following day. we planned to fly to Tinker AFB in Oklahoma City, Oklahoma. After takeoff, we were wandering all over Texas, having a ball. We landed at Tinker, got a bite to eat, and headed back to Corpus. We flew at 500 feet right between Dallas and Ft. Worth, with no radio contact and no radar service. It was the future home of DFW International Airport and in 1968 it was open prairie land. The day after our flight, we were called into student control. They asked,

"Where is your Navigation Log?"

"I didn't know we were supposed to do a Navigation Log. We received no instruction on cross-country flight planning,"

We were told we would get two unsats on the flight. One for no preflight planning and one for no in-flight navigation tracking. I told the Training Officer,

"The flight was great fun. Let me do it again."

"No. Continue in phase."

I received no D stage below averages (BA) but ended up with two unsats. Even with the two unsats, D stage was my second-best phase in VT-31. In one week, they gave me four unsats and said to continue training. This inconsistency reflected the intensity of training to get pilots out of training and into fleet squadrons at the Vietnam War's height.

LANDING ON A CARRIER AGAIN

On Wednesday, February 21, I did a D stage #14 IFR student cross-country to Pensacola. We were going to make our aircraft carrier landings on the USS Randolph, CVS-15. They put us in rooms at the BOQ and on February 22; we did one FCLP pattern at Sherman Field. Then, much the same as the T-28s, we stood a loose schedule around the jet carrier landing. On February 23, 1967, we were in the snack bar at Sherman Field, standing by for our time to go to the boat. In midafternoon, at 1500, they told us to launch. I do not remember how many airplanes went. Two or three is my best recollection.

The sun was setting when we got into the pattern for my landings on the USS Randolph in the TS-2A. The environment was dusk in marginal weather, with low ceilings and low visibility. I remember how small the WWII aircraft carrier looked in the fading light. While flying a TS-2A, I noticed it seemed almost equipped with an auto land feature. Of course, they never installed an auto land feature on the TS-2A. But the Instructor Pilot in the right seat was all over the controls with me to make sure he set me up for my landing. He just wanted to get it done. We did one touch and go and four arrested landings. Like the T-28, the TS-2A deck launched without using catapult assistance, which sped up the process. We flew back to Sherman Field, and it was dark when we landed.

The six of us Carrier Qualified that day. We went to the BOQ to change and clean up. We wanted to celebrate and went to downtown Pensacola for dinner. I remember drinking Martinis and eating oysters. No longer feeling like a student pilot, I felt like a fleet pilot in an operating squadron. Going out with my fellow Naval aviators fulfilled my dream. This pilot's world was exactly where I wanted to be and wouldn't have traded that moment for anything. It filled me with confidence and a sense of accomplishment unequaled in my life. How lucky was I to be living up to my childhood dream? The moment was almost "pinch me." I thought, *Am I dreaming?* We would all be getting our wings of gold that signified we were Naval aviators in the next couple of weeks.

ST ELMO'S FIRE

Late the next afternoon, we took off on a student night instrument cross country instrument flight back to Corpus Christi. It was IFR and turned dark shortly after takeoff. Over Houston, we flew into icing. The icing striking the airplane produced static electricity and produced sparkling blue lights know as St Elmo's fire. The St Elmo's fire started dancing around the edges of our windshield. Static filled the radios, and we could not communicate with ATC. Next, the dancing blue electrons came into the cockpit. They started rolling down the instrument panel to the center console while getting brighter.

As student pilots, we were having a WTF moment. Neither of us had ever seen or heard of St Elmo's Fire before. Intense static roared on the radios, and we couldn't talk to anyone. We were on our own, no one could help us. Our anxiety rose as we continued flying in the icing. I was flying from the left seat and suddenly there was a bang with a blue flash in the cockpit. The dancing blue light vanished and the heavy static in our radios stopped. Then the VHF comm and VHF Nav radios came back online. Things were semi back to normal. However, the TACAN and UHF Radio quit working. We stayed on the airways using our VOR and elected to continue to NAS Corpus. Then I looked at our hydraulic pressure gauge and saw there was no pressure.

Oh! Oh! We got out the emergency checklist; and looked at the landing without a hydraulic pressure checklist. We would have to pump the gear and put the flaps down. We would have no brakes. I declared an emergency, and I decided I wanted the long runway at Corpus. It had arresting gear. Planning my stop, I intended to drop the tail hook to catch the arresting gear. It was nighttime IFR; the weather was close to landing minimums, with a 400-foot ceiling and one-mile visibility. The airplane's TACAN was not working, therefore I couldn't do a TACAN approach the runway I wanted. A radar approach was the only solution, and

I asked for a GCA to land on the long runway with the arresting gear. They informed me that the long runway was not set up for a GCA. We would have to do a Surveillance Radar Approach (ASR) to the long runway with the arresting gear. In 1968, the Navy ASR controllers gave the pilot target altitudes every mile from touchdown. I would have limited glide path information on my approach.

A real-world emergency would test us as never before. Unlike grading by our instructors whose "grades" don't always match capability, we were being tested in the real world. Here, our training and competency as pilots would test us in a life and death situation, with the ultimate measure of success being a successful outcome. We got set up and pumped the gear and flaps down. Then, following the checklist, I turned on the rudder augmentation switch. It gave a hydraulic boost to a panel forward of the rudder. But with no hydraulic pressure, the augment panel turned into a free-floating panel. It acted as a huge uncontrolled trim tab for the rudder. Instead of assisting me in flying, it acted in the opposite direction. If I pushed the left rudder, the airplane should have yawed left, but now it would yaw right. Differential engine power now became my yaw control. I took my feet off the rudders and used differential power for small direction changes. Our ASR approach set us up for a landing in the touchdown zone. I broke out at minimums, saw the runway and put the plane down in the touchdown zone. We coasted down the runway without brakes and caught the arresting gear. Now our emergency landing closed the duty runway.

There was a P-3 from VP-45 waiting to take off. They could not take off because of our emergency approach. NAS Corpus shut down the runway when we took the arresting gear. We could not taxi without brakes. So, we sat and waited for a tug to come out and tow us back to the VT-31 ramp. The runway remained closed until the tug pulled back to the VT-31 ramp.

The P-3 had to wait for us to be towed off the runway. A year later, when I was in VP-45, I was telling the story to a pilot I was flying with. He said "Oh! That was you? We wondered who screwed up our flight." The small world of Naval Aviation.

Because I had declared an emergency, I had to file a safety report with the squadron safety officer. He forwarded it to the Naval Safety Center. The Navy Safety Center wrote us up in their monthly digest and gave us an "Atta Boy," Navy term for good job, for our headwork in handling a compound emergency. The experience was a real confidence builder for a new pilot. My above average performance in instrument training had paid off in spades. I felt I was in charge the whole time; I had a plan, and it worked. Not only was the Navy training me to fly an airplane, but they were also instilling confidence in me to take command.

WINGS OF GOLD

I only needed a few more flights to complete my training, and I did my last flight on Tuesday, March 5. On my final grade sheet for VT-31, I ended up with above average grades. And my best stage was the B stage. The one with the heaviest weight was Instrument flying. The following morning, Wednesday March 6, 1968, the Navy would award me my Navy Wings of Gold. In those wartime days, they did not prioritize formal ceremonies as they do today. Pumping pilots into fleet squadrons drove the agenda. Mom and Dad flew down to Corpus Christi to see me get my wings. Mom stayed with Lou and me in our mobile home. In a brief ceremony on the NAS Corpus Christi Admin building steps, seven of us received our wings that day.

The Base Commanding Officer, a Navy Captain, gave a short speech recognizing us as the future of Naval Aviation. He noted the challenging program that those receiving their wings had completed. We would now go to our fleet squadrons and play our part in the nation's defense.

Next, we went indoors to take pictures, getting our wings pinned on our uniforms. Lou had pinned on my shoulder boards in Pensacola at my commissioning, so with my dad watching, I had my mom pin on my wings since she flew in for the ceremony. Mom flew home, going through Phoenix to visit her father, Grandpa Meakin. His health was declining, and he died the next month.

Reflections on Navy Flight Training. I was good when I was good. But I was inconsistent. My proficiency suffered when I experienced extended breaks in training, but when I flew regularly, I easily mastered the training requirement. I received six unsats while going through training. Yet they still graded me ahead of my contemporaries. I benefitted from the Navy's desperate need for fleet pilots. Two years later, with President Nixon's Vietnamization of the War, the military drawdown started, and the demand for pilots dropped. The Navy started looking for any excuse to drop pilots from the training program.

The elements of luck and timing play roles in our lives that are hard to understand. Why did I see that ad in the Michigan State student newspaper announcing the Navy Aviation Recruiter would be on campus? Why did Tommy bring Lou to my apartment? Am I lucky, or is a greater force guiding our lives? It has touched me in so many ways.

Chapter Six
Training Squadron Twenty Nine VT-29

NAS Corpus Christi

In 1968, all P-3 pilots, just like WWII patrol plane pilots, started out as navigators. Before I left Corpus Christi, I had to go through Celestial Navigation Training at VT-29. When the P-3Cs came into the VP squadrons in 1970, pilots no longer attended navigator training. After I got my wings, I went into a pool waiting for a class at VT-29.

PILOT'S LICENSE

With my free time, the one thing I wanted to do was take my Military Competency Test and get my civilian pilot's license. The FAA allowed military-trained pilots to get their commercial pilot's licenses by demonstrating knowledge of civilian aviation rules. The Military Competency Test was a 40-question test on FAA Regulations. When I passed the test, the FAA would issue me a Commercial Single Engine Land and Multi-Engine Land Airplane Instrument (COMM. SEL/MEL, INST) pilot's license. I studied the FAA regulations for about three days. Then I drove down to Alice, Texas, Flight Service Station to take the test. The test was easy and didn't take long. An FAA Inspector, who had an answer sheet full of punched holes, graded it. I could see he had used his answer sheet many times and issuing the pilot's license was nothing new to him.

He issued me my COMM. SEL/MEL, INST license. My license was the same license carried by new airline pilots in 1968. Now that I had my civilian pilot's license, I joined the NAS Corpus Christi Flying Club. The club checked me out on the C-172. I could not believe how underpowered it was and how feather light the controls felt. Then I gave Lou her first airplane ride with me as the pilot. The airplane rented for $7.50 an hour, which included gas.

I went to Student Control on Friday, March 15, and found that the Navy had promoted me to lieutenant junior grade. My new rank made me the senior man in the pool. Student Control appointed me as the class leader and mustering officer, i.e., do headcount, for the group in the VT-29 pool. The new position meant nothing since I would never hold a muster. Everyone in my pool had orders to report to VT-29 on Monday, March 18.

NAVIGATOR GROUND SCHOOL

On Monday, March 18, I checked into VT-29. Before we started flying, we had three weeks of ground school. The course covered sextant use, how to do navigation logs, use Sight Reduction Tables, and how to find the stars in the heavens. Navigation began with "class one" stars. In the Northern Hemisphere, there are 16 class-one stars. We were required to locate these stars. Not all stars are in sight all the time. Class one-star locations varies with the seasons. In the observatory, the instructors showed us the seasons and associated stars.

They gave us gouges to help locate the stars such "Big tit, little tit, Arc around to Arcturus" and "Orion's Belt." They then tested us on star locations. I had a 142 hours of ground school that ran through May 3. I received a grade of 69.01, almost two standard deviations above the mean of 50. The score put me in the top 97 percent of everyone who took the class. On the final exam, I applied a little-used navigation solution, called a Local Apparent Noon (LAN). I received the highest grade ever given on the final, an 80, the highest score the Navy gives in training. I was not alone; others also made the top score.

NAVIGATOR FLIGHTS

Navigation was right up my alley. I really enjoyed my role as Navigator directing the airplane through the heavens. It filled me with a sense of satisfaction. On April 8, I took my first flight in the T-29 navigator trainer. These were long flights averaging about six hours each. I did nine flights and logged 55 hours as a navigator student along with five other navigator students on the flight. We would take turns being the lead navigator. When not navigating, we would track the lead navigator's work. We did day and night flights.

My college math came in handy. Celestial Navigation made perfect sense to me. The Solid Geometry class from college came in handy. I easily mastered the concepts of Celestial Body Subpoint, Azimuth, and Declination. Because of my math background, I did not have to use a calculator to do addition and subtraction in the Sight Reduction tables. I could quickly work out the navigation problems. In every phase of navigation flight training, I scored the highest grade they could give. I got 80s in all three phases. Three standard deviations above the mean, or the upper 99 percent of everyone who had gone through the training. I whizzed through Navigator Training. My performance confirmed I had taken the right path in pursuing my goal of becoming a Navy pilot. My Nav School grades would land me the job as VP-45's Navigation Officer and assignment to the XO's crew as navigator.

LEAVING CORPUS CHRISTI

When I finished, I had 10 days off before I started more training in Norfolk, Virginia. I would move around often in the next five months, and we decided Lou would stay at home with her parents. She would go to school at Eastern Michigan University and work on her degree. We put our trailer in storage at our trailer park in Corpus Christi until we found a place to set it up in Jacksonville. On May 10, we pulled out of Corpus towing the English Ford back to Michigan. I would leave the 1967 Ford Fairlane with Lou in Michigan. The Cortina would go down to Norfolk with me. Little did I know I would spend less than four weeks with Lou in the next year.

Chapter Seven
Fleet Avionics and Electronics Training Unit Atlantic Fleet (FAETULANT)

NAS NORFOLK

Now that I had my Navy wings, I had to learn to fly the airplane assigned to me by the Navy. The training would include not only how to fly, but also how to use the airplane's on-board equipment to employ it as a "Weapons System." In late May, I started at Fleet Avionics and Electronics Training Unit Atlantic Fleet, better known as FAETULANT. I drove down and showed up on Sunday night, May 26, 1968. The main BOQ had no rooms, but they told me I could voluntarily accept a room at no charge in the old WWII BOQ currently not being used. When I said "Sure," they gave me sheets and towels. I found an empty room with two bunk beds with the head, Navy term for bathroom, down the passageway. I had to make my bed. The bunks and sparse living reminded me of Batt I at AOCS, but there would be no inspections like two years earlier.

The first day in class, I met up with some pilots I knew from VT-29, Jon, who would join me at VP-45, and Don, a trailer park neighbor from Corpus Christi. We were all getting a basic housing allowance and elected to find a place to rent for six weeks. We found a three-bedroom place on the Willoughby Spit right across the bay from NAS Norfolk. Again, there was a camaraderie and instant acceptance found amongst Navy pilots. It made doing something like renting a place together a decision requiring little thought.

GROUND SCHOOL

At FAETULANT, the Navy would introduce me to Anti-Submarine Warfare systems, tactics and weapons used in anti-submarine operations. We learned about the various sonobuoys the Navy employed to detect and track submarines. We learned about the SOSUS, a highly classified system. In 1968, even saying the word SOSUS outside of a secure area was a security violation. Weapons training included conventional depth charges, homing torpedoes, and nuclear depth charges.

The nuclear weapons training was a weighty experience. The nuclear training room was inside a double-barbed-wire-barrier-protected compound. Armed Marines were at each gate inside the barbed wire. We did double ID checks to gain access. We learned all about how to employ the Mk-101 and B-57 nuclear depth charges. They showed us settings for yield, depth of detention, and how the bomb worked. With highly classified training, we took no notes and received no handouts. We learned by pure exposure and memory. I still feel funny talking about that training because of the warnings the instructors gave us about being punished for disclosure of information learned during those classes. But today, anyone can go on the internet and find out how bombs work.

The Navy cut the course to five-weeks so we could make our class date at VP-30 for P-3 pilot training. They made

FAETULANT a low-pressure program, and I ended up #8 in a class of 9. The material encompassed a collection of unrelated rote content to be memorized. The subjects were classified, and we could not study it away from the classroom. This hurt my performance.

A WEEKEND AT NEWPORT

The first weekend at Norfolk, I elected to see if I could catch a ride as a space-available passenger on an airplane up to Navy OCS at Newport, Rhode Island, to visit my cousin, Jim Beall, and my college friend, Dave. I checked in at NAS Norfolk Base Ops and found a P-3 going to Boston. I hitched my very first ride on a P-3 as a passenger, not a training crew member. It excited me. I would get a ride in my future aircraft. I sat on the radar console behind the pilot. The P-3 rapidly accelerated, and I had to hold on to the pilot's seat to avoid being thrown on the floor. We were climbing at 4,000 feet per minute at 250 kts; I couldn't believe it. What an impressive airplane! I thought, *"The Navy is going to let me fly the P-3?*

The crew told me about a missing nuclear sub. A nuclear submarine, the USS Scorpion, disappeared near the Azores. The sub's loss generated a lot of flight activity on the east coast. Airplanes were prepared for flights to the Azores and search for the sub. We got to Hanscom Field near Boston. I elected to hitchhike down to Newport. An airport employee dropped me at the entrance to the expressway. Dressed in my Tropical Khaki uniform with my brown leather flight jacket, I started hitchhiking down to Newport. Soon a cop pulled over, and I thought *Oh! Oh! Am I in trouble? Maybe hitchhiking isn't allowed in Massachusetts.*

He asked where I was going. I told him about Newport, Rhode Island, Naval OCS. He said to hop in, and he drove me to

Newport. Really nice guy. When I got to the Naval Station, I tried to find Jim and Dave. I was now a lieutenant junior grade and was wearing wings on my flight jacket. The gate guards treated me like someone who has some authority and went out of their way helping me locate Jim and Dave. Again, I thought, *Wow! What have I done to receive such special treatment?*

Being an officer outside the training environment, where my rank wasn't commonplace and signified some level of expertise and authority, was a unique first-time experience. Until now, as a student, I had little interaction with the Navy outside of training. I just followed instructions for everything. After I found Jim and Dave, we went out to dinner. Now I needed to get back to Norfolk. I caught a bus to NAS Quonset Point, then found a C-130 heading back to Norfolk. I was exhausted and found the bunk in the cockpit where I slept on way back.

FREE TIME

I had a fair amount of free time, so Don talked me into going sailing. I had fun until the sail boom came across the boat and smacked me on the head. Don, a USNA graduate, laughed his head off about my seamanship. Later, Jon wanted to go to the beach, and I said I had nothing to do, so I went. We went down to Oceana Beach but didn't stay long because the crowd was large.

Lou came down to visit me on the weekend of June 15. I remember truly little about the weekend, but I remember her leaving the Norfolk Municipal Airport. In 1968, at smaller airports, there were no concourses, no boarding ramps. I could stand by the fence and watch people get on and off. She was going to fly her first leg to Washington National on a United DC-6, among the last piston-powered airliners still in use. I watched her board; watched the engine starts and the takeoff. I missed her. For Lou and me, it was the longest time we had been apart since we were married 16 months prior. I did not want her to leave Norfolk.

SMALL WORLD

Naval Aviation is a small world. I was in the casual snack bar at the O'Club in my shorts and, as I walked out; I saw my AOCS roommate and locker mate, Steve Gillis, in a phone booth. He was now attached to a Search and Rescue Squadron, HC-2 at Lake Hurst, New Jersey, flying the HU-2 helicopter. He flew "Plane Guard" on aircraft carriers. Plane Guards flew next to aircraft carriers during flight operations in case a pilot ejected and went into the water. The helicopter would pick up the downed pilot. Steve was in town for a tennis tournament. He didn't have a car, so I loaned him my Cortina because I could mooch rides off Don and Jon.

While Steve was in town, we went to see *2001 A Space Odyssey* with my roommates. One thing I remember about the movie was the multifunction flat screen displays shown in the future cockpit. They got one thing right. I wonder about HAL2000? We fell into easy into our friendship when Navy buddies' paths crossed.

We had to do a survival swim at FAETULANT. AOCS had prepared us well for the class. Navy swim instructors introduced us to a new procedure called the Concussion Swim. I floated on my back in the water with my legs crossed, feet and head out of the water. We then had to swim 75 yards in the Concussion Swim configuration using only my hands.

We finished FAETULANT on June 28, and the Navy gave me leave until the 9th of July, before I had to report to VP-30. The gap in reporting gave me a week off, and I went back to Detroit to spend the Fourth of July with Lou and my family. We drove up to my grandparents' Canadian home in Lion's Head, Ontario, for a couple of days. Since Jon and I were going to VP-30, Jon went up to Patuxent (Pax) River and found an apartment near the base. We moved in together when we got to Pax River.

Chapter Eight
Patrol Squadron Thirty VP-30

NAS PATUXENT RIVER

Patrol Squadron 30, VP-30, at NAS Pax River in Maryland, known as the Replacement Air Group (RAG), was where pilots learned to fly the P-3 Orion. I would learn to fly the newest patrol airplane in the Navy inventory. The P-3 would take off at 127,500 pounds, fly 5,000 miles and could remain airborne for up to 20 hours. The Navy would fly the P-3 Orion for over 60 years. The same as with my other new training reports, there was limited space available in the BOQ. The Navy gave me a housing allowance to pay for my part of the apartment with Jon. Another VP-30 student going to Brunswick, Maine, who was in a class with us in Norfolk, would join us. The three of us from FAETULANT lived in a two-bedroom apartment without air conditioning near the base.

GROUND SCHOOL

In ground school at VP-30, new pilots who had just earned their wings would mix with experienced fleet pilots. These pilots were coming into the P-3 after up to 12 years in the Navy making a broad mix of experience in the classroom. We had four weeks of ground school prior to our first flight in the P-3. The class included two weeks on the engine and propeller taught by P-3 Flight Engineers, who really knew airplane mechanics better than anyone. The propeller class was three days long, probably because the prop was a complicated mechanism. Time spent taking cars apart in the garage on Beach Road gave me an advantage in understanding all the mechanical parts in the engine and prop. I quickly figured it out. A senior guy in our class said to his buddy, "Randy seems to have this thing figured out. We should sit next to him for the final exam."

Their confidence in me was quite an honor. I did well in the engine and propeller portion of training and scored above average in my class of 16 pilots. Throughout my time in the P-3, I would get good grades on systems knowledge.

After the engine and prop school, we moved into the VP-30 hangar on the old seaplane ramp down on the river. Instructors set the classroom up in a horseshoe, with tables around the edge. The instructor would walk up and down inside the horseshoe. We studied the P-3 Naval Aviation Training and Operating Procedures (NATOPS) manual, checklist use, and the emergency and abnormal procedures found in the NATOPS. Our ground school instructor had flown the P-3 on Market Time missions in Vietnam. He talked about the loss of an airplane there as a lesson in emergency procedures. Here I learned about Patrol Squadron 26's P-3 loss on April 1, 1968, flying a Market Time mission. The Cambodians shot down and killed our next-door neighbor from Whiting Field, Brain Matheson. I grasped the reality of flying in combat. Flying around Vietnam would not be a routine operation. I decided not to tell Lou about our neighbor's P-3 being shot down. It might unnecessarily raise her level of anxiety. (See Appendix A).

The heat and humidity at Pax River in the summer was stifling, in the 90s all the time and sometimes close to a 100, and being near the water, it was always humid. I shared an upstairs room with Jon Dalton. With no air-conditioning, it was nasty and made sleeping difficult. To cool off, I took a cold shower, jumped into bed, fell asleep and, hopefully, slept all night. A neighbor locked his dog outside all night, and it would bark and howl. The barking often killed my sleep, waking me up and leaving me in a state of continuous exhaustion.

One of our VP-30 classmates, Lance, was a Naval Academy graduate, and he was getting married at the Naval Academy Chapel on the weekend of August 17. He wanted an Arch of Swords at his wedding with his classmates in Choker White uniforms. Lance asked me to join his wedding party. It honored me to raise a sword for him. The rehearsal and dinner were a fun time with my Navy buddies. Lou came down for the weekend and attended the wedding and reception with me.

Before we could fly the P-3, we would have three Operational Flight Trainers (OFT) sessions in the cockpit to prepare us for our first flight. During the OFTs, we spent our time in the cockpit of a P-3 going over checklists, starting engines, addressing abnormal systems operations and aircraft emergencies. I had a great instructor, Lt. Merrical. Per Navy procedures, all my training was in the left seat. No trainees fly in the left seat in the civilian world until they are ready to become captain.

FLYING THE P-3

On Tuesday, August 13, I had my first flight as a pilot in the P-3. An unusual feature of VP-30 was its location on the old seaplane ramp. Our P-3 had to taxi up a steep incline, known as the "Hill," to climb to airfield elevation. The "Hill" required a high-power setting to climb off the seaplane ramp up the taxiway. I used my left hand on a little steering wheel to guide my airplane down the taxiways and my right hand on the power levers pushing up the power to climb the Hill. I had a "big time" feeling. Here I was in the left seat in a new airplane.

How lucky can one guy get?

We flew a steady schedule of nine flights in 16 days. The training started out in the bounce pattern, making 6-12 landings per flight. I got 50 landings in seven days. The flights included landings with one and two engines simulated out, plus no flap approaches and landings. Our instructors introduced us to refusal speed, the maximum speed that allowed the airplane to stop on the runway. After refusal speed, the pilot continued the takeoff. To show an emergency, on one takeoff, the instructor popped open the smoke removal hatch in the cockpit's ceiling. A rejected takeoff after refusal speed would be encountered again in a year. For a 300-hour pilot, it was a little like learning to swim in the pool's deep end. Airline pilots with 1,000s of hours would not experience these maneuvers in training until they became a captain.

I had to learn to flare again: no more carrier-style landings. On my command, the Flight Engineer would set 200 horsepower as the proper power setting for a good landing. On Friday, August 23, I took my pilot Familiarization (Fam) Stage check ride, and that final task completed my aircraft Fam training. We used the new Dulles International Airport in Washington DC for our bounce pattern because there was little activity there, yet. I got average grades in the Fam stage.

Next, I went into the Instrument Stage, where I shot 20 instrument approaches in five days. One of my exciting flights in the P-3 was a long IFR cross-country flight. We flew non-stop, 2,500 miles, from Pax River to NAS Los Alamitos in California. The flight was an exciting new experience. I relished being in the P-3's cockpit cruising at Flight Level 280 at over 380 kts. We talked on the same frequencies as the airliners; I really felt like a professional pilot.

Of course, that feeling abruptly ended when I got caught with my head up my ass. On takeoff from Los Alamitos, I did not check compass heading with runway heading and took off and turned to the wrong heading. The instructor brought it to my attention. My mistake didn't put us in danger, but I was really embarrassed. I became a little defensive, one of my weaknesses trying to cover up my screw up. But it was a great lesson, one that has stuck with me the rest of my life. When I got back from California, I took my Instrument Stage check on Friday, August 30.

A day later, the Training Officer called me into his office. He told me that student control elected to transfer me to another instructor. Lieutenant Merrical was one of their better instructors and, since I was not having any problems, they gave me another instructor. The switch would allow Lt. Merrical to work with the student having difficulties. I could only think of my VT-2 instructor change and the memorable 1st Lt. Tyc USMC. This time, though, the new instructor was also good, although I had to adjust to his instructional method. Most of the people I had been training with would be on my crew when I reported to VP-45. It frustrated me that the move separated me from all the VP-45 crew going through training. I had got to know them and wanted to stay with them.

Friends we met while in flight training at Whiting Field, Bob, and his wife, lived at Pax River. The Navy had assigned Bob to VP-49, and deployed him to Vietnam where he was flying Market Time missions. His leased house near Pax River was not being used. He said Lou and I could stay there. Lou finished summer school and came down for a couple of weeks over Labor Day. We went back to Michigan for me to stand as a groomsman at Cousin Jim Beall's wedding. Jim married a woman named Bev. She had also been in the 2000 ½ crowd. Jim, now an Ensign in the Navy, attended Mess Officer's school at Pax River before going to Point Mugu in California.

NAVIGATING ACROSS THE ATLANTIC

A big event at VP-30 was a transoceanic navigation flight. We would go to Stavanger, Norway. My Grandmother Hotton, who died in 1967, was born in Norway. I was excited to see this part of my ancestry. Planning the flight was a time-consuming exercise of preparing a great circle route. The great circle route was the shortest route between two points. Then we laid out the courses on several shorter-range charts. Plotting a straight line on a Global Navigation Chart (GNC) would project a great circle route. Every five degrees of longitude, we identified points on the great circle route. The points plotted in latitude and longitude transferred to large-scale Mercator Projection Charts.

We then entered the data into our navigation logs. Navigation school had prepared me well for the exercise, and I had no difficulty putting it together. Three navigators were getting their first exposure to transoceanic flight planning. When we completed preparing the charts and logs, we put them into a Navigation Bag. It looked exactly like the ones I used two years earlier at AOCS with the "Up bookbags, up" routine, explaining why they were called Nav Bags.

We planned the flight on the weekend after Labor Day, which meant we left just a little too late for me to spend my twenty-fifth birthday in Norway. The day the flight arrived, we got the forecast winds for our flight and finished filling out our navigation logs for the overnight crossing. We would have the stars visible for celestial navigation. I grabbed the Nav Bag, and we took off in the late afternoon. Crossing over St. Johns, Newfoundland, I set up for the first leg of navigation. I opened the navigation bag, and, to my shock, it was the wrong bag. It was the one we used for planning. All our completed approved navigation materials, charts, and navigation logs were still in another bag back in the training room at Pax River. My brain scrambled, *Boy, have I screwed up. Would we now have to turn back because of me?*

I told the Naval Flight Officer (NFO) Navigator Instructor, "I don't have the right charts, they are back at Pax River."

"What do you have for charts?"

"We just have a GNC with the great circle route."

"That is good enough," he said. "Use it."

There was no one who wanted to turn back since we were going to Norway. I thought of my VT-31 instructor who said, "Sometimes you just gotta do what you gotta do."

On the chart, it is only about 24 inches from St. Johns to Stavanger. The pencil line was 20 nautical miles wide. I gave a heading to the flight crew as I assumed navigation and computed my first celestial start shot.

When I stuck the sextant through the porthole in the fuselage's top, I was almost blinded by how many stars were in my field of vision. At 24,000 feet over the North Atlantic, the sky was as clear as anyone could expect to find: no obscuration. Unlike the skies over the Gulf of Mexico and Southern Texas that I had seen back at VT-29, where the haze limited the stars I could see, over the North Atlantic, they all looked bright. I picked my three stars and did my shot. The three celestial plots lines crossed at the same point, a near perfect three-star triangle. My shots impressed the instructor. On a normal chart, the pencil line would be only about a mile wide and much more difficult to get a perfect three-star fix. I often wonder if I had a regular chart where the pencil line was not 20 nm wide, would I have gotten the same near perfect three-star fix? The Navigator Instructor relieved me of my navigation duties. I signed off on the navigation log and another navigator took over the navigation. I went to the cockpit and got to log some flight time.

We spent two nights in Stavanger. The Norwegians were buying P-3s and were interested in looking at ours. The Norwegian Air Force assigned us an airman as a guide. He spoke excellent English, and he took us around the countryside in his car. We toured the Norwegian countryside. I remember the high taxes made everything expensive. At VP-30, I got my best grades in the Navigation phase. VT-29 had done a good job of preparing me. The phase was good, other than a below average for the navigator bag to screw up on the flight to Norway.

CRAB CAKES

Jim and Bev moved to Pax River to attend Mess Officer's school. They rented a house from another deployed VP-49 pilot close to our house. One thing we discovered was crab hunting in the marshes around Pax River. We would collect a bushel basket of crabs and have crab cookouts. Eating crab was a messy deal because it created so much scrap. More trash came from the crab than what we ate. We would cover the table with newspaper and when we were done, just roll all the trash into the giant paper ball. Having Jim and Bev at Pax was great, like college days again. But in mid-September, Lou went back to EMU, and Jim and Bev left for California. I was lonely without them around. My loneliness wouldn't last long. I would soon go on my camping trip to Maine, known as SERE (Survival, Evasion, Resistance, and Escape) school.

My last flight at VP-30 happened on Wednesday, September 25. They canceled our scheduled night tactics flight because a Navy F-8 had gone into the ocean near Norfolk. Search and Rescue was a P-3 mission, and the Navy diverted us to a Search and Rescue mission. We were now involved in a real-world mission where one of our fellow pilots needed our help to be rescued. I spent hours looking out the observation windows, searching for anything that might help find the downed pilot. I looked for flares, strobes, and other lights to find the pilot in the middle of a dark ocean. After seven hours, we approached minimum fuel and called off the search. We did not find him, and they declared the pilot missing. I did not know the pilot, but he faced the danger of flying over the ocean and its associated threats. The moment was sobering to consider being lost at sea after bailing out of an airplane. A challenge I hoped I would never have to face. I finished my training at VP-30 and was now a designated P-3 pilot. I was on top of the world. How lucky was I to reach this point?

Chapter Nine
Survival Evasion Resistance and Escape (SERE) School

NAS BRUNSWICK, MAINE

I finished flying at VP-30, and the Navy needed to get me on my way immediately. NAS Brunswick was my next assignment, and I had a deadline for starting Survival, Evasion, Resistance, and Escape *(SERE)* school. Since my squadron, VP-45, was going to be flying in Vietnam, all aircrew had to complete SERE to fly in the theater. SERE is a program that provides U.S. military personnel with training in evading capture, survival skills, POW interrogation skills, and the military code of conduct. On a tight schedule, I checked out Friday morning, September 27, with orders to report NLT Sunday, September 29. The Navy had cut my original orders for two weeks of SERE school. But thank goodness, the school shortened it to one week because deer hunting season was starting.

On the way to Brunswick, I dropped by NAS Lakehurst, New Jersey, to visit my AOCS classmate Steve Gillis. I drove up to Brunswick on Sunday and checked into the BOQ. For the first time, the BOQ had room. I met a bunch of people from VP-30, including some of my VP-45 squadron mates who were going through SERE. We went out Sunday night for what we jokingly called the "Last Supper." We found a nice seafood restaurant in Brunswick. Of course, we all had lobster and beer.

POW TRAINING

On Monday, they gave us a classroom presentation primarily about the POWs that were currently in North Vietnam's Hanoi Hilton. The Navy had established covert communication with the POWs. One of them, Cdr. Jim Stockdale, was sending letters to his wife with secrets written in invisible ink in the letters. The class received detailed information on what we could expect if the enemy captured us. We learned of John McCain's refusal to be released early and how he adhered to the Military Code of Conduct. The instructors gave us techniques we could follow to resist while being interrogated and how we had to respect the chain of command.

After an early Tuesday morning wake up, we climbed on a bus with only our flight suits and a survival kit. The SERE camp was in Rangeley, Maine. The bus dropped us in the woods. They told us we had all just bailed out of our airplane into the People's Republic of North America (PRNA). The instructors gave us a lecture on surviving and living off the land. Normally SERE would have us spend a day evading, but Deer Hunting season was starting the coming weekend. They wanted to clear the woods by Friday. About 1500, a green army truck showed up. Men in green uniforms with funny patches jumped out and started shooting blanks into the air. They informed us PRNA had captured us. The PRNA soldiers ordered us into the truck. They stacked us like cordwood.

At the camp, they ordered us into a locker room and told us to strip. Then the POW camp guards lined us up outdoors, naked belly button to butt and sprayed with freezing water, in the cool Maine afternoon, as a delousing wash down. They gave us wooden tags with a number. They gave me the number five. It marked me as the fifth most senior man in the compound. Number five would come into play when I became the senior leader in the camp. Since we had eaten that morning and slept the night before, we were in decent shape the first day. Still, the uncertainty of what would happen next and how I would respond dwelled upon me.

THE BAD GUY

They ordered me into the POW camp admin building. Then they took me to a small room off the hallway's right side, not much bigger than a large closet. The room had plain walls with no windows and a single bright light bulb hanging from the ceiling. An insignificant dilapidated table with some papers on it was the only furniture. Most importantly, an intimidating man dressed in an unfamiliar green uniform with a strange unit patch was waiting for me there. My interrogation started. I had met the "bad guy." We were both standing, and he, inches away from my face, demanded I confess my crimes against the people of PRNA. I played the tough guy, like John Wayne, and gave the standard name, rank, serial number, date of birth. He ridiculed me for being a stupid American and described my indoctrination into the falsehoods of American greatness.

The "bad guy" screamed at me I did not fully understand the nature of my crimes. The interrogator stood on a large U.S. flag. I avoided stepping on the flag because over the years I had learned to respect it and all it stood for. He turned his back to me and produced a stream of yellow fluid to imitate urine like he was peeing on the flag. His actions revolted me. I was out of my comfort zone and unsure of how I should react to the flag's discretion. The "bad guy" grabbed me and again demanded I confess my crimes. In the small room, there was nowhere to escape. He started bouncing me off the wall, grabbing my coveralls by the lapels, pulling me toward him and then pushing me back against the wall. He demanded I give him more information beyond name and rank. I refused. He beat me some more. After about a half hour of this process, the "bad guy" routine was over. I had stood my ground and had disclosed nothing beyond my name, rank, and serial number.

The "bad guy" took me out into the hallway and turned me over to a guard sitting at a desk outside the interrogation room. He told the guard that I needed to consider my crimes against the peace-loving people of PRNA. The guard was told to put me in the punishment box. The box was maybe 3 feet by 4 feet by 3 feet. I had to squat to get into the box. They instructed me to respond when I heard him knock on the box, with a return of my knocks from inside the box. A safety precaution to prevent possible injuries. The guard closed the lid and left me confined in the dark. I fit into the box with a little room to spare, and not that bad. Every five minutes, the man would knock on the box to see if I was all right. I returned his knocks. After a while, the guard released me from the box. He told me to sit on a bench for further integration.

THE GOOD GUY

After sitting on the bench for a time, I saw a man coming toward me who called me into his office. This time there was a desk with a chair behind it. He offered me a seat in a chair opposite the desk. The room had windows, and the desk had a picture of a woman with a child. I assumed they were his wife and kid. The interrogator played the "good guy" role. He offered me some tea and biscuits; I ate the food immediately. In our one-day ground school, the SERE instructors told me to never turn down food or drink. After the encounter with the "bad guy," I was looking for a friend and I relaxed with the "good guy."

He told me he was an anti-war activist; however, the draft had pushed him into the PRNA Army. The camp commandant's POW treatment did not agree with him. He asked how the camp officers treated me. I elected not to comment. He said PRNA's Army had separated him from his wife, and he missed her. Then he asked if I had a wife. I answered yes. He commented that most US pilots went to college and that he was a college graduate. He asked what school I went to. I told him about Michigan State, and how I majored in Industrial Arts education. I had opened up to the "good guy." He then started asking questions about my airplane and mission. I recognized this technique as intelligence gathering and stopped giving him information, but he had already learned too much about me. He had gained all he was going to get from me.

The "good guy" took me back out to the guard in the hallway and told him to take me out to the compound. The guards at the gate outside the admin building opened it and escorted me into the compound. Immediately, a short guard, about five feet two inches tall, found me. They had assigned him to harass anyone wearing the wooden number five. He grabbed me and bounced me off the outhouse wall. He demanded I apologize for my war crimes.

After a while, he put me in a coffin-like box laying on the ground in the compound. The box was long, and I could lie down. They filled it with rocks. However, I was thin and fit into it with room to spare. I pushed the rocks aside to uncover the bare wooden floor and found it was not bad. With the sun shining on it. The inside was warm. A pleasant change from Maine's cool fall air. The time there did not last very long, and they released me from the box. Prisoners could not stand up, and we could not sit. They forced us to keep moving and had to crawl around the compound. They covered the hard earth with pea gravel. I could not rest my knees on the ground because of the pea gravel's discomfort. I had to crawl around on my toes and hands; it was very tiring. If I stopped crawling, immediate harassment followed.

SOMETHING TO EAT

One of my VP-45 squadron mates, Jon, was also crawling around the compound. Approaching me, he reached into his crotch and pulled out a half-eaten apple. He said, "Here, Randy, I saved this half for you." The training's harsh nature meant we were now going on 36 hours since we had eaten, and I welcomed any food. We learned in training, *refuse no food*. I grabbed it and wolfed it down. Seed, core stem, everything, gone in about two gulps. I was afraid they would confiscate it if someone saw me eating. The short guard saw me, ran over, grabbed me, and started banging me off the outhouse wall again. He demanded I tell him where I got the food. I told him I found it on the ground. He had probably set the whole thing up and watched it happen. I do not recall being fed, but I guess the guards fed us, and we must have had something to drink.

SENIOR OFFICER

The second night in the compound, I became the senior officer in the camp. All the officers senior to me were in isolation. They called me into the admin building. I doubt I had slept over two hours in the last 48 hours. I was a zombie filled with fog in my thought process. My mind was running like I just finished six beers. The interrogation started again. I was the senior officer present, so they asked me to confess for the entire camp our crimes against the people of PRNA. I refused and said I had no authority to do so.

The demands for a confession continued, and I refused to confess. I was called chicken by the guard; he said I was afraid to assume command in the POW camp. The guard threatened me with firm punishment, but I could avoid punishment if I pretended I was an American Chicken. Too tired to endure further punishment, I agreed to be an American Chicken. They posted me outside the admin building near the compound gate. My fellow POWs could see me. I walked in a circle flapping my arms and clucking, saying, "I am an American Chicken." I was thinking. *My DIs back at AOCS would have been ashamed of me and would have screamed at me for my DOR.*

My behavior embarrassed me, but it was a lesson learned. A real SERE school lesson was when well fed and rested, I had a higher level of resistance. But after just two days with little sleep and almost no food. I was a mere shadow of my former self. If I ever became a POW, that would be the test of my survival.

They sent me back to the compound. We were told we could now rest. They moved about forty of us into a hut off to the right in the compound. They allowed us to stretch out on the floor and left us alone for about 30 minutes. Some prisoners had escaped from the compound. They needed a roll call, and we were all roused for a muster. The sun was now coming up in the compound; it was Thursday morning, the second night's end. The guards said if we wanted to, we could play football. We picked teams, but we were all worn out, exhausted and had little energy. Our simulated POW conditions had zapped our strength quickly.

We were shuffling around, pretending to play the game while wondering if we could just eat the old pig skin, when we heard a truck roaring toward the compound. Coming down the road toward the entrance to the compound was a truck full of Navy Seals. They busted down the compound's entrance by driving the truck through the gate. Gunfire erupted and the blanks never sounded so good.

RESCUE AND ESCAPE

The Navy Seal team came to rescue us. The guards all played like they were dead. The Seals told us to get into the trucks and they would take us to freedom. With whoops, we piled into the trucks and about a mile down the road; the truck "broke down." The guards, not simulating death, were streaming from compound in hot pursuit with guns blazing to recapture the POWs. The Seals said head for the hills, and they would hold them off. Pure Hollywood, but a real motivator to take to the hills. Off I went. The Seals gave us an escape map and told us our rescue point was a logging camp. We would hear a chain saw running on and off for about five minutes every 15 minutes.

A Navy Commander, an A-7 pilot, joined me. The Navy had recalled him from the Reserves, and he was in his mid-30s. We worked as a team. He told me to slow down, he could not keep up with me. I remember the PRNA truck going up and down the road, which we could still see, but we made sure they did not see us. It had a loudspeaker asking us to surrender and we would receive humane and lenient treatment.

Humane and lenient treatment. No fucking way!

After about four hours, we heard the chainsaw and found the logging camp. The man in the logging camp gave us cheese sandwiches. I had lost about five pounds in the three days in the compound. The cheese sandwich was one of my best meals ever. The man gave us a sleeping bag and told us we had to camouflage ourselves because PRNA would look for us that night. Dead beat tired, I dug my trench. Then I got some pine branches to cover the trench and climbed into my bag. We were told if they found us, the PRNA soldiers would fire their guns near our heads. I fell sound asleep. Later, I heard gunshots from all over where we had hidden. Including one near my head. I went right back to sleep. It started raining that night, a chilly rain. My trench started filling up with water and it collected at my feet. I just pulled my legs up and went back to sleep.

DEBRIEF

On Friday morning, the Navy gave us bacon and eggs for breakfast, and we climbed onto the bus to go back to NAS Brunswick. We cleaned up and, after lunch, the SERE school instructors debriefed us on our performance. I was told the American Flag was just a piece of cloth if it was not being respected and my reaction to the flag played into the interrogator's plan. I gave the good cop a lot of information because I fell for his friendly interrogation style. They said my eating the apple was the right thing to do. When I looked in the mirror after taking a shower at NAS Brunswick, my chest and arms were all black and blue from the fists pounding into my chest while being bounced off the outhouse wall. Bruised, beaten, with loose teeth, the SERE school guards had gotten to me.

We went out to dinner on Friday night, and I had one beer. It wiped me out, and I was ready for an early bedtime. I went to bed and got up at 0400 on Saturday to drive back to Detroit. I got back to the house on Beach Road at about 1800 that night. The day was one long drive through the US and Canada. I remember coming down Long Lake Road at Coolidge. The old Hilly Acres Dairy Farm barn on Coolidge Road, a Troy landmark from younger days, had burned down. The structure was still smoldering. Troy was changing. When Lou saw the black and blue bruises all over my chest, she burst into tears. She could not fathom why they treated me this way.

HOME

I would be home for about 10 days in early October, and the Detroit Tigers were in the World Series. The Tigers were down three games to one, and it did not look good. The games glued my mom to the TV. She was the ultimate Tiger's fan and lived and died on every pitch. The Tigers made a great comeback and won three in a row, including the last two on the road against St Louis Cardinals to win the series. Detroit went crazy.

Lou was going to Eastern Michigan University in Ypsilanti, so I spent a lot of time with her at the Strader's home in Garden City. We spent the weekend at the house on Beach Rd. During this visit, Lou became pregnant. A month later, after I had reported to VP-45 in Jacksonville, she told me we were expecting. The news excited me. I was so happy. We wanted to start a family when I finished flight training. We planned to have a large family. Her pregnancy was fantastic news.

On October 16, 1968, I left Detroit and drove to Jacksonville in my 1966 Ford Cortina. I would drive as far as Atlanta. I-75 was an incomplete project with many detours onto two-lane roads. It took a long drive of over 12 hours to get to Atlanta. While driving through the city, a car whizzed by me on I-75. About two minutes later, the State Police pulled me over for speeding. I explained a car had screamed around me about two minutes ago. My English Ford was not capable of going that fast. He gave me a ticket, said I could tell that fact to the judge, and let me go. I spent the night in Atlanta. On Thursday afternoon, I pulled into Jacksonville. The city was beautiful. I waited until the squadron had secured for the day before I checked in. I went to the BOQ, got a room, and had dinner. I reported to Patrol Squadron Forty-Five and had my orders endorsed at 1953 hours on Thursday, October 17. I was where I wanted to be a real Navy pilot in an operational squadron scheduled to fly in direct combat support in the Vietnam War.

Now, I had become one of those Navy pilots I idolized. That kid part of me who watched Victory at Sea *in the '50s cheered me on.*

PART 3
The Active Navy

Chapter One
Patrol Squadron Forty-Five VP-45

NAS JACKSONVILLE (BEFORE DEPLOYMENT)

In the summer in 1968, Patrol Squadron Forty-Five (VP-45) moved into the new VP Hangar, Hangar 1000, at NAS Jacksonville. It had three hangar bays, with offices on the second deck. NAS Jacksonville had only three VP-squadrons: VP-5, VP-16, and VP-45. Because of my accomplishments at Navigation School, VT-29, in Corpus Christi, the squadron designated me as Navigation Officer. They assigned the VP-45 flight crewmembers to 12 different numbered crews. They sent me to Crew 20 belonging to the executive officer (XO), Cmdr. Ralph Mason. The co-pilot was a lieutenant named Bob Hartl. He was also a qualified Patrol Plane Commander (PPC). When the XO could not fly, I would fly as Bob's co-pilot. Bob was a fantastic mentor, and I benefited from his lessons.

Lou would not be joining me in Jacksonville since it was already late October, and I would deploy to Vietnam in early December. She was now living at home while attending Eastern Michigan University, working on her nursing degree. I lived in and took my meals at the BOQ. One thing I had to do was find a place somewhere near the base to park our mobile home. One of my squadron mates was living in the Walker Mobile Home Court. It looked nice to me. I found a lot and signed a contract. I could now have our mobile home moved into Jacksonville, about a ten-minute drive to the base. It differed from most parks in that we parked the trailer parallel to the street, so it looked more like a normal home.

The trailer located across the street had a car parked there with Michigan tags on it. It belonged to Bob and Karen from Southgate, Michigan. The Navy assigned Bob to VA-105, an A-7 squadron at NAS Cecil. They deployed to Vietnam on the USS Kitty Hawk about the same time as my own squadron, VP-45.

When I checked into VP-45, the squadron designated me a Patrol Plane Non-Qualified Pilot (PPNP). As a PPNP, I had not qualified for any pilot position and was in training to become a Patrol Plane Third Pilot (PP3P). The squadron required me to clear a constant set of hurdles to advance as a first tour pilot. For the next two years, I would be in training to become qualified as a Patrol Plane Commander (PPC). The PPC qualification was a continuing evaluation process. Not everyone would become a PPC, there were no guarantees. To qualify as a PPC, not only did I have to show airplane knowledge and flying ability. I also had to master Antisubmarine Warfare Tactics and crew leadership. I flew graded training flights with squadron pilots in Transition, Familiarization, Instruments, and Tactics.

At Jacksonville, the squadron issued me a green Nomex, read fire retardant, flight suit. These flight suits were standard allocation for crews flying in S. E. Asia. On Thursday Oct 24, I took my first flight with VP-45, a 1.5-hour night instrument flight. In October and November, I flew a lot and logged 50.5 hours. I had 90 days to prepare for my PP3P check ride. The Navy had not yet set up squadron instructor standardization, so any PPC could be an instructor. On October 31, I had my first training flight with a lieutenant junior grade. He gave me above average grades. One flight comes to mind on November 15, Lt.

Cmdr. Andy Anderson, Admin Department head, and I flew back from Norfolk. He let me shoot a Ground Controlled Precision Radar Approach (GCA) into NAS Jax. I had it wired on glide path, on course, on speed and I used the Flight Engineer effectively to set approach power. Lieutenant Commander Andy complimented me on how well I had flown the GCA Approach. Word spread about my flying; I was off to a good start.

Since Lou was not with me, I would get together with our friends, Jerry, and Helen. The Navy attached Jerry to VP-5 at NAS Jacksonville. We would go out to dinner occasionally. One question they would often ask us was, "When are you guys going to start a family?"

When I found out we were expecting, I couldn't wait for Jerry and Helen to ask their question again. We went out to dinner and the question never came up. After dinner, I said to them, "Aren't you going to ask me when we plan on starting a family?" They had a strange look on their faces and said OK we will ask the question. I told them I just found out Lou was pregnant. They were so excited for us. Lou having good friends when she came to Jacksonville was a blessing when I would be far away from home.

On Friday, November 22, 1968, I flew my first over-water navigation flight in VP-45. We went down to NAS Roosevelt Roads in Puerto Rico. VP-18, a recently decommissioned P-2 Squadron, had been based at there and left behind surplus equipment. VP-45 wanted to pick up some cruise boxes to ship our equipment overseas. We loaded the cruise boxes into our bomb bay. One thing I remember is that we went to the Class Six store, the military term for a liquor store. Bacardi Rum was a $1.00 a one-liter bottle. It was such a bargain, I bought a case, and I don't even like rum. Writing these words in 2024, I still have an unopened bottle of Bacardi Rum from the trip to Puerto Rico in 1968. Not really saved, just avoided.

In that same year, the Navy lost at least one P-3 to enemy action. The Navy decided the P-3 needed an offensive capability for self-defense. The AGM-9 Bullpup, a radio guided Air to Ground Missile, was added to the P-3 weapons inventory. All pilots had to take training on a computer-like device to practice firing the Bullpup missile. The system was the first video game I ever played. The computer had a large, 30-inch round screen. An instructor would set up airspeed, launch altitude and arm the missile. When launched, the missile would come from my left or right side. My input to the missile went through a little joystick, where I gave up/down, left/right pulses to guide the missile to the target on the screen. The Navy assigned some practice bullpups with dummy warheads to the squadron to use in live fire exercises. I was not lucky enough to be chosen to fire a live missile in practice.

We had to bring our medical shot records up to date. The Navy gave us all the shots for deployment, including a thick fluid, called Gamma Globulin, which was shot into my butt. Since I would not be flying over the weekend, the squadron did the shots on Friday afternoon. It felt like I was carrying a bowling ball in my rear pocket. I would not want to be sitting in a cockpit with that lump in my pants.

LOU'S VISIT

Lou came down for the four-day Thanksgiving weekend. I kept my room at the BOQ, while Lou and I lived in our trailer. Lou met Karen Bondy, our neighbor across the street. They hit it off and became best friends. Bob and Karen had a newborn baby. With Lou's pregnancy, baby talk quickly became the hot topic. We would become lifelong friends with them. This time was solemn for Lou and me. She was pregnant. I was going away to fly in an unpopular war. To ensure there would be no legal complications if I did not come back, we all had to fill out what they called "I love you" wills. We owned nothing; therefore, it was not a complicated document. I wrote a little addendum to the will where I said such things as who would get my 1963 Comet and tools. The future had many unanswered ifs. We were no longer a couple of college kids living together and having fun.

We shared a solemn Thanksgiving dinner in our trailer. We cooked two Swanson Turkey TV dinners in the small oven. So much for the big Thanksgiving meals we had both celebrated with our families up to this point. Lou and I talked about baby names. We would call him Andrew, after my father and great grandfather, if it was a boy and Sulette, after Lou's sister, if it was a girl.

The Friday after Thanksgiving was a normal workday, and I flew on an ASW training flight. On Sunday, December 1, I took Lou to Jacksonville Airport so she could fly home. The next week I would deploy to Vietnam. We would not see each other again for six months. Once more, I lingered at the gate as her airplane pulled out. Then I went back to our trailer. *Signs of her presence were everywhere in the trailer, but she was not there.* I was really going to miss her. Before we deployed, I stayed in the trailer. When I left for Vietnam, I closed it and made it ready for Lou. She would finish her winter semester at Eastern Michigan and come down in the spring during my deployment to Southeast Asia. I gave a set of keys to Helen, who said she would come by a couple times a month and check it out. Lou would have friends in Karen and Helen when she came home. Knowing this made me feel better. She would not be alone.

Chapter Two
Deployment

CROSSING THE PACIFIC

The commanding officer, Cmdr. William Sanders, split the squadron into three wings: Wing 10, Wing 20, and Wing 30. He made this change to establish crew and plane rotations for the upcoming deployment. We would fly most of our missions from Utapao, Thailand. Four crews and three airplanes comprised each wing. Every wing would spend a 10–12-day rotation period flying missions out of Utapao. They assigned the XO's crew to Wing 20. Our assigned airplane was P-3A Bureau Number (Navy serial number) 151363, marked as LN-20. LN was the tail marking assigned to VP-45. The 20 showed which crew manned the aircraft, in this case crew 20.

Monday, December 9, we started our transit to the Philippines. Our transit would be a four-day, four-leg flight through Moffett Field, California, Barbers Point in the Hawaiian Islands, and Guam. Terminating at NAS Sangley Point on Manila Bay in the Philippines. The CO wanted the individual wings to fly in a three-plane formation all the way to the Philippines. In the transit to the Philippines, the fourth crew did not have an assigned airplane, so they flew split up among the other three crews and airplanes. We were on the last flight to leave Jacksonville. Cmdr. Ralph Mason, my PPC, was acting as the VP-45 OINC (Officer in Charge) at NAS Jacksonville until the squadron deployed.

We flew on Jet Routes Airways non-stop to NAS Moffett Field. One thing I remember after leaving NAS Jacksonville, we were flying over NAS Whiting Field in the panhandle of Florida near Pensacola at 24,000 feet. I looked down and saw the T-28s in the pattern. I saw our house in Pace, and my mind flashed back to eighteen months ago. Then I was in VT-2 flying those patterns, but now I was in a squadron on my way to Vietnam. My training at Whiting played a part qualifying me to fulfill the Navy's mission. When I saw the T-28s flying around southern Alabama, it was like a replay of something I contemplated when flying into Pensacola over these same fields on June 29, 1966, on my way to AOCS.

The loop was complete. I was now a Navy pilot on his way to the unknown of an unpopular war.

Wing 20 flew 7.5 hours of three-plane cruise formation into NAS Moffett in San Jose, California. We landed at Moffett Field early in the afternoon and checked into the BOQ. The officers wanted to go to town and check out a place called the Ore House. The ultimate strip bar where the girls only wore Band-Aids over their crotches. I needed to check this place out, so I said, "Let's go." After a couple of beers, I went back to the BOQ and turned in early. Tomorrow our crew had a long flight to Barbers Point in the Hawaiian Islands. I would be our crew's navigator directing our flight across the Pacific.

In the morning, after breakfast at the BOQ, the officers caught a crew bus out to the flight line, and the ride was filled with ongoing nervous chatter about our upcoming adventure in Vietnam, including jokes about hoping Randy didn't get lost on the way to Hawaii. We met the enlisted crew at our airplane and prepared to cross the Pacific. I was excited to pick up my first oceanic crossing as a navigator in an operational squadron. A visit to the meteorologist for a last-minute weather briefing gave me the winds on our route to Barbers Point. My charts and navigator's logs were ready, prepared back in Jacksonville, and I only had to plug in today's winds. I wanted to do a good job. On the flight to Hawaii, I spent most of my time back in the Tube. The airplane's back was referred to as the Tube. It is where the equipment operators had their stations, including radar, EMC, navigation, tactical coordinator, and acoustical data processor. The Tube had a familiar and comforting smell that was a combination of JP-5 (jet fuel), exhaust, decaying plastic, and sweat. We took off and 7.9 hours later found the Hawaiian Islands. The navigation turned out to be a piece of cake. We had continuous Loran Alpha signals, and the Sun remained in sight on a cloudless day for the hourly Celestial shots. The engine drone added to the magic of going through the air. We landed at Barbers Point on Oahu. I stayed on base and turned in early. Most of the other officers went down to Honolulu. They got in late, which worked out for me, because they all wanted to rest en route to Guam and as a result I got more time in the cockpit.

P-3s had a NATOPS Max Gross Weight Takeoff (MGWTO) of 127,500 pounds. On takeoff out of Barbers Point, I made my first MGWTO. We used Water Alcohol Injection to boost our horsepower on takeoff. The XO, Cmdr. Mason, quizzing me on why we used the water injection. Even with the extra power, it was slowly accelerated. It seemed to stagger into the air, unlike aircraft I had flown at training weights. When the water injection stopped, our airplane became even more sluggish. Over the next six months, the MGWTOs became routine. Often, we were over NATOPS MGWTO with max fuel and ordinance. Commander Sanders said the 127,500 weight was a peacetime NATOPS limits and since we were flying in combat, we could use higher takeoff gross weight numbers.

The flight to Guam was 11.2 hours. Commander Sanders wanted us to go from Hawaii to the Philippines without staying overnight in Guam. It would be a late arrival in the Philippines and the XO elected to spend the night in Guam. After the long flight that day, it was dinner, a couple of beers and hit the rack for another day of over-ocean flying. We took off early the next morning for NAS Sangley Point in the Philippine Islands. The quick 4.2-hour flight was easy, and the TACCO did the navigation across the Philippine Sea. I got to fly in the right seat on this leg. I remember the lush green vegetation and white beaches of the east coast of the Philippines rising out of the deep blue sea in the morning light. We flew over the Philippines to the South China Sea on the west coast and landed at NAS Sangley Point. Commander Sanders didn't like the overnight in Guam. Cmdr. Mason got a "Talking to" about not following his orders to fly to Sangley Point the night before. Most of us thought spending the night in Guam and not arriving at an unfamiliar airport in the dark after a 22-hour day was a good idea. The CO and XO were off to an adversarial relationship.

THE PHILIPPINES

Immediately after we landed, they loaded us into a semi-trailer that looked exactly like a trailer used for moving animals. Like a subway train, there were no seats and only handheld loops coming out of the ceiling. We knew it as a Navy cattle car, the standard way to move people around the base. They took us straight to our VD (Sexually Transmitted Diseases) lecture at the base gym. An overweight Navy Corpsman started talking about the diseases we could catch in town if we slept with the bar girls. He had slides of women's crotches with ugly sores and guys' private parts with puss dripping out. It nearly turned my stomach.

To make his point, he told a "Sea Story." The difference between a Fairy Tale and a Sea Story is a Fairy Tale starts out "Once upon a time" and a Sea Story starts out "This is no shit." His sea story was about a new STD called the "Black Clap." The disease had no cure. If they diagnosed anyone with the "Black Clap," they moved them out to a ship anchored off the south coast of Vietnam. The Navy listed them as Missing in Action (MIA) and would inform their family of their loss. *I knew that story was semi-bullshit, but he got his message across.*

Guys were going into Cavite City. They reported the city was just fine. Cheap drinks and entertainment were available at the clubs in town. So, on my first day off, I went to see the city. I walked into town in the daylight. About a block from the Sangley Point gate, a kid tried to pick my pocket. Not exactly the welcome I expected. I figured going into town alone might not be a good idea and went back to the base. In the future, I would visit Cavite City with a group of my buddies. We would take colorful, customized Jeeps called "Jeepneys" from the gate into town.

We had monthly Personnel Inspections at Quarters. Sanders would walk by us and attempt to grab hold of the hair protruding under our hats. If he could hold any hair between his fingers, we had to get a haircut. Not wanting to get Sander's attention, we went to the barbershop every week; besides, haircuts were only a quarter. He also wanted no chest hair protruding from our T-shirts. If we wore a V-neck T-shirt, we had to shave a V on our chests to pass inspection. I wore crew-neck T-shirts.

Commander Sanders had a reputation as a demanding CO. The JOs (Junior Officers) avoided any unnecessary contact with him. An incident stands out in my memory. At Sangley, the hangar was about three-quarters of a mile away from the BOQ. Even in the early morning, I would break a sweat walking this distance. One morning, as I made my way to the hangar with a few of my buddies, we saw the CO's pickup truck coming down the road. My buddies all jumped into the bushes and told me to flag him down for a ride. He stopped for me, and I got into the cab. We made idle conversation. Meanwhile, all my buddies jumped into the pickup truck bed. No one else wanted to be in the cab with him. I didn't mind the CO.

Chapter Three
Operation Market Time

THE PATROLS

In 1965, the Navy instituted Operation Market Time to set up a sea-based and airborne barrier. Our barrier was to prevent North Vietnamese supply ships from entering South Vietnam's waters. Resupply ships supported the North Vietnamese Army (NVA) and Viet Cong (VC) units operating in South Vietnam. The Navy divided Market Time patrol areas into a near-shore area out to 20 nautical miles and a long-range area out to 120 nm. Small Navy boats conducted the near shore patrols and P-3s conducted the long-range patrol portion of Market Time. The P-3s flew five flights a day, two out of Utapao Thailand, VP-45's base, and three out of Cam Ranh Bay, South Vietnam.

The P-3s provided coverage 24 hours a day, seven days a week. Just before VP-45 arrived in SE Asia, the Navy started what we would know as Daisy Chain Operations for Market Time. Every five to seven hours, a P-3 would show up off the Vietnam coast just south of the DMZ. Then they would fly an over-water route to the Vietnamese Cambodian border. Soft on-station times were used to confuse the enemy. We could arrive on station up to an hour before or one hour after our designated-on station start time. Our flexibility in on station times limited the NVA's ability to understand our schedule. We patrolled a strip of water from 20 nm off the coast to 120 nm off the coast.

The commander of Market Time required a speed of advance along the Position of Intended Movement (PIM) of 150 kts. We could cover the search area looking for gun runners in seven to eight hours. Descending onto the station, we would loiter shut down our number one engine. It saved gas without affecting our speed at low altitude. In case we needed to get the engine running on short notice, we ran the engine relight checklist to the point of starting the engine. Most of the time, we were on three engines down below 2,500 feet. We did radar run-ins on all contacts.

To cover the search area, we would often need to fly at 250 to 300 kts as we moved amongst radar contacts in our surveillance area. The Missions were overt: Find and Identify. We wanted the NVA to know we were watching for their ships. These patrols were like regular open ocean patrols. We rigged every ship. Rigging a ship included flying by both sides of the ship to take photos, while plotting their course, speed, and position. We then filled out a rigging log to capture the information. We turned these reports over to Naval Intelligence at the end of our flights. The 45,000-ton SS Tokyo Muru was not a gun runner, but as part of our mission, we rigged it, anyway. Later, operations would ignore these large, friendly cargo ships.

As a pilot, I enjoyed flying rigging runs. I hand flew down to 200 feet off the water at 250 kts and maneuvered to get the best photo shoots of the ship. Making the P-3 perform under my hands to accomplish the mission gave me a sense of satisfaction. Our enlisted radar operator in the Tube would call out the contacts found in our search area. He would then give the pilot radar vectors toward the target. The TACCO and navigator would start plotting the contact's position on the Dead Reckoning Tracer Mod-4 (DRT-4) based on the bearing and distance given by the radar operator. Working as the navigator, I could then determine the contacts course and speed which we passed to the pilot. Based on course and speed information, the pilot would then set up a non-threating pass to look over the ship. During our six months of flying Market Time, we did not intercept one resupply ship. We were spinning our wheels.

125 GROUP

The squadrons flying Market Time missions in 1969 did not know about the North Vietnamese 125 Group operations. Only revealed later in the war, 125 Group was a highly classified dedicated North Vietnamese Infiltration unit. The NVA made this elite unit a "need to know only" within North Vietnam. They equipped the 125 Group ships with modern Russian Electronic Counter Measures (ECM) capability. Ships from 125 group could easily track the P-3's distinctive APS-80 electronic radar signature. The NVA supply ships could abort missions upon detection of a P-3 when outside the 120 nm search zone. The CIA knew of 125 Group operations. They received intelligence reports on ship movement from SR-71 photo recon flights flown over North Vietnam. The CIA passed the information to Military Assistance Command Vietnam (MACV).

But MACV elected to not share this information with Commander Seventh Fleet, our boss, because it was too sensitive. The crews flying these interdiction patrols did not need to know about the resupply ships in MACV's eyes. *All part of a screwed-up war.* The messy communication was like a game of "I have a secret, and I will not share it with you." Maybe the Air Force didn't trust the Navy. After we left in June 1969, MACV started sharing the information with Seventh Fleet. The Navy changed the Daisy Chain Ops into non-routine patrols based on intelligence coming out of North Vietnam. It then started having successful intercepts of the NVA "Gun Runners."

SIHANOUKVILLE

The NVA didn't need to run the resupply ships into South Vietnamese waters because, in December 1966, the Cambodians opened Sihanoukville to communist bloc nations. The NVA set up supply bases on the Cambodian side of the Cambodia/Vietnam border. This move provided logistic military support to the VC/NVA forces in southern end of Vietnam. Intelligence sources have said the same level of supply for the VC/NVA flowed through Cambodia, as came down the Ho Chi Minh Trail. Communist ships were off loading in the Cambodian port of Sihanoukville because the open port eliminated any great pressure for NVA sea infiltration.

Now the NVA could transport supplies into the Delta from Cambodia with impunity. The Navy told us Cambodia was a neutral country. What took place in a neutral country was none of our business. We could not patrol in Cambodian waters. They gave us instructions that if we saw a ship going into Sihanoukville; we were to take no photos or make any log entries of the names and location of these ships. These instructions were one of the goofy things about the Vietnam War. We knew the Russians were unloading in Cambodia. The Russians knew we knew they were unloading. But we officially ignored the supply operations in Cambodia. *Part of the craziness of a crazy war.* VP-26 lost two P-3s and crews in 1968 in the Cambodian waters, including my former next-door neighbor. In the summer of 1969, Sihanoukville was closed, and the North Vietnamese had to redouble their sea-based resupply.

UTAPAO, THAILAND

Before Crew 20 rotated to Utapao, Thailand, for our first Market Time mission, I had a couple of local trainer flights in the Philippines. On Thursday, December 19, my crew flew our first Market Time Mission from Sangley Point to Utapao Thailand. The flight was 10.3 hours in daylight. We flew airways toward Danang, Vietnam. Approaching Danang, we canceled IFR and descended to a point 70 nm from Danang TACAN on the 045 radial.

While I was in the right seat, our PPC, Paul Dykeman, me set up for a lesson. Our Radar Operator, William Campbell, used to be a short-order cook and with the last name of Campbell, the name "Soupy" fit him perfectly. He loved cooking and made sure he provided our flights with great meals. In the very back of the P-3 was a fully equipped galley with a refrigerator, convection oven, hot cups, frying pans, and a coffeemaker. "Soupy" would run it like a restaurant. He would take orders by asking, "How would you like your eggs? What kind of meat?"

He took my order and soon brought me my meal. It was the first instance where someone served me a meal while I was flying. I slid my seat back and started my chow. We were at 1,500 feet on three engines. When I should have been monitoring the aircraft flight path, I was eating a meal.

Incensed at me foregoing my co-pilot duties, Paul yelled, "What the hell do you think you are doing? Get out of the seat, get out of the seat."

He was right. Eating my meal while flying at 1,500 feet on three engines was not a good idea. I should have waited until I swapped out with another pilot to have my meal. *Another lesson learned.*

The Market Time Operations staff had divided the coast of Vietnam into designated search sectors about 150 nm apart down the coast. We followed our Market Time track and flew through the search sectors. They assigned beer names to each sector station. The beer names made the stations memorable. While in transit, we would check in via unsecured UHF radio with each sector. We exchanged information in plain voice communication. "Perky Beer, Perky Beer, this is Fine Art 20." Fine Art was VP-45's Navy code name for our squadron as designated by Commander Patrol Wings Atlantic.

We would pass on any contact information we had developed. The station would pass us any intelligence about potential infiltrator traffic in their area, plus, offer idle chitchat while making fun of talking to a beer station. Comments such as "How much beer to you have" and "I'll a have Bud draft" crossed on the airways. Perhaps we fooled the NVA, and they thought we were talking in code. The patrol continued to our off-station point. Our first Market Time mission was complete. We had launched out of the Philippines and recovered in Utapao.

After landing at Utapao, we taxied to the Navy Detachment Ramp at the south end of the runway. The Navy duty driver took us to the BOQ. The squadron assigned us four to a room in the three-story prefabricated concrete BOQ. The rooms were air-conditioned, had four single beds with dressers and nightstands. For meals, we went to the Thai Military Officers' club. The club had a dirt floor, and we ordered our meals off the menu by numbers. The waitresses did not speak English. Meal options of about a half dozen choices were available to include a combination of western and Thai food.

We would be at Utapao for 12 days and we would fly a 10-11 hour mission every other day. One day flight would be followed two days later by a night flight. We flew another 10 hours daytime Market Time flight on December 22. While flying, we tuned in Hanoi Hannah on our HF radio. She played popular American music with anti-American propaganda commercials. Stories of unfaithful wives and greedy capitalists profiting from our unappreciated efforts were part of her repertoire. She filled the broadcasts with how the peaceful Vietnamese people hated Americans.

Hanoi Hannah gave us a warning that Ho Chi Minh had ordered the base at Utapao destroyed at Christmas. The base posted soldiers with machine guns outside our BOQ. I found this guard force unnerving because I did not like the possibility of being shot at. She had issued four warnings that month about the destruction of the base. Nothing happened, and the threats of the base being destroyed became routine.

PUT IN HACK

Commander Sanders wanted to set records for the most hours flown and the least number of aborts. An aborted flight is when a flight launches but cannot complete the mission. In December, we had two aborted flights with a Return to Base (RTB). In December, during Wing 20's Utapao rotation, Paul Dykeman aborted a flight for a mechanical generator failure. The NATOPS manual directed a mandatory engine shutdown and RTB. Paul followed the NATOPS procedures. Commander Sanders said we were flying under combat conditions. Losing an engine was not an abort criterion in his book. We flew on three engines all the time as part of our regular procedures, so we would not abort a mission if we lost an engine. To make a statement, Commander Sanders put Lt. Dykeman in "Hack." Hack was an unofficial punishment.

In Hack, Paul had certain liberties removed for a short time, so he could avoid having anything put in his official records. He was stuck in his room except to fly and eat for the duration of this Utapao rotation. If Paul officially protested the loss of privileges while in Hack, the CO would make comments in Paul's official records. The joke amongst the JOs became that the only acceptable abort criteria under Sanders's command was an uncontrolled wing fire inboard of the outboard engine. We only had two more aborts in the next five and half months. The Navy recognized Sanders for setting a record for the least number of aborts on Market Time missions.

CHRISTMAS EVE

We flew our first night Operation Market Time mission on Christmas Eve, 1968. The U.S. had arranged a "Peace Stand Down" with North Vietnam. During the Peace Stand Downs, the NVA would not launch any offensive operations and the US would reciprocate. However, the NVA would use the time out during the war to resupply their units in South Vietnam.

A time out during the war?

But that odd way of thinking was the way it worked. During our mission briefing, the Intelligence Officer, Denny Westwood, alerted us. He said North Vietnam used Peace Stand Downs to resupply the south. Be alert for the potential of increased infiltration activity. The routine patrols would continue during the Peace Stand Down because they were not of an offensive nature. Our route was from Utapao, over Korat AFB, Upon AFB, and over to Danang. It took us across the Ho Chi Minh trail in Laos. A spectacular fireworks display awaited us going over the trail that night. A-4s, A-6s and A-7s flying through paraflares to deliver ordinance with enemy Anti-Aircraft Artillery (AAA) coming out of the ground. An unreal experience on Christmas Eve. I had spent every Christmas Eve for my entire life up till now in church with family singing Christmas Carols. I was watching the death and destruction taking place in the skies and the ground below me. Yet I was thinking of my family back home at church celebrating Christmas.

So much for "Peace on Earth."

The mission was ten hours. After we landed and debriefed, we had a little Christmas celebration in the enlisted barracks. The enlisted crew members had made a Christmas tree out of the cut-up beer cans.

Very symbolic.

We sang "Silent Night," and another song. The experience was kinda weird. We had just flown on a combat support mission and now we were singing Christmas carols.

The next day, December 26, we flew another 10-hour daytime flight. Bill Dailey got sick on the Patrol and couldn't stay at the TACCO station. I took over on the TACCO's ASA-16 scope and built "Fly To" points on targets. "Fly To" points were electronic waypoints passed to the flight station so the pilot could read bearing and distance to the target. I was doing both the TACCO's and navigator's job. The emergency on-the-job training at the TACCO station helped me understand the TACCO's role and operation of the ASA-16. The cross training made me appreciate how jobs integrated into the mission. They scheduled us on another night flight on the 28th.

On the 27th, Bob Hartl, Crew 20s other PPC, and I flew LN-20 up to Bangkok to have our airplane washed. The salt air collecting on the airframe at low altitude was hard on the airplane. Washing it off would help prevent corrosion. We had four hours off while our airplane got washed. Bob and I went downtown to have lunch at the Air Force Resort Hotel. We did a little shopping. I had my first exposure to a taxi driver in Bangkok. He drove like a madman. The driver was on the sidewalk, wrong way on one-way street, running red lights and always on the horn. He was crazy, like he was practicing for a demolition derby. People flooded the sidewalks and were no more concerned about the crazy drivers than seeing a stray dog.

Food carts were everywhere, with their pots sitting in boiling water. The vendors would sell the food on sticks. The person buying food would point to a pot and the vendor would place a scoop of the stuff in that pot on the stick. I elected to bypass these Thai sidewalk food vendors.

When we got back from Bangkok, I picked up SDO duties from 2000 to 0800 the next morning. The duty was a phone watch in the briefing building. While I was on my watch, I was the primary contact person in the Detachment at Utapao. I would take phone calls, read message traffic, then decide if anything needed to be done that night. I had an enlisted assistant, one of my crewmembers, who could run errands, and otherwise help me on the watch. The squadron issued personal survival weapons to the flight crew. One of my duties included handing out short-barreled Smith and Wesson 38 Specials to crews going out on Market Time missions. I had a bunk in the briefing building and got some rest. We would fly another night patrol on the 28th and I went back to the BOQ and got some sleep.

BOB HOPE SHOW

The Bob Hope Show came to Utapao that evening. The show started at 1700. We did not have to show up for our mission briefing until 1900. Our schedule allowed us to go to the performance. Bob Hope had an advance team come in before the show. They checked out the local stories. Then they would prepare jokes unique to Utapao. Bob Hope came out carrying his trademark golf club and wearing a VP-45 ball cap. He made a joke about the Navy taking over an Air Force base. Everyone laughed at this one. He then started telling jokes. One of them was about the church on the base's main street. Everyone on the base referred it to as "Howard Johnson's" because the steeple looked like a Howard Johnson's restaurant tower. Bob Hope made a joke of the similarity and said, "The base here at Utapao is so Americanized that it has a Howard Johnson on Main Street." Everyone roared at that joke.

After he told a few more jokes, he introduced the highlight of the show, Ann Margret. Ann Margret was a famous, popular singer and movie star in the early 60s. We all knew about her. She was a hot number wearing a soaking wet, skintight body stocking that left little to the imagination. That night we did a 10-hour Market Time flight. After a day's rest, we flew a 7.8-hour open ocean surveillance flight en route back to Sangley Point. I would rack up over 100 hours of flight time in December 1968.

At the Utapao detachment, there was no break in the routine. Every day was just a day. Weekends or holidays did not differ from any other day. A way I kept track of time was filling out log pages and putting the day's date on the page. The missions around Vietnam rapidly faded into a series of almost identical flights. The monotony made it difficult to distinguish one flight from another. The Navy awarded us two points toward an Air Medal for every flight across Laos with a Combat Flight Purpose Code (FPC). They assigned 1V4 Combat Reconnaissance, as our FPC. After 10 flights under this code, the Navy would award us a Strike Air Medal.

Chapter Four
Other Duties

NAS SANGLEY POINT

Back at Sangley, I flew a pilot training flight on New Year's Day, which was a five-hour flight with eight landings. The New Year's Day flight would prepare me for my PP3P check. They scheduled my check ride two days later. The PP3P qualification would allow me to fly missions listed as a pilot and not just as a navigator. The squadron could then put me on schedule as a required crewmember in the pilot position. I wanted to do a decent job and was studying hard, but the flights kept getting canceled. One day there was no check pilot available, and they rescheduled my training for two days later. Then there were no airplanes available. Trying to peak for the check ride and then having it canceled was very frustrating. The schedule changes were discouraging. Around the 14th of January, we were also supposed to get four days of R&R in Hong Kong. To buy stuff in Hong Kong, I borrowed $625, a month's pay, from Navy Federal Credit Union. Before our departure, I wanted to finish my PP3P check ride to make our trip more enjoyable.

An advantage of a Philippines deployment was US submarines availability to conduct ASW training exercises for the P-3 crews. So, we flew a lot of Anti-Submarine Warfare (ASW) training flights. On these ASW training missions, I flew little. In my role as the tactical navigator, I spent most of my time at the Nav station. These flights allowed VP-45 to gain ASW qualifications, known as quals. After a crew completed all ASW qualifications, they became an "Alpha" Crew. Earning "Alpha" Crew status was like earning Blue Ribbon status in ASW.

Sanders wanted all his crews to get "A" status by the time our deployment was over. Each crewmember had to show ASW skills unique to their position. The Nav was a key crewmember position. As Nav, I was the source of the documentation to support our success in these ASW training exercises. My skill at the Nav station boosted my reputation in the squadron. When a new navigator came to the crew, the crew lost all ASW qualifications held by the navigator. Since I held the navigator's qualification position, even though I qualified as PPC in July 1970, the squadron still listed me on the master crew list as Crew 20's navigator in order to maintain the crew's Alpha status. I remained as the XO's then CO's navigator until he left the squadron in August 1970.

At 2230, on January 12, we returned to Sangley from an ASW training mission. The schedule had us on another ASW training flight on January 13, at 0430. So much for crew rest rules. Then at 0430, on January 13, we showed up for the brief and found out the squadron canceled our ASW flight, my PP3P check ride, and the trip to Hong Kong. We had a new mission. The squadron would establish a detachment on Guam. *So much for making plans, just for one good deal after another.* The breaks of Naval Air.

GUAM DETACHMENT

We went back to the BOQ, packed our bags and early in the morning flew two P-3s to Guam for a three-day detachment. Out of Guam, we would fly an ASW Screening mission for the USS Enterprise, CVAN-65, battle group during transit to Yankee Station. The XO stayed back a Sangley to act as Officer in Charge (OIC) and Bob Hartl acted as PPC. In hindsight, despite being pissed off at all the changes, I am glad we did it.

I enjoyed the visit to Guam. On January 14, we flew our scheduled 11-hour ASW barrier patrol ahead on the USS Enterprise's transit path. About four hours into our mission, we got a call that the USS Enterprise had a crippling uncontrolled flight deck fire. The Enterprise fire started when a Zuni Rocket detonated under the plane's wing. It ruptured the plane's fuel tanks and started a fire. The fire spread to more munitions that exploded, blowing holes into the flight deck that allowed burning jet fuel to enter the ship. The fire killed 28 sailors, injured 314, and destroyed 15 aircraft. Six years later, I would get orders to be part of the ship's company on the USS Enterprise. One of my duties on the Enterprise would be zone inspections where I did a tour of certain areas on the ship. On these inspections, I would visit the area damaged by the fire and see the repaired spaces. The ship turned around and headed back to Pearl Harbor for repairs. Our mission was over. We went back to Guam.

PP3P

We had the 15th off, so Bill Dailey and I rented a Honda sports car, did a tour around Guam, and drove around the island's southern end. The jungle was untouched and completely unpopulated. Later, the US discovered there was still a WWII-era Japanese soldier living in the jungles on the island's southern end. The Japanese soldier did not know the war had ended. He surrendered to the US in 1972. Luckily, we did not encounter him. Later that day I found out, because of the Enterprise's fire, we would not fly our scheduled mission on January 16. The squadron said I would take my PP3P check ride with Lt. Cmdr. Jack Pleasure. The flight went well. He gave me four above average scores and told me I prepared well for the check ride. That positive experience alone made the Guam detachment a good deal.

On the 17th, we had to get back to Sangley. The crew would leave for our second Market Time rotation on the 18th. We flew a 10.7-hour ASW Patrol to the East of Guam and then turned back to the Philippines. During this night's flight, we picked up a radar contact with no lights north of Guam. We illuminated it with a para flare. It turned out to be a Russian AGI trawler, an intelligence gathering ship. We reported it, but everyone knew its location. The Russians stationed an AGI off Guam to report when the B-52s took off for their missions over Vietnam. The Russians had these AGI ships all over the world keeping track of our military. I picked up the navigation crossing west of Guam into the Philippine Sea. Brilliant stars filled the sky. Much the same as my trip to Norway the previous September. I could not figure out which stars would give me good a celestial fix. I got good fixes but was unsure of which stars I used for my celestial sighting.

Unsure of my position, I had lost confidence in my navigation.

In over my head, I confessed my concern to Bill Dailey, my TACCO, that I was not sure of my navigation. Bill gave me some good advice. He advised me, "Never admit you are lost as a navigator; you will get a reputation that will follow you forever." He said we were holding a steady course, and it was only a couple of hours to cross the Philippine Sea. We would find the Philippines with no problems. It didn't worry him, and it shouldn't worry me either. Sure enough, we hit our coast in point in the Philippines within about 10 nm, a good standard for celestial navigation. I maintained my navigator's reputation in the squadron. *A lesson learned here, even if I was not sure of what was going on, never admit it.*

BACK TO UTAPAO

We had little time off. Our schedule was unrelenting. The next day we went back on Market Time flights and flew a 10-hour daytime mission into Utapao. We taxied onto the VP ramp on the south end of the runway. After the FE shut down the engines, Cmdr. Mason announced we had just ditched. Everyone needed to execute their ditching duties. This included taking the rafts out of the over-wing emergency exits. It was a lot of work after an already long day, and we still had to debrief. The drill was a pain in the ass. On the 20th, we flew a 9.5-hour daytime Market Time mission, followed by a 9.5-hour nighttime mission on the 22nd. We flew a 6.7-hour flight back to Sangley on January 26. Sometimes we wondered why we were doing these missions. We spent a tremendous amount of time and energy on a mission that accomplished little, like spinning our wheels.

I remember things we saw on patrol, such as finding a Polish cargo ship heading into Hanoi. It had live pigs running around on the decks. The crew's food included these live animals. They would butcher the pigs as they sailed across the oceans. Or a Moravian registered ship with decks full of trucks going into Hanoi. If we were serious about preventing supplies going in the North Vietnam, stopping these ships would be the easiest way to do it. It would be three more years before Richard Nixon acted to curtail supplies going into North Vietnam by mining the harbors in 1972.

On a bulletin board near the USAF Officers' Club's entrance, the Air Force posted their flight schedules for bomber and tanker crews. Air Force schedules were inside a locked, glass-covered display case to prevent pilferage or tampering. The USAF detailed the crew composition and scheduled events to the minute. The crew list would name every crew position, name, rank, and serial number, such as Aircraft Commander, Lt. Col. Jones, Fred, A. Serial Number 1234567. Line-item times included Wake-up call: 0534, Crew bus pick you up: 0557, Breakfast: 0607, Bus to briefing: 0641, etc. As a rub against the USAF, VP-45 posted their schedule on a handwritten cocktail napkin taped to the schedules board. Our schedule contrasted with the USAF schedule. It read, "Morning Flight Crew 20, evening Flight Crew 22." We did not have strict times like the USAF; instead, our flexible on-station times were aimed at confusing potential gun runners.

READY ALERT LAUNCH

We got back to Sangley on the 26th and picked up the Ready One Duty on the 28th. It meant we had to be airborne within one hour after being alerted. To prepare for this immediate launch, we would preflight our assigned airplane in the morning, and fuel it to 30,000 pounds. Then go into crew rest at the BOQ. The squadron gave the crew the Ready One pickup truck so we could get to our airplane as fast as possible. Upon receiving the signal to fly, the PPC and TACCO would attend the briefing. The FE fueled the airplane, the other enlisted crewmembers would prepare their equipment for launch. In my role as the navigator, I would pull the charts needed for our patrol area.

While we were in crew rest, a report came in that North Vietnamese trawlers had gathered in the Paracel Islands. These islands, in the middle of the South China Sea, were about 200 miles off the coast of Vietnam. China has since moved into these islands and turned them onto military bases. But in 1969, many countries claimed them, and they were unoccupied. Our Operational Commander, CFT 77.2, elected to launch the alert airplane to investigate the ships. In our briefing, they ordered us to get good pictures of these ships, but still observe the 12-mile international standoff. We did not have a hi-resolution camera with a long-distance telephoto lens.

The only way to get these pictures was to fly within 1,000 yards of the target and take pictures. So much for the 12-mile international limit. The 1,000-yard standoff were the Rules of Engagement (ROE) limits when encountering a potential hostile ship. The VP-26 airplane lost in Cambodian water in 1968 had violated the ROE limits. We were very aware of our 1,000 yards standoff distance. Sometimes you just gotta do what you gotta do.

The ships turned out to be Vietnamese or Chinese fishing boats. We took our photos and continued our open ocean patrol to the north. We flew up toward Yankee Station and back toward the Philippines as the sun set. Visibility was going down, and we did a radar run in on a target. Turned out to be a Russian AGI again. While passing by, the Russian crew came to the ship's side and waved. I waved back. So much for the evil Russians. They were guys doing their job just like us. The mission lasted 12 hours, my longest flight yet in a P-3. January was another 100-hour month for me. The deployment was a great time to be a junior officer in the squadron. All we did was fly: we had no preparation for inspections and only limited office duties. Flying, drinking, and resting. Flying, drinking, and resting. I was getting comfortable in the P-3.

DUTY CREW SANGLEY

February came, and we picked up the Duty Crew rotation at NAS Sangley Point. As Duty Crew, our crew performed administrative duties. We would stand watches, work in the offices, and not fly for a week. During our duty week, we filled out the squadron watch bill to include Squadron Duty Officer, Command Duty Officer, Duty Driver, etc. I had demonstrated above average proficiency in ASW tactical navigation. So, the squadron gave me another additional duty. They wanted me to review every crew's ASW qualification logs and charts to ensure the crew would receive credit for the qualification. Even though the crew had properly executed an ASW qualification event, sometimes the logs did not support a successful conclusion. I would detect errors, and the navigator log pages often needed to be rewritten to meet wing grading criteria.

Assignment as the duty crew meant lots of time to visit the O'Club in the evening, since we were not on schedule. The O'Club was off Sangley runway's side. We could sit there and watch airplanes coming and going. We drank a lot. Five drinks in a couple hours was normal. After a few drinks, my mouth would start running with my world thoughts as I viewed them. Then a senior officer offered me some kindly advice, "No one cares what you think. Stick to what you're good at, which is navigating. *I had yet to learn that building a solid reputation as an officer was based more on squadron interpersonal relationships and acceptance than tactical skill.* Here I was, operating under a misguided assumption that my job was to know my airplane, be tactically proficient, and execute our airplane's mission.

On February 5, Bob Hartl and I flew a squadron operations team up to NAS Cubi Point just north of Sangley for a meeting. The VFR flight was quick, and we flew by the Corregidor Island and the Bataan Peninsula, the sites of early WWII battles in the Philippines. We spent a couple of hours on the ground at Naval Air Station Cubi Point while the ops team went to an ASW exercise conference. I took the time to go to the Navigation Chart Office at Cubi Point and drew charts to resupply our squadron stock. Since I was there, I got all the charts for the South Pacific, some places where we had extraordinarily little chance of operating. But I had read so much about the battles in the Solomon's I wanted to have these charts.

DUTY CREW UTAPAO

On February 9, we started another busy Market Time flight schedule. We flew a 10.5-hour Market Time mission during the day, from Sangley into Utapao. After a good night's rest, and no sleep during the day, on February 11 we launched at 2100 on a 10-hour nighttime mission. Then after 24 hours off, on the 13th, we flew another 10-hour daytime mission. The schedule took us out on a 9.9-hour nighttime mission on the 15th. Over the course of six days, I logged 40.4 hours flying four Market Time missions. The schedule's intensity took its toll on the crews. Upon returning to Utapao, Cmdr. Mason again ran one of his emergency evacuation drills. He simulated the airplane's nose wheel collapsed. It was necessary for us to exit the main cabin entrance by sliding down the escape rope. I guess this was the reason for the rope drills at AOCS. After flying a demanding, all-night Market Time missions, there was no need for these stupid emergency evacuation drills. What a pain!

On the 15th, our crew would have enough points for our first Air Medal. The award ceremony for our Air Medal would take place at NAS Sangley Point next month. On February 16, Crew 20 became the Utapao duty crew at Utapao for the next two weeks, until February 27. I found out Stan Wainwright, who had been our fourth pilot, was transferred to another crew. I enjoyed flying with Stan because he shared the navigator duties with me, which let me log time in the cockpit. His replacement was going to be a lieutenant commander who wouldn't pick up any additional crew duties, which meant I would spend more time at the Nav table.

On the 17th, Bob Hartl and I flew some heavies, read senior officers, over to Cam Ranh Bay, Vietnam, for a Market Time conference. We flew around the south coast of Cambodia and picked up an IFR clearance to fly up to Cam Ranh Bay. The base housed the Market Time operation's headquarters. We parked on the Patrol Squadron ramp. The maintenance trailers at Cam Ranh Bay, beat up old camper trailers, looked the same as the ones we had at Utapao. We were there about four hours, and we got lunch at the chow hall. Bob Hartl and I did not go to the conference. Instead, we borrowed a jeep to explore the base. We drove down to the beach: beautiful, white sand, clear water. Just like Pensacola. I thought, *This is exactly the place the Hilton would build a resort hotel.* We were back in Utapao before dark.

I met my flying partner from VT-31, Rob Strayhorn. The Navy had assigned him to VP-9. I took his picture with a Cam Ranh Bay sign in the background. In 2002, doctors diagnosed me with prostate cancer. My photo would come in very handy in 2012. I discovered during a meeting with a veteran's benefit counselor I was eligible for VA disability compensation. The VA linked exposure to Agent as a probable cause of prostate cancer. My photo confirmed my presence in Vietnam and that I met the VA's definition of being in Vietnam and qualified me for a VA disability. The military also used Agent Orange in Thailand to remove foliage around air bases, such as Utapao. I suffered much more exposure to Agent Orange at Utapao than I did at Cam Ranh Bay. But in 2011, exposure to Agent Orange outside of Vietnam didn't qualify for VA disability compensation. In 2022, the VA expanded the definition of exposure to cover air bases in Thailand as they rightfully should have done in when they set up the definition of exposure.

On the 20th, the squadron gave me three nights of R&R in Bangkok. I stayed in the USAF resort hotel downtown. The Air Force hotel had tours arranged for me, visits to jewelry stores, where I bought bracelets and rings for Lou. One thing I remember is going to the movie theater and seeing "Bullet" where Steve McQueen raced around San Francisco in his Mustang. The engine noise brought back memories of my 1963 Comet sitting in my mom's garage back in Troy. The movie had Thai subtitles on the screen while actors spoke English.

When I got back from Bangkok, we were still the duty crew. I got an assignment from the Executive Officer, Cmdr. Mason. At the morning meeting, he said that he wanted a volleyball net set up by our BOQ. The squadron had a volleyball net, but no posts from which to suspend it. Nothing had happened when he asked another officer to do it. The XO wanted to know if I could get the job done. I said I'd try. After all, being a trained shop teacher, it would be a "piece of cake." The task was no big deal. I found the volleyball net. Base supply gave me a couple of 4 x 4 beams, some concrete mix and an empty 55-gallon drum. They were very easy to deal with. I just asked for it and they gave it to me. Supply never asked for any forms or purchase requests. A maintenance guy back at the squadron cut the drum in half with an acetylene torch. I mixed the concrete with my hands. Then, I set the 4 x 4s in the concrete and waited for the cement to set. I painted the uprights black with white reflective tape for a contrast.

By that afternoon, I had a working volleyball net. I set it up in the asphalt parking lot next to the BOQ. We chose teams, and we played a lot of volleyball. The guys really enjoyed the diversion from the constant Market Time flights. It became a place where the crews could blow off some steam while waiting for their next mission. I even got a thank you with free beer at the O'Club. Not that 10 cents can be such a big deal.

On the 27th, we did an IFR airway flight over Laos and Danang, where we started a 10.9-hour open ocean patrol in the South China Sea. But since we did not have a Combat, Flight Purpose Code, (FPC), it did not count as points toward our Air Medal points. The next day we went out for an ASW exercise, but the sub we were supposed to track had broken down and nobody bothered to let us know. After flailing around for a couple hours, we turned it into a night ASW tactics training flight where I flew as pilot, applying ASW tactics.

We had a quick turnaround before we had to go back to Utapao on March 7. I had one pilot training flight with Bob Hartl. Bob gave me good grades on this flight. Then I went back to my ground duty of cross checking ASW qualification logs pages. All the February duty crew assignments at Sangley and Utapao limited my flying time to only 69.3 hours. February was my lowest deployment flying time month. I had averaged over 100 hours a month since deploying to Southeast Asia.

We had a ceremony at morning quarters the first week of March, where we were all awarded our first Air Medals. The day/night patrols around Vietnam on Market Time patrols continued. On March 7, we returned to Utapao for an eight-day rotation. The crew flew a 10.5 daytime mission into Utapao.

Chapter Five
My Adventures

THE BAD LANDING

During our Utapao rotation, I had an embarrassing moment. We were inbound to Utapao, coming back from one of our day patrols. When we started our approach, it was dark. The winds were light, and the airplane handled steady as a rock, and we were landing to the south on runway 18. Red lights illuminated the cockpit, and the runway was clearly visible through the windshield. The visual approach glide slope lights showed us on a proper glide path. Off to my left were the illuminated B-52 revetments. To the right was the brightly lit transient ramp. At the runway's, the Gulf of Thailand appeared as a black hole and completed my visual picture. The FE held a steady 700 HP on all four engines.

I was on speed and had my approach nailed. It would be a piece of cake landing. The runway was 11,800 feet long and our turn off was at the far end near the Gulf of Thailand. Pilots used a long landing technique and left extra power on the engines. That way, the airplane would fly further down the runway before touching down. When the plane landed, it would be closer to our turn off at the runway's end. It saved taxi time to our ramp.

During my landing, I wanted to end up closer to our ramp. As I entered the flare, I told the FE to set 400 HP instead of 200 HP. I carried the extra power into the flare and held it off, and I had the landing wired. My crew will buy me drinks tonight for this one. However, I touched down so smoothly I did not know I had landed. I never pulled the power off. The runway's end was approaching rapidly. Thinking I had not landed, I called "Go Around Power" and pushed the power levers up to maximum power. Cmdr. Mason in the right seat turned toward me with a puzzled look.

"What are you doing? You already landed?"

"I'm going around."

He told the tower we were doing some pilot training, and we went around for another landing. My next landing was firm, and I knew I had touched down. At the BOQ bar, I had to buy all the drinks. With cheap drinks, it did not cost me much. Over drinks, my crew teased me about not knowing how to find the runway. Everyone had great fun with my embarrassment over my unknown landing.

On the 9th we flew a 10.4-hour nighttime mission. On the Market Time missions, a day flight followed a night flight that was followed by another day flight. We were always out of our circadian rhythm. Getting enough rest was always a problem; we rarely got a good night's sleep. Making it even worse were our sleep interruptions. Our BOQ was near the ramp where the USAF tested their KC-135 tanker jet engines at night. Even though we flew with an augmented crew composed of extra pilots and flight engineers, fatigue was still an issue.

FATIGUE

The impact of fatigue stands out. On one nighttime flight, we were busy along the southeast coast of Vietnam, flying in the shipping lanes. A lot of contacts and the crew's chatter on the intercom kept us alert and on the go. But when we turned northwest up the west coast of Vietnam, there were almost no contacts. Chatter died down over the airplane's intercom. We had no tasks. It became quiet as the workload dropped off. One time, around 2 or 3 in the morning, we were at 1,500 feet on three engines, autopilot on and locked into the Radar Altimeter Altitude hold. The sky was black: no stars, no horizon.

To keep our night vision at its peak, dimmed red instrument lights illuminated the cockpit. Our flight deck was nearly dark, so we only saw shadowy shapes for crew members. Fatigue set in. The engines' hushed hum filled the cockpit. I was fighting off sleep. White noise filled our cockpit. Micro-napping started where minutes felt like hours as I was fighting off sleep. Then I nodded off.

I awoke with a startle, not knowing if I had been asleep 30 seconds or 30 minutes. I looked across the cockpit from the right seat. Bob Hartl, in the left seat, was asleep, and the flight engineer was also sleeping. I turned over my left shoulder and looked back down at the tactical stations in the Tube. Everyone back there was asleep. I just woke up, and I was the only person conscious. *Holy Fucking Shit! I needed to think of a way to wake them without saying,* "Hey wake the fuck up." Yelling "Wake Up" might have introduced a startle factor and unexpected results as the pilot and FE discovered they were asleep.

Thinking it over, I called the galley for some cockpit coffee. An off-duty crew member in the galley responded in a surprised, yawning voice. When Bob and the flight engineer heard my call on the PA, they also woke up and asked for coffee. I got my coffee and lit up one of my Chesterfields shorts. Then I sat back to enjoy the rest of the night. Bob bummed a cigarette from me and lit it up. I was smoking three packs a day. They were only a dollar a carton, ten cents a pack. *Yeah, it might be unhealthy, but any unhealthier than flying in Vietnam?* An incident like that really woke me up for a while. Fatigue on this day/night schedule was always an issue.

SMALL WORLD

One of those small world incidents happened after our 9.8-hour nighttime flight on March 13. I was in the O'Club for breakfast. After an all-nighter, I couldn't think straight, when up came this USAF pilot in his green flight suit. He grabbed me by the shoulders and said, "Randy, it's the Hump."

Fatigue set in, and my brain was running half speed like I had just sucked down a couple of beers. My mind was going, *What the hell is a hump?* It turns out he was my former MSU roommate and almost fraternity brother, Joe Heywood. Joe was the guy who ribbed me for having my MSU block S letter blanket back in our dorm at MSU eight years earlier. He put on about 50 pounds, and I didn't recognize him. We were in AFROTC together, and I found out he was a KC-135 navigator flying out of Utapao. Here I was, as far away from MSU as I could get, and I ran across my college roommate. On the 15th, my crew flew a 9.7-hour flight back to Sangley Point.

THE DREAM

We operated at airplane weight limits, always close to or over MGTOW. Takeoffs in the high temperatures and high humidity resulted in low engine power, even when using water injection. No leaping into the air like I experienced when flying at training weights. Shortly after liftoff, the water injection would run dry, and the engines would drop to an even lower power setting like we had lost an engine. The airplane was slow to climb and accelerate.

The inescapable stress of continuous day and night extended flying was getting to me. In mid-March, I started having P-3 crash dreams where I crashed on takeoff. We would approach the Rotate speed, and the other pilot would call out "Rotate." At "Rotate," I would pitch my nose up to the takeoff attitude and the plane does not want to fly. I would wake up with a startle and realize thankfully it was just a dream. Not exactly nightmares, but vivid dreams I remembered after I woke up. I would have these dreams regularly. Even today in 2024, I remember these dreams vividly.

The squadron gave me another one of those Shitty Little Jobs (SLJ). They wanted data collected on the functional capabilities of gyro-stabilized binoculars. These binoculars were the size of a shoebox, weighed about eight pounds, and had a gyro that stabilized the lens. They cost over $8,000, more than a year's wages for me. They were supposed to let us check out a target from a longer distance. I passed the binoculars among the crews at Utapao to get their input on the binocular's practicality. I prepared an evaluation form and had them fill it out with their comments.

The binoculars were cumbersome, had a too-narrow field of vision, constant demands to adjust the focal distance and were a distraction while flying at low altitude when the user should have been concentrating on altitude control. They were not good for an airplane traveling at 300 kts. Based on the feedback, I submitted a recommendation to the Operations Officer. I said the gyro stabilized binoculars were more of a nuisance than useful tool. Based on our squadron's evaluation, the Navy elected to not adopt the binoculars for our use on Market Time patrols.

TOKYO

When we got back from Utapao, we picked up alert duty. We stood the Ready 1 and Ready 2 alerts for five days. Our crew was told we would go to Hong Kong in April to make up for the canceled trip in January because of our Guam deployment. Rumor had it the Navy was considering mining Haiphong harbor, and CTF 77 wanted all crews current and qualified on the P-3's mining mission. They ordered us to the mining range up at Okinawa to get qualified for our mining mission. Mining in a hostile area was not a suitable mission for a P-3. Thankfully, no one ordered us to mine the North Vietnamese Waters. Three years later, President Nixon would use A-6's and A-7's mining North Vietnam's harbors.

When we completed our mining qualification, we recovered at NAS Atsugi in Tokyo, Japan. We spent two nights in Tokyo before returning to Sangley. In Japan, the U.S. military issued Military Payment Certificates (MPC). We exchanged our dollars for MPCs. A one-dollar bill had a picture of Grace Kelly. MPCs were the currency we used when shopping in Tokyo. We did the tourist things: visited the Emperor's Palace, shopped on the Ginza, and had a fancy meal. According to the junior officers, one requirement of a western Pacific deployment, besides flying missions in Vietnam, was to load up on stereo audio equipment, available at discounted prices in Japan. I bought a Sansui 2000 tuner, which still plays great tunes today. Plus, a Sony reel-to-reel tape recorder and phonograph combined with two sets of Sansui speakers. All this sound equipment was for around $300, $2,500 in 2024 dollars.

On March 26, on the way back to Sangley, they tasked us to conduct a 9.7-hour open ocean patrol. The plane had to be steered in different directions, altitudes, and speeds to collect data on the ships we encountered. We entered the ship's name, type, course, and speed into the rigging log pages and forwarded the information to 7th Fleet Naval Intelligence. I became frustrated because I could not keep up with all the changes. I was trying to run a normal transoceanic Navigation Log. Ralph Mason gave me a tip. He said "Don't worry about it. Occasionally, take a Loran A fix, make an ASA-47 DR computer update, log our ASA-47 position. That's sufficient." He, like all patrol plane pilots, had also been a navigator once upon a time and shared how he had done his tracking in a similar situation.

Oh! What an easy learning event.

Of course, when we got back to Sangley, Cmdr. Mason ran one of his silly ass evacuations drills. He simulated the right wing was on fire and we had to evacuate out the left-over-wing exit. Such Bullshit!

During an All-Officer Meeting at Sangley, our Flight Surgeon briefed us on a recent P-3 accident and its implications for flight crew members. On March 6, 1969, a VP-31, P-3 crashed at Crow's Landing Auxiliary Field in California. A hard landing resulted in the wing breaking off, and the airplane turning into a fireball. When the fire entered the cockpit, the flight crew could not escape. The flight crew were not wearing their fireproof Nomex Flight Gloves. They also had their flight suit sleeves pulled up above their elbows. When the fire flashed in the cockpit, it seared their hands and forearms and rendered them useless. Their hands no longer functioned. They couldn't open the exits and burned to death in the airplane.

The story chilled me and was beyond my comprehension the thought of being trapped in a burning cockpit and unable to escape. I never wanted to find myself in that situation. The proper way to wear your protective gear was to put the Nomex gloves on. Then pull the flight suit sleeve over the glove at your wrist and tighten the Velcro fastened around your wrist. This gives you maximum protection from fire, to ensure you have use of your hands and arms. This story stuck with me the rest of my career.

HONG KONG

On March 28, we flew a 10.2-hour daytime mission back to Utapao. Then on the 30th we flew a 9.7-hour nighttime mission. In March, I flew on twelve flights and got over 106 hours of flight time. In all that flying, I had no training flights to practice landings, and I only got five landings. I needed to make more landings. The more I did, the better I got. These long missions combined with splitting landings between the four pilots limited landing opportunities. Such is the intensity of operational flying. April started with Crew 20 doing a normal Utapao rotation flying four missions. We finished our rotation and flew back to Sangley on April 5. Two days later, we flew to Hong Kong to spend four nights.

We flew our P-3 into Hong Kong's airport. It was tricky. The pilot had to land on the side of a mountain as he came off the harbor. If the pilot didn't land, he faced flying into the mountain's side. We stood there talking about how tricky the approach and landing were at the Hong Kong Airport. Then we watched a DC-8-63, in 1969, one of the largest commercial airplanes in the world landed. So much for our superior talents on getting into Hong Kong's Airport. With no military facility, we had no place to park our P-3. Instead, the crew coming off their Hong Kong R&R would fly the airplane back to Sangley. We had a hotel set up for us by a tailor. He arranged tours for us around the town. He would make us custom hand-tailored suits. The tailor had us come by his shop every day for fittings.

Bob and I visited the Chinese Communist Embassy in Hong Kong. It reminded me of SERE school, with armed guards wearing a Red Star on their uniforms. They had a picture of Mao on the wall, and we picked up Mao's Little Red Book of sayings. I was happy to get out of that building.

The tailor treated us to a fancy dinner. There, I had my first encounter with caviar. The restaurant had some black lumpy stuff in the buffet. I put some on my plate. The little balls were salty and fishy tasting. I did not like it. "What is this stuff? I asked Bob Hartl.

"It's caviar."

Yuk, this food was supposed to be a delicacy, but not for me.

I purchased three nice, hand-tailored suits for $100: a wool two-piece suit, a silk sport coat, and a gabardine three-piece suit. I packed the suits up and did not plan on wearing them again until I returned to the States. Unfortunately, the last fitting was the only time I wore them. I would lose them during our transit back to the States. We got back to Sangley on April 11.

Chapter Six
Winding UP

YANKEE STATION
READY ONE LAUNCH

The squadron assigned our crew Ready One on Friday the 13th. Lucky for us? We had only two pilots assigned to the ready crew, Bob Hartl and me, because of a pilot shortage. Two NFOs, Bill Dailey and Tom Lesko, filled the TACCO and navigator positions in the back. If they launched us, we wouldn't have a relief pilot available on the crew. They allowed us to stand the ready alert with a short crew, because they would never launch the Ready One. *Well, unless they do, like this time.*

That afternoon, we received an alert to launch and to fly a night Yankee Station radar surveillance patrol. Yankee Station was a geographic operating point for aircraft carriers off the coast of North Vietnam. We would spend our time on-station in an active radar search looking for enemy surface craft. Primarily PT boats, which might try to make a run on the aircraft carriers. We came out of Sangley at round 132,000 MGTOW. Our airframe had a published MGTOW of 127,500. We had paraflares on four stations, plus full fuel, adding to our takeoff weight. To top it off, we had a full ASW "C" load, at 3,600 pounds just in case we found a sub on Yankee Station.

On a 95-degree day, with light winds, we would use water injection to increase engine power. We would need every inch of Sangley's 8,000-foot runway to get airborne. The takeoff roll started, and everything looked normal. At 95 kts, the water injection system failed. One of the two water injection pumps stopped working. With only one water injection pump, the system auto shutdown. Losing water injection caused engine horsepower to drop. We did not have adequate horsepower for a normal takeoff. 6,000 feet down the runway. The plane had only sped up to 100-kts. Rotate speed was in the 130-knot range. We didn't have enough room to abort, and it looked like we didn't have enough left to take off. Approaching the end left us no choice.

The short distance forced us to rotate well before we reached rotate speed. The plane staggered into the air and wouldn't climb and was slowly speeding up in ground effect at only about 50 feet off the water, putting us on a trajectory straight toward Manila International Airport. We finally reached flap retract speed and got the flaps up to reduce our drag so we could speed up and start our turn. I smiled, looked over at Bob and said, "Good job" He raised his eyebrows with a false bravado like everything had been under control. Bob called for climb power, and we were on our way to Yankee Station.

We spent 7.5 hours orbiting Yankee Station doing a radar search for PT boats. After dark, on a sweep up the west coast of Hainan Island, we picked up a small target on our radar. To identify the target, we would have to drop a paraflare to make a visual identification. To say I was a little nervous on this radar run would be an understatement. The boat was off the coast of China, and I was thinking of VP-26's run-in on a small boat off the coast of Cambodia. P-3s burn profusely when shot at. After our briefing the previous month, I preferred not to be in a burning airplane. One of my fears was being trapped in a burning airplane. To cover my unease, I lit up a cigarette to show I was cool with everything. After all, I had to keep up my smoking to go through a pack of cigarettes on one flight.

Bob appeared very much in charge and followed Soupy's radar guidance for proper standoff distance. We flew by and dropped a para flare and made a 180-degree turn. After the turn, we were on the contact's opposite side, looking across at the boat being illuminated by the para flare. The contact was an unarmed Chinese fishing boat. We would see these boats all over the world. Bob impressed me with how he handled this radar run in. In his role as PPC, he was also playing a role as a mentor to me. A couple years later, when I was a PPC and thrust into an uncomfortable situation, I would think, *"What would Bob do?"*

About forty years later, I would cross paths with Bob Hartl again and tell him how his performance on that run in impressed me. I commended.

"I was nervous."

"I don't remember it."

"It scared me shitless."

"It never showed, or I would have remembered,"

If I had shown my worry, it could have been a much more unnerving experience for both of us.

UTAPAO AGAIN

I got a landing pattern practice flight on the 17th with Lt. Cmdr. Taylor. Then a six-hour ASW qualification flight mission on the 20th. Then back over to Utapao on April 21. We would have one more Utapao ration before we returned to the States. Our deployment was near the end. On the 25th, I had earned enough points for my second-strike, Air Medal. But Seventh Fleet told the squadron when they applied for our second award that P-3s on combat support flights did not qualify for Strike Air Medal points. We would only get one Air Medal for our Vietnam support operations.

I did a lot of different flying in April from bounce flights to ASW qualifications to Market Time missions. They kept me busy. A flight I remember included when they scheduled us to fly the reverse of our normal route. After taking off from Utapao, we flew south to the Vietnamese/Cambodian border. Then around the southern tip of Vietnam, north towards Danang. We discovered after takeoff we had no radar. Radar was mission-essential equipment and would result in a mission abort. But we continued our flight because of the JO's interpretation of Cmdr. Sander's abort criteria as an uncontained wing fire, Bill, the TACCO, had a copy of "Lloyd's of London" sailing orders.

The sailing orders book gave us the name, type of ship with departure and arrival port that was operating in the Southeast Asia area. To avoid the CO's ire for aborting a mission, we picked out the ships, leaving Bangkok and Singapore. Then we plotted the ship's dead reckoning positions on our route. We filled out our logs, documenting radar run-ins on the imaginary targets. We filled out rigging logs based on the information found in Lloyd's sailing orders. The logs looked good.

The weather provided unlimited visibility that day. We were sure no bad guys slipped in during our flight since they were using the port Sihanoukville in Cambodia and had no reason to penetrate our barrier. Bill and I submitted our logs to the Intelligence Officer and never heard another thing. On the 23rd we flew a 10.2-hour night mission, followed by a 10.0-hour daytime mission on the 25th. We finished our Utapao rotation on the 27th with a 10.0-hour nighttime mission. We flew back to Sangley on April 29. With our visit to Hong Kong, I only flew 15 days in April, but still logged over a hundred hours.

GOODBYE PHILIPPINES

May would be my last stay in the Philippines. It seemed like we had been there forever, and it felt like home. But when I packed up this time, I would not be coming back to Sangley. We would end our deployment and return to the States from Utapao.

Meanwhile, I started training for my PP2P check ride. I went into the landing pattern with Bob at NAS Cubi Point. On this flight, we were practicing engine failures after refusal. On an engine failure after the refusal maneuver, the instructor simulates an engine failing during takeoff, and I continue the takeoff on three engines. Bob had pulled the engine on the left wing three times in a row. Then, on the fourth engine failure, he pulled a right-wing engine; I jumped on the right rudder as I had done for left engine failures. The response was automatic based on the previous simulated engine failure; I should have waited for the drift to develop before jumping the correct rudder to stop the drift. My bad! We went into a skid and were looking down the runway out the side window. We recovered and stayed on the runway with no airplane damage. Bob gave me an UNSAT, a down. A down was a training failure. I now had to go to a squadron review board. *Could this be the end of me becoming a PPC?*

On May 16, I flew as navigator up to Naha, Okinawa, with a stop in Taipan, Taiwan. We spent the night in Okinawa and flew back to Sangley. Again, I spent most of the time at the Nav table. On May 19, I had my last flight at Sangley. I flew as the navigator on Crew 13 with my Sangley BOQ roommate Walt; he could not master an Alpha-32 (A-32) Qualification. To earn full qualification as an ASW crew, the crew satisfactorily completed a series of training events identified as A-1 through A-34. A-1 was the radar tracking of a ship. A-34 was a tracking of a submerged submarine using MAD. The Alpha-32 used a method called "Julie," the Explosive Echo Range system of sub tracking.

We would drop a Practice Depth Charge (PDC) that contained about 2 ounces of explosive. The PDC would detonate and generate a sound wave. The sonobuoys would record the sound wave bouncing off the submarine to determine its distance from the sonobuoy.

I had no problem keeping up on an A-32. So, they assigned me to this flight to help Walt out. I sat at the Nav table and Walt ran the A-32 from the TACCO's ASA-16 scope. We found, tracked, and successfully simulated an attack on the submarine. The PPC threw a carrot at me by letting me fly back to Sangley and make the landing. The successful completion of an A-32 gave Crew 13 their Alpha qualification and made the squadron 100 percent Alpha qualified. Few squadrons achieved this level, and this qualification was a big deal. We were all very proud of our accomplishments.

On the morning of May 20, we left Sangley and flew a 10.0-hour daytime mission. Our last rotation started at Utapao. Before this Utapao rotation, days really meant nothing. A day was a day, and all days were something that came before the next day. But now I could count the number of flights I needed to before it was over. Now, for the first time, thoughts of going home, seeing Lou again, and putting Vietnam behind me filled my mind.

On the 22nd, we flew a 10.0-hour night flight. Just after going on station south of the DMZ, we picked up a target, a good-sized radar return, and we began a radar-guided run in on the target. The target had no lights, and we could not identify it. Thinking it might be a Navy ship, we called Fleet Common, UHF frequency, 277.8, but got no response. We elected to illuminate the target. We set up our paraflare run and dropped the flare. Starting our turn to identify the target, the ship came up on UHF Guard 243.00 and broadcast, "This is the USS ABC. We are friendly. Do not shoot, do not shoot." We looked at the ship with a flare in the background, only to see a US destroyer escort. They assigned the ship to the Market Time force.

LAST MISSION

May 24 was another routine 10.0-hour daytime mission. Then on the 26th we flew our last nighttime Market Time mission another 10.0-hour flight. On May 28, we flew our last patrol of our Market Time mission. Having these flights behind us was good. We had a sense of satisfaction; we had done our job. The squadron set a record for the least number of aborted missions by any squadron flying in Market Time. Our crew had never missed a mission. We had done our jobs. They wouldn't assign any more Market Time missions to our crew on this deployment. The squadron planned a flight ramp party for each crew member when they completed their last mission. Beers were waiting for us on the ramp along with lots of backslapping and "High fives."

Chapter Seven
Going Home

LEAVING UTAPAO

In six months flying around Vietnam, I had logged over 630 hours of flight time. I had flown 29 Market Time missions and logged 294 hours of direct combat support. My entire experience was a dream come true. I became part of a Navy Patrol Plane flight crew. As I longed to be when reading Gordon Forbes *Goodbye to Some*. A series of mentors had helped me grow in my role as an officer and pilot. I became proficient in flying P-3s on these demanding day/night missions. My DIs at AOCS had drilled discipline into me to live up to the intensity of Combat Support Operations. It filled me with a sense of satisfaction. I still had lots to learn, but my first deployment was a success. What a rewarding time for me.

VP-6 out of Barbers Point Hawaii would relieve us. They arrived at Utapao, and we went into a three-day turnover with our relief squadron. After our turnover, we would fly home to Jacksonville. Instead of going through Guam and Hawaii like Wings 10 and 30, we would take a shorter route going through Japan and Alaska to San Francisco. Wing 20 had three VP-45 airplanes at Utapao. On May 31 we flew to Iwakuni, Japan. We spent two nights at Iwakuni before we left on our next leg to

Adak, Alaska, near the Aleutian Island chain's end. While at Iwakuni, we took a train up to Hiroshima to visit the site where America dropped an atomic bomb. I toured the museum and signed into the visitors' log. May was another month when I flew over 100 hours.

ADAK, ALASKA

On June 2, we made our flight to NAS Adak, Alaska, where we spent the night. Since we crossed the international date line, we landed in Adak on June 1st. Everyone was in high spirits to be back in America. We had been flying around Vietnam for six months and our deployment was behind us. At the O'Club, we toasted with drinks, celebrating our combat support flying's end. Adak marked the end of our journey before returning to "The World." Our spirits were high because our combat tour was over. Tomorrow we would be back in the lower-48 states after a short seven-hour flight. In twenty-four hours, I could call Lou. Then one more night in Frisco, and I would be home with my wife in her eighth month of pregnancy. We could relax on one more routine over water flight to the states. I couldn't wait.

TAKEOFF

June 2, 1969, in Adak, Alaska at 0600 local, we taxied toward the runway for takeoff. Commander. Mason, our PPC, was in the right seat and I was in the left seat, making our takeoff. Our smoke hatch was open, and we were flying our "Crew Pride" flag out of the top of the cockpit. The silk flag we had made in the Philippines celebrated our achievements during our deployment and showed decorations with all our awards and accomplishments. We referred to it as our "Fuck You" flag, showing what we achieved that others didn't. Despite the overcast skies at 400 feet, the visibility exceeded three miles, offering a full view of the runway. The gray cast of the early morning sun gave a gloomy setting. In keeping with maximum personal protection, I was wearing my Nomex flight gloves with sleeves Velcro fastened around my wrist. Although I had fewer than 1,000 total hours of pilot time, I had over 400 hours in the left seat over the last six months. In the Navy, I never made a right seat takeoff or landing until I became an instructor pilot in 1971. Compared to previous months where we flew with maxed out fuel, with only 47,000 pounds on board this day, we were well under MGTOW at 120,000 pounds. The cool Alaskan temperatures provided full power availability, with the engines being torque limited at 4300 horsepower. What could go wrong?

The P-3 had an engine protective device called Pitchlock. If the engine overspeeds, the Pitchlock system locks the propeller's blade angel, turning it into a fixed-pitch propeller to prevent further overspeed. In order for the props to go into reverse, there was another system called the Pitchlock Reset, which allowed the engine to overspeed going into reverse. Adak's forecast wind the night before was over 50 kts. The MRC (Maintenance Required Card) for parking in high-wind conditions directed the flight engineer to feather the props, which would prevent engine damage from a windmilling prop. The Flight Essential DC Bus that powered the Pitchlock Reset system had electrical power any time the battery was in the airplane. Feathering the props and keeping the power levers in ground range would activate the Pitchlock Reset and run down the battery. To protect the battery life, the Flight Engineer (FE) followed the guidance found on the MRC card and pulled the Pitchlock Reset Circuit Breakers (CB).

In my element, I felt comfortable making this "piece of cake takeoff." I was flying the same P-3 I had flown around Vietnam for the last six months. The tower cleared us for takeoff on runway 5. With my left hand on the nosewheel steering wheel, I directed the airplane onto the runway. Frenchy, our second FE, was observing the takeoff from the unofficial cockpit seat atop the radar console behind me. He reached up and pulled in our "Crew Pride" flag and closed the Smoke Removal Hatch. We turned toward the foreboding Bering Sea off the end of the runway. With the overcast skies, the water had a gray ominous appearance and blended with the horizon in the distance. White caps broke off the runway's end. Off to the right stood the VP-ramp and hangar with its brilliant lights shining down on the ramp in the early morning light. On the left side of the runway stood a mountain, and about half down there was a deep drainage ditch that separated the runway from some abandoned WWII hardstands. Once I aligned the aircraft on the runway, I pushed the left set of power levers forward and called out to the FE, "Set takeoff power." The FE pushed on the right set of power levers further forward and set 4300 HP. With my left hand on nosewheel steering, I guided the airplane down the runway's centerline. My right hand rested on the top of the left set of power levers in case I needed to abort the takeoff. As we passed 80 kts, Cmdr. Mason called out, "80 knots." I released the nosewheel steering as the rudder became effective. My left hand moved to the yoke. At 120 kts, the PPC made the "rotate" call. We were now beyond abort airspeed. I released my right hand from the power levers and moved it to the yoke. Now I had both hands on the yoke. Releasing the power levers and placing both hands on the yoke meant we were now committed to takeoff. I pulled the nose up to seven degrees, our takeoff pitch attitude. As I rotated, the nose wheel left the runway, and we assumed the takeoff attitude. While rotating, I heard a "WHAM, Woosh." The cockpit overhead, smoke removal hatch popped open. The engineers designed the smoke hatch to be opened and closed in flight during emergencies for smoke evacuation. Despite the smoke hatch's accidental opening, I continued the takeoff as VP-30 trained me a year before.

ABORTED TAKEOFF

Commander Mason announced, "Abort, I have the controls," and took the controls. My hands let go of the yoke and I took my feet off the rudders. He pushed the nose back onto the runway. In an instant, he pulled the right set of power levers into full reserve to perform an aborted takeoff. Commander Mason, a Test Pilot School graduate, had performed P-3 fleet acceptance testing, and conducted 142,000-pound, three-engine aborted takeoffs. Our aircraft would operate outside of its envelope, and he knew it. As he pulled the power levers into reverse range, the engines oversped, and the props should have gone into reverse. But the Pitchlock Reset system failed during the aborted takeoff because the Flight Engineer had deactivated it the night before. He did not reset the circuit breakers in the morning. His actions disabled reverse thrust. The engines had gone into Pitchlock because there was no Pitchlock Reset protection. Our propellers became locked in a fixed pitch with forward thrust.

On our abort when the engines pitchlocked, no one looked for the little green "Beta" lights on the engine annunciator panel at the top of the engine instruments. The "Beta" lights would show the prop blade angle was in the reserve range. No "Beta" lights indicated reverse thrust was not available. Navy P-3 crews did not receive the same training as civilian crews flying the Electra. In the civilian world, the FE called out "Four Betas" before the pilot pulled the power levers into reverse range. Our FE was not required to, nor did he call out the "Beta" lights absence before Cmdr. Mason pulled the props into reverse. A "No Beta lights" call would have alerted us to the pitchlock situation. The confusion grew because of the blade angle setting and power lever position caused low horsepower, low TIT (Turbine Inlet Temperature), 100% RPM, and reduced fuel flow, classic de-couple indications. A de-couple meant the prop and engine were no longer connected, resulting in zero thrust. Contradictory information quickly overwhelmed us.

Only the noise of tires thumping on runway cracks filled the dead silent cockpit. Commander Mason assumed we had decoupled the props and tried to stop using brakes. As we slowed during the brake application, our horsepower increased because the fuel control scheduled more fuel to maintain the engines' RPM, increasing the airplane's forward thrust. When he released the brakes, the airplane would accelerate. He jumped on the brakes again and blew out the tires. Now the airplane thumped and rumbled down the runway on its wheels and flat tires. We could not stop and only 3,000 feet of runway remained. While all this chaos was happening, the FE reached down under his seat and reset the circuit breakers, but it was too late. Frenchy saw the smoke hatch blow open and reached up to close it. When he saw we couldn't stop the airplane, he jumped up and said, "Oh shit!" He ran out of the cockpit to his ditching station in the radio compartment.

We knew if we went straight ahead into the Bering Sea, everyone on the plane would die of exposure. To the left side of the runway, beyond the culvert, was an abandoned taxiway that led to a couple of old WWII aircraft hardstands. The PPC stood on the left rudder, and we went toward the runway's left side. Our airplane went into a severe right yaw, skidding sideways on the blown tires. We departed the runway's left side at 110 kts with about 2,500 feet of runway remaining. As we left the runway, Cmdr. Mason called out for the Emergency Engine Shutdown handles (E-Handles) to be pulled on engines #1 and #4. The FE pulled the E-Handles.

We departed the runway into the drainage ditch and unprepared terrain. The airplane would most likely disintegrate into a ball of fire, much like VP-31's P-3 at Crow's Landing, when we departed the runway. My fear of being trapped in a burning airplane raced through my mind. I realized I might die. A helpless feeling overcame me as I thought, *"Peace of God that passes all understanding."* My life was in the hands of a higher power. There was nothing I could do. My mind raced, "This is not fair. I have done my time in Vietnam. I am supposed to go home. My wife has a child on the way. Why me? Why now?" Were these the thoughts of a man about to die? I did not plan on dying that day. Just like the ending in Gordon Forbes's book *Goodbye to Some*. The book's lead character crashes on a Pacific Island while going home after flying patrols around Vietnam's coast. I purchased the book in East Lansing four years before.

PREPARE TO DITCH

Commander Mason shouted, "Alert the crew, tell them to prepare to ditch."

I picked up the mike, looked over my left shoulder and turned the intercom selector to the Public Address position: "This is not a drill. Prepare to ditch, prepare to ditch."

While going through the gully, Cmdr. Mason ordered E-handles #2 and #3 be pulled to shut down engines. We left the runway's pavement about 30 degrees to the left of the runway, heading into the dirt near the drainage ditch. When the plane hit the gulley in a 15-degree right skid, it tore our right wing off. The severe deceleration forces associated with wing breaking off caused the microphone to fly out of my hand and bang into the windshield. The violent wing separation smashed my shoulder harness into me. Deceleration forces were so brutal they produced bruises in the exact pattern where the shoulder harness came across my chest, like someone had tattooed the straps under my skin. I could even see the shoulder harness adjustment buckle's imprint. The right wing ripped open and spewed fuel all over the ramp, which ignited and turned into a giant fireball.

I remember the FE pulling out the E-handles and I saw him looking at the #3 E-handle in his hand. The #3 E-handle pointed straight up at the ceiling. Attached was a long cable going back into the instrument panel's top. The right wing was no longer attached, and the cable no was longer connected to #3 engine. With the FE's distraction, he failed to pull #2 E-Handle. The #2 engine continued to run.

The airplane emerged from the fireball. The right wing's separation forces spinning the airplane to right combined with #2 engine still running spun the airplane around about 270 degrees. We came to a stop facing the flames, which were about 75 feet away. Smoke filled the cockpit. In the early morning sunlight, the smoke reflected the fire's orange brilliance right outside our windshield. I couldn't figure out where the flames were coming from. Was the cockpit on fire? We seemed engulfed in flames.

Panic set in to get my ass out. Pure "Get the Fuck Out of Here" engulfed me. I released my seat belt and shoulder harness, but did not move my seat back nor lift my armrest. Immediately, I leaped out of my seat and walked across the center console's fuel panel. The cockpit emergency exit was right behind my seat, but I could not get to it. My hand was inches away from the emergency exit, yet as hard as I tried, I couldn't reach the exit. I was stuck in a Twilight Zone of lost reality. Why couldn't I reach the exit? I was trapped in a burning airplane. *Is this a bad dream? Am I already dead? What the fuck is going on?*

In an instance, my mind flashed back three years to my water Dilbert Dunker training at AOCS. If I was trapped, they taught me, I should go back to my last position and verify I was clear of all obstacles. When I checked my last position, I saw I forgot to raise the armrest before getting out of my seat and it hooked onto my Mae West. It was holding me back. I sat in my seat again and undid the life vest. Then I turned back to the cockpit emergency exit. Now I could reach it, so I pulled it open. All this took only seconds. I was the first person to leave the cockpit. The exit was a good eight feet off the ground, and the evacuation was like jumping headfirst out of a second-story window. But away I dove. I was 25 years old and indestructible.

Luckily, the arm rest interference delayed my evacuation. I could have jumped into a spinning propeller. When the airplane came to a stop, the #2 engine was still running, and it was inches away from the cockpit emergency exit. Crew members going out the left side over the wing exit reported the #2 engine was still running and blew them off the wing. Because the #3 E-Handle had broken off, the FE never finished pulling out the #2 E-Handle. Before I exited, Cmdr. Mason pulled the #2 E-Handle to shut down the engine, and in following procedure, probably saved my life again. Only 25-30 seconds had elapsed from the time I started to rotate until I escaped the burring airplane. There were 21 people on board. Everyone escaped in 15 seconds. Did Cmdr. Mason's "silly ass" evacuation drills over the past few months make a difference? Hell yes.

THE BUS RIDE

After our escape, we gathered at our predetermined rendezvous point a hundred yards off the tip of the left wing. Commander Mason accounted for everyone with a head count. We watched black smoke billow out the open emergency exits as our plane burned. Our personal possessions were going up in flames. My three custom, hand-sewn suits from Hong Kong would turn to ashes.

One of the crew said, "I lost my jewels."

A couple other crews members grabbed their crotches and said, "Man, I am glad I still got mine."

Laughter broke out and relieved the tension.

While we were standing there, a gray Navy school bus came by on a road by the end of the runway and stopped. The driver asked if we wanted a ride back to Base Ops. We thought they had sent it to pick us up, so we climbed on. Small world incident. Shaking with adrenaline from the crash, I saw my cousin Dave as the bus driver. He was my Uncle Bob's adopted son, and we hadn't seen each other in years.

Base Ops didn't send the bus; it was just making a routine run back from a school on the base. We departed the scene before the Crash and Rescue trucks got to the fire. Adak's Crash and Rescue crew searched the smoke-filled burning aircraft interior. They did not find any sign of people. They radioed the tower and said they couldn't find anyone, and our status was unknown. Without their knowledge, we had boarded the school bus and began our journey back to the hangar.

THEY ARE ALL DEAD

We were the first airplane in our three-plane flight to takeoff. When we started our takeoff roll, the other two P-3s were holding short, watching us takeoff. They watched our airplane swerve off the runway's left side and disappear into a ball of fire. The fireball obscured their view of our P-3 after it left the runway. The other crews did not see us as we emerged from the opposite side of the airplane. They did not know we had escaped the burning wreck. These crews thought they had just witnessed their close friends "buying the farm" in a burning airplane. "Bought the farm" is a WWII saying that refers to the survivors' $10,000 death benefit that allowed beneficiaries to pay off the family farm. Everyone feared the worst.

The two other P-3s taxied back to the VP Hangar ramp and shutdown. While taxiing, they asked the tower if they knew anything about the crew's fate. The tower told them that the Crash and Rescue crew had not yet located anyone. Everyone assumed the worst. With no words about what happened to our crew, many of our squadron mates thought we were dead. The school bus dropped us off at the hangar's back door. I would not see my cousin, Dave, again for years until my uncle's funeral in 1986. When we walked into the hangar, the other VP-45 crews were standing around chatting. Many had their back toward us. One by one, they turned our way and stopped talking. When they saw us, there were looks of shock and disbelief. Their faces exploded in joyful smiles as they ran toward us, hugging, backslapping, and handshaking. They were so glad to see us alive. Dick Dolson ran toward me with tears of joy in his eyes. He grabbed me tightly and told me how happy he was that I was alive. *Me too!*

THE PHONE CALL

Lou dreamed about the squadron returning. The squadron P-3s would show up, and I would not be there. She was worried about me not coming home. The anxiety of having a loved one in a combat zone was always there. Any time the phone rang or there was a strange car in the neighborhood, shivers ran down her back. Then she got the phone call. The person calling from the Wing Headquarters in Jacksonville said, "Your husband won't be coming home, his airplane crashed in Alaska."

She never heard the words "He is alright and will call you later."

In her mind, her worse fears had come true: she was pregnant, her husband was gone, and her baby would never know its father. When I called later that afternoon, she was still in tears. I tried to console her. I told her I was all right and I would be home soon.

The question is whether the event was preordained or a random event under chaos theory. Takeoff crash dreams had been hitting me about once a month. The right wing broke off the P-3 model I built. Did I jinx my plane? Lou dreamed I would not be coming home. *Anyone believe in Voodoo dolls?* Were those dreams too much of a coincidence? Maybe a premonition?

FINALLY, HOME

I spent five days at Adak for the accident investigation. With the baby due soon, I was eager to get home to be with Lou. The flight engineer and the three pilots on the plane gave individual statements. We had been at the O'Club until nearly midnight the night before. The official rule was eight hours with no alcohol before takeoff. While flying around Vietnam, the bottle-to-throttle rule was no big deal. No one flew under the influence, but we had little awareness about the cutoff time before a flight. Not sure of the Navy's bottle-to-throttle rule, I had four or five drinks between 1900 and 2300. Our briefing for our flight would take place at 0500. I had an off-the-record interview with the Fight Surgeon assigned to the accident investigation. He asked about our drinking. He said drinking was not a causal factor and he would not mention it.

The accident investigation board closed the hearings at Adak. Then the squadron deployed to Adak, VP-47, flew us on a P-3 to NAS Moffett Field in San Jose, California. Bob and I sat in the airplane's galley seat and were all white knuckles on that take off. We stayed overnight at NAS Moffett. A VP-5 P-3 picked us up the next morning and took us back to NAS Jacksonville. Now, being a nervous flyer, it floored me when the PPC elected to turn on the water injection during the climb to FL290. At

FL270, without reducing power, he turned it on and all four red TIT over temperature lights came on. The TDs, the Temperature Datum system on the engines that provides over temperature protection, started trimming fuel to protect the engine, fuel flow and horsepower were dropping. My mind was going *Holy fucking shit. I am about to witness a four-engine flame out at FL270 and end up crashing in the Nevada desert.* Fortunately, the engines quickly corrected the situation and returned to normal operation.

But we got home, and there was Lou. I had left her with a flat tummy, now her belly protruded with the baby. The change made me love her even more than before. I missed almost her entire pregnancy. The demands of service separated me from her during one of the most significant events in our lives. I was never so happy to see someone as Lou that day. Her six-month burden of having a loved one in a combat zone was over. I was safely home.

I hugged her around her massive belly, content to wait for our child to arrive while flying non-combat missions at home.

Epilogue

Why would I write this memoir? It started out as a project for my grandchildren and great grandchildren. I wished my grandparents, and great grandparents had written about their lives. Oldsters are hesitant to tell their stories, maybe out of embarrassment or a feeling that they would just be boring the listener. But we can learn so much about how they dealt with the struggles and rewards of life. I have set up trust funds for my grandchildren and great grandchildren. I thought it would be nice if they knew more about the people who set up the trusts.

Preserving our love story is part of my goal. Lou's decision to drop out of college, marry early, and endure the turbulent times in the late 1960s needs to be told. Our marriage would test her with extended separations. She loved someone flying in a combat zone, and the anxiety associated with not knowing if I would return. Loved ones, like Lou, who waited at home, have their own, little-known heroic courage. I married a great gal who supported me, raised our family, put up with deployments, unemployment, moved every 3 years, and never threatened to bail out on me. Among her many superpowers, she can pack up a household in one day to move to the next job. I am so glad she chose me.

Much the same as I would have liked to know more about my ancestors, I'm hoping my own line will be interested to us. I started this memoir strictly as a family project, but after showing it to a few friends, they encouraged me to publish it. This story tells about my transformation from a directionless civilian kid with a dream of becoming a Naval Aviator into the man who fulfilled that dream.

To sum up my motivations and a bit of my story, I am including a snapshot of my life found in my introduction into the Michigan Aviation Hall of Fame. I am deeply humbled by the honor they gave me when it seems as if there were many other people who were much more deserving.

Michigan Aviation Hall of Fame induction for Ralph "Randy" Hotton:

Nothing distinguishes Randy from the others who have been admitted to the Michigan Aviation Hall of Fame. He like those nominated is now a member of the Hall of Fame. He has pursued a passion and dedication to flying and aviation in the state of Michigan. Like stories found in the memoirs of John Glenn and Neil Armstrong, his passion for flying, airplanes and aviation started at an early age. Like his heroes, he built the models, went to the airport, hung around pilots, and tried to mooch rides in airplanes. Because of his dedication to the country, he volunteered to serve in the US Navy as a pilot during the Vietnam conflict. His dedication to the country continued for 26 years of active Navy and Naval Reserve service. In his civilian career, his leadership had a major impact on the airline management at Drummond Island Air and USA Jet Airlines. His love of flying had been reflected in his role as a mentor to a new generation of flyers. Randy's role in shaping the future of the Yankee Air Museum has played a key function in the museum's growth and stability. Perhaps Randy's most significant contribution to Michigan's aviation history is the writing of his book on the Willow Run Bomber Plant. His passion for aviation has led to 55 years of continuous pursuit of excellence in aviation.

I have read several Vietnam era pilot memoirs. I found them all engaging. Pilots have unique stories about their careers and adventures. As a P-3 multi-engine "puke," I have not endured the trauma seen in the memoirs of my Attack and Fighter "puke" comrades. I claim nothing close to hero status. But these memoirs are important pieces of American history. One hundred years from now, some student or historian may want to dig into my personal experiences flying in the Navy during the Vietnam War era.

My memoir will be a valuable resource to save these stories, along with the details of Navy Flight Training in the 1960s. In 1968, demands for record pilot production pushed the system. The Navy had a production goal of 3,500 pilots: a record since the Korean War that still stands today. These Vietnam-era memoirs will add a personal touch to the experiences of those military people at the food chain bottom who executed the orders given to them. These stories will augment the history books, much the same as reading the memoirs of Civil War and WWII veterans.

As an average Navy pilot, my story is of an unspectacular kid who grew up with the pipe dream of being a pilot, even more so a Navy pilot. But, as is common with many children, these dreams were only dreams. Throughout my childhood, my life had little purpose and remained unremarkable. I played no sports and never belonged to any clubs in high school. I enrolled in college prep courses because I didn't know what I wanted to do. If I had any claim to fame, it might have been that I had the fastest car in the parking lot. I loved tinkering with cars, a gift from my father. I enjoyed taking them apart and putting them back together. In my day, I would classify as a "Greaser" as opposed to "College Preppy." My grades were ordinary, and I graduated with a 2.9 GPA. Of course, in 1961, a 2.9 put me in the top 15% of my class. I went to college because my mom went to college. Then, through happenstance, I seized on an opportunity to pursue my childhood dream of becoming a Navy pilot.

I refer to the "breaks of Naval Air" in my book. Many would refer to these as the breaks of life. Naval Air is a casino of sorts.

Those people doing the job may face unfavorable odds while fulfilling their Navy roles. Naval Aviators face so many encounters with random events beyond their control. For example, two planes go out on a mission, only one comes back. Rather than dwell upon the loss, they are shrugged off as the "Breaks of Naval Air." Perhaps a coping mechanism to hide that the disaster could have been for me. Are these breaks because of chaos theory or preordained events?

The words *"FUCK," WTF*, and other four-letter curses appear many times in my story. These words, if used at home while growing up, would get my mouth washed out with soap. We understand in 2024, the "f" bomb has become a common word that carries truly little offensive shock value. Nowadays, it's impossible to watch a cable TV program and not hear the "f" bomb dropped many times. But in 1960, people rarely used the word, and when used, it caught people's attention. Hearing Sgt. Sanders scream at me while using the "f" bomb shocked me as nothing ever had before. It underwrote the transition from the comfortable world where I had been living into the unknown new military world.

I have divided my life into two parts. A time before 2:30 p.m. on Wednesday, 6-29-1966, and a time after I heard Sgt. Sanders scream at me, "GET THE FUCK OFF MY QUARTER DECK!" His words introduced me to the most formative eleven weeks of my life. A chance encounter with a DI at the AOCS reunion clarified their role. Three of us from class AOCS 25-66 attended the September 2021 AOCS reunion. We got to dinner late and sat at the only open table. A couple of AOCS DIs from the 1980s were sitting at the table. A limited conversation took place. Maybe I was still a little intimidated, fearing I might screw up and bring down their wrath on me. But conversation became open and went to asking them "What drove you to be a DI?" His answer floored me.

"I wanted to ensure those who made it through the program would turn out like you guys," he said. "Guys who made it through flight training served their country with honor and made me proud of my contribution."

Who me? The screw up who fumbled through AOCS. I failed inspections, picked up demerits, and spent weekends marching off demerits on the Grinder. Hats off to those DIs who shaped men into Naval Aviators. The DIs who terrified us had a mission. They molded us into a cohesive collection of men dedicated to our fellow service members and our country. We would strive to fulfill our obligations and there would be no hesitation in answering any call to duty. They determined who had the "Right Stuff" to serve the country as a Naval Aviator.

I think John McCain's words given at his son's winging ceremony at Pensacola captured my feeling about service:

What I wish every American understood is, despite its attendant risks and sacrifices, military service even for one or two enlistments or for a career is one of the most rewarding experiences you could ever have. Make no mistake, those risks and sacrifices are great and daunting even in peacetime. But few other occupations completely invest your life with importance, even historic importance, and so well develop your character along lines of excellence. It is an advantage and a satisfaction you will always have that others will never know. You develop as strong a bond, as deep a concern with those who serve beside you, as you will ever have with anyone outside your family. And you will discover an insight that many people never will. That your life is bigger and more satisfying the more that it is part of something beyond your self-interest.

I found the satisfaction John McCain described in his speech.

What are these little understood forces that guide our lives? Is there a Divine plan or is it chaos theory, where a series of random events intersect with our lives? I do not have an answer, but too many things have happened in my life that I believe point to a master plan in our lives. I use the term "a bullet dodged" many times in this memoir. Encounters with random events that, if they had a different outcome, could have vastly changed my life. I have no regrets. My life has been complete.

Look for the rest of Randy's story in a book called *Livin' the Dream* which continues Randy's aviation career. Follow along as Randy fulfills his Naval aviation dreams. He excels flying the P-3 Orion, recruiting Navy pilots, and becoming qualified as Officer of Deck Underway on the USS Enterprise. Ride the rollercoaster of disappointment with him when his career comes to a screeching halt in the service-wide Reduction in Force following the Vietnam War. He, along with more than a thousand other Vietnam-era, military-trained pilots, are thrust into the civilian job market. Struggle with him and his supportive wife in the era of airline deregulation and his bumpy adventure through the minefield of dead-end flying jobs. Experience his joy resurrecting his military career in the Naval Reserve. Grasp his ultimate career achievement when he reaches into a garbage can and pulls out a job at USA Jet Airlines. Join the satisfaction of living his dream.

GLOSSARY

A

A-3	A twin engine carrier-based jet attack airplane used in Vietnam.
A-7	A single engine carrier-based jet attack airplane used in Vietnam.
A-32, A36, A37, etc.	Antisubmarine training qualifications. A series of training events needed to qualify an ASW crew to perform their mission.
AA	Above Average flight grades
ACRAC	Aviation Cadet Recreation and Athletic Club, a place for AOCS candidates to get drinks and relax.
AFB	Air Force Base
AFROTC	Air Force Reserve Officer Training Corps
AGI	Russian Auxiliary Intelligence Gathering Trawlers
AGL	Height above the ground or water
AOCS	Aviation Officer Candidate School, an 11-week school leading to a USNR commission.
APU	Auxiliary Power Unit, an internal power unit on an airplane to provide electric and pneumatic power to the aircraft.
ASR	Surveillance Radar Approach, a radar guided instrument approach providing directional information without glide slope
ASW	Anti-Submarine Warfare
ASW "C" load	Complete set of anti-submarine search

	ordinance, sonobuoys, PDCs, etc.
ATC	Air Traffic Control Center.
ATL	American Thought and Language, freshman English class at MSU
AWOL	Away without Leave, being away from your military unit without approval.
AVROC	Aviation Reserve Office Candidate (AOCS school split into two six weeks summers for candidates still in college.)

B
| BA | Below Average flight grades |
| BOQ | Bachelor Officer Quarters, housing on base for single officers |

C
C-172	Single-engine four seat Cessna airplane used for pilot training.
C-182	Hi-performance version of C-172, with variable pitch propeller
CAPT	Captain, O-6, Sixth level of officer rank in the Navy
CAP	Civil Air Patrol, a USAF civilian organization
CB	Circuit Breaker
CDR	Commander, O-5, Fifth level of officer rank in the Navy
CFT	Commander Task Force
CO	Commanding Officer

D
DC-8	A 150-passenger four-engine jet airplane built by Douglas Aircraft
DI	USMC Drill Instructor
DOD	Department of Defense.
DOR	Drop, Own Request, used by an AOCS candidate when they elected to remove themself from AOCS.

DMZ	Demilitarized Zone, border between North and South Vietnam.

E

ECM	Electronic Counter Measures, passive collection of electronic signals
EMI	Extra Military Instruction, marching off demerits on the grinder.
ENS	Ensign, O-1, Most junior officer rank in the Navy

F

FAA	Federal Aviation Administration, Federal governing body for civil aviation
F-4	Navy Phantom, a twin-engine carrier-based jet fighter airplane used in Vietnam.
FCLP	Field Carrier Landing Practice, practice carrier landings on a shore-based airport.
FE	Flight Engineer
FL	Flight Level such as FL230 which is 23,000 feet above sea level.
FPC	Flight Purpose Code defines the purpose of an aircraft's flight.

G

GCA	Ground Controlled approach, a radar guided instrument approach conducted by an operator talking the airplane down. Provides both directional and glideslope information.
GNC	Global Navigation Chart, used for plotting great circle routes in flight planning.
SGT	USMC Sergeant, E-5 fifth level of enlisted rank
SSGT	USMC Staff Sergeant, E-6 sixth level of enlisted rank
GYSGT	USMC Gunnery Sergeant, E-7 seventh level of enlisted rank

H

HP	Horse power, P-3 engines were set by calling for horse power
HC-2	Helicopter Composite Squadron based at Lake Hurst, New Jersey, flying the HU-2
HRD	P-3 engine fire extinguisher with a High Rate of Discharge
HU-2	Search and Rescue helicopter flown off aircraft carriers.

I

IO-435	225 HP, Six-cylinder horizontally opposed piston engine used on the T-34B.
IAS	Indicated Airspeed, the airspeed reading the pilots see in the cockpit.
IFR	Instrument Flight Rules, allows flying without outside visual cues.

J

JO	Junior Officer, officer rank of LT and below

K

KC-135	Four-engine USAF inflight refueling tanker jet.
KIA	Killed in Action
kt	Knot(s) or nautical mile per hour

L

L-188	Lockheed Electra, cargo airplane civilian version of P-3
LCDR	Lieutenant Commander, O-4, Fourth level of officer rank in the Navy
LT	Full Lieutenant, O-3, Third level of officer rank in the Navy
LTJG	Lieutenant Junior Grade, O-2, Second-lowest officer rank in the Navy
LOCBC	Localizer Back Course, an instrument approach using the opposite side of the approach.

LOFAR	An ASW sonobuoy with a wide frequency band omni-directional sensor for passive tracking of submarines.
Lockheed 12A	An 8-passenger twin engine airplane built by Lockheed Corporation.
LSO	Landing Signal Officer, the officer who observes and directs aircraft landing on aircraft carriers.

M

MACV	Military Assistance Command Vietnam
MAD	Magnetic Anomaly Detector, ASW tracking device to locate submarines.
MGWTO	Max Gross Weight Takeoff
MIA	Missing in Action
MOT	Mark on Top
MSU	Michigan State University
MPC	US military issued Military Payment Certificates, a substitute for US Dollars
MRC	Maintenance Required Card, provides maintenance procedure guidance.

N

NAAS	Naval Air Auxiliary Station
NAF	Naval Air Facility, a Naval Air support facility located at a non-NAS airfield.
NAMI	Naval Aviation Medical Institute
NAS	Naval Air Station
NATOPS	Naval Aviation Training and Operating Procedures manual, pilots' operating guidelines for each airplane
NDB	Non-Directional Beacon, a radio homing device
NFCU	Navy Federal Credit Union.
NFO	Naval Flight Officer, officer flight crew member who is not a pilot.
nm	Nautical Mile, a measure of distance that is one minute, one sixtieth of a degree, of elevation of a celestial body on a great circle.

NVA	North Vietnamese Army

O

OFT	Operational Flight Trainers, stationary airplane cockpit used to familiarize student with aircraft controls.
OINC	Officer in Charge
OLQ	Officer Like Qualities, Class rating on a candidate's officer potential
OPCON	Operational Control Center, manned 24 hours a day as a call center for operation control of fleet assets.
OV-10	North American twin-engine turbo-prop attack airplane used in Vietnam.

P

P-2	Navy Neptune, a two-engine piston-prop Patrol Airplane.
P-3	Navy Orion, a four-engine turbo-prop Patrol Airplane.
PDC	Practice Depth Charges, mini depth charges with 2 oz of explosive.
P-47	A single-engine WWII fighter bomber airplane built by Republic.
PIC	Pilot in Command, the pilot in charge of the aircraft.
PIM	Position of the aircraft's Intended Movement.
PPNP	Patrol Plane Non-Qualified Pilot
PP3P	Patrol Plane qualified as third Pilot.
PP2P	Patrol Plane qualified as second Pilot.
PPC	Patrol Plane qualified as Patrol Plane Commander
PR	Public Relations
PRNA	People's Republic of North America, an imaginary enemy country used at SERE school to train aircrew members in POW resistant technics.
PB4Y-1	A WWII Navy patrol airplane, the Navy version of the B-24 bomber

PBED	Pay Base Entry Date, day one of joining the Navy and starting pay longevity.
POW	Prison of War
PT	Physical Training, pushups, sit ups, jumping jacks, flip flops, etc. often used as punishment for minor infractions of AOCS rules.

R

R-1820	1425 HP, Reciprocating nine-cylinder piston engine with a displacement of 1,820 cu. in used in the T-28, C-1A, and TS-2A.
R-3350	3,000 HP Reciprocating 18-cylinder piston engine with a displacement of 3,350 cubic inches used on the Lockheed Constellation
RAG	Replacement Air Group, a training unit that prepared crews to fly their fleet-assigned aircraft, i.e., P-3, F-4, A-7 RAGs.
RDO	Runway Duty Officer, Navy student pilot duty to observe runway safety.
REO	Rules of Engagement, standoff distance with potential hostile encounters.
RLP	Room Locker and Personal Inspection, a scheduled inspection by an AOCS DI
R&R	Rest and Relaxation, relief from operational flying
RM	Regimental Messenger, an officer candidate assigned duties to carry a satchel of messages between buildings at AOCS.
RTB	Return to Base, aircraft aborts the flight and returns.
RV	Room Violation, a violation found during a RLP that resulted in demerits.

S

SAT	Scholastic Aptitude Test, college entrance exam.
SDO	Squadron Duty Officer, A designed officer who is the point of contact for a squadron, i.e. phone watch.

SEATO	Southeast Asia Treaty Organization, a mutual defense organization of friendly Asian nations.
SERE	Survival Evasion Resistance and Escape School, POW training
SLJ	Shitty Little Job, miscellaneous collateral officer duties.
SNAFU	Military term for "Situation Normal, All Fucked Up"
SPDB	Student Pilot Disposition Board, "Speedie Board," an official review of a student's performance after an unsatisfactory grade.
STB	Starboard, right side of a ship or plane

T

T-28	US Navy North American Aviation single engine piston basic trainer used for acrobatics, instrument flight and aircraft carrier landings.
T-34	US Navy Beechcraft single engine piston primary trainer used for new students in Navy Flight Training
T-29	US Navy Convair twin engine piston Navigation trainer used for new Navigators in Navy Flight Training
TS-2A	US Navy Grumman Aviation twin engine piston advanced trainer used for instrument flight and aircraft carrier landings.
TACAN	Tactical Air Navigation Ultra High Frequency Radio Navigator station providing bearing and distance.
TACCO	Tactical Coordinator, an NFO flight crew officer who ran the mission in the back of the airplane.

U

U of M	University of Michigan located in Ann Arbor Michigan.
UA	Unauthorized Absence, being away from your military unit without approval.

UCMJ	Uniform Code of Military Justice, a class at AOCS
UHF	Ultra High Frequency communications radio
UNSAT	Unsatisfactory flight grade
USAF	United States Air Force
USNA	United States Naval Academy
USNR	United States Naval Reserve, Commissioned status of all AOCS graduates
USN	United States Naval, Regular Navy Commission as career officer

V

V-5 program	A WWII. Pilot training program, the precursor of AOCS.
VC	Viet Kong
VD	Venereal Disease, Sexually Transmitted Diseases
VFR	Visual Flight Rules, flying in clear weather.
VOR	Very High Frequency Omni-range Radio Navigator station
WNC	Weapon Not Clean, a cause to earn demerits for rifle not clean.
VPB-111	Navy Fixed Wing Heavier than Air Patrol Bomber Squadron 111
VP-5/6/7/30/45/49/93	Navy Fixed Wing Heavier than Air Patrol Squadron 5/6/7/30/45/49/93
VT-1	Navy Fixed Wing Heavier than Air Primary Training Squadron One that flew the T-34B as NAAS Saufley Field
VT-2	Navy Fixed Wing Heavier than Air Basic Training Squadron Two that flew the T-28 at NAS Whiting Field.
VT-5	Navy Fixed Wing Heavier than Air Basic Carrier Landing Training Squadron Five that flew the T-28 at NAAS Saufley Field
VT-29	Navy Fixed Wing Heavier than Air Navigator Training Squadron Twenty-Nine that flew the T-29 at NAS Corpus Christi

VT-31	Navy Fixed Wing Heavier than Air Advanced Multi-Engine Training Squadron Thirty-One that flew the TS-2A at NAS Corpus Christi

X

X-C	Cross-country flight, student pilot's flight between two airports more than 50 nm apart
XO	Executive Officer, second in command of a squadron

Y

YAM	Yankee Air Museum, a non-profit museum at Willow Run Airport

Appendix A

Official Navy Report on the loss of the VP-26 P-3B.

On April 1, 1968, a U.S. Navy P-3B Orion (#153445) was on a routine coastal surveillance patrol as part of Operation Market Time, this was the Navy's effort to stop troops and supplies from flowing by sea from North Vietnam to South Vietnam during the Vietnam War. The aircraft, operating out of Utapao, Thailand, received requested assistance in establishing visual reconnaissance of a large Cambodian landing support ship (LSSL) that was reported to be off-loading cargo to sampans near the Cambodian Island of Hon Doc in the Gulf of Thailand. The Orion responded to the request and moments later reported to the Coastal Surveillance Center at A Thoi that it had received hostile fire from a .50 caliber antiaircraft gun. The P-3B was hit in the starboard wing, knocking out the #4 engine and starting a fire. All attempts to extinguish the flames were unsuccessful. Flying too low to bail out, the crew had to choose between ditching in hostile waters or attempt to make an emergency landing at Phu Quoc airfield less than 20 miles away. Within sight of the runway, and with their wing still aflame, the crew prepared to land their stricken aircraft. As the plane banked left onto its final approach, the starboard wing tore off between #3 and #4 engine, and the P-3B tumbled into the sea with no survivors.

About the Author

Randy Hotton is a retired Navy Captain who spent 26 years flying in the active and reserve Navy. As a Navy pilot, he flew the P-3 Orion aircraft in Vietnam and conducted anti-submarine patrols during the Cold War. Randy grew up in Troy, Michigan and has a bachelor's degree from Michigan State University and a master's degree from Central Michigan University. Randy has been inducted into the Michigan Aviation Hall of Fame. He and his wife, Lou, still live in Michigan. He continues to work in aviation and has never lost his love of flight.

Note from Randy Hotton

Word-of-mouth is crucial for any author to succeed. If you enjoyed *Get the F*#k Off My Quarterdeck!*, please leave a review online—anywhere you are able. Even if it's just a sentence or two. It would make all the difference and would be very much appreciated.

Thanks!
Randy Hotton
https://www.randyhottonpilot.com/

We hope you enjoyed reading this title from:

www.blackrosewriting.com

Subscribe to our mailing list – *The Rosevine* – and receive **FREE** books, daily deals, and stay current with news about upcoming releases and our hottest authors.
Scan the QR code below to sign up.

Already a subscriber? Please accept a sincere thank you for being a fan of Black Rose Writing authors.

View other Black Rose Writing titles at www.blackrosewriting.com/books and use promo code **PRINT** to receive a **20% discount** when purchasing.

www.ingramcontent.com/pod-product-compliance
Lightning Source LLC
Chambersburg PA
CBHW072150070526
44585CB00015B/1076